UNIX Secure Shell

McGraw-Hill Tools Series Titles:

Maxwell	*Unix Network Management Tools*	0-07-913782-2
Medinets	*Unix Shell Programming Tools*	0-07-913790-3
Ross	*Unix System Security Tools*	0-07-913788-1
Fisher	*Red Hat Linux Administration Tools*	0-07-134746-1

To order or receive additional information on these or any other McGraw-Hill titles, in the United States please call 1-800-722-4726, or visit us at www.computing.mcgraw-hill.com. In other countries, contact your McGraw-Hill representative.

UNIX Secure Shell

Anne Carasik

McGraw-Hill

New York • San Francisco • Washington, D.C. • Auckland • Bogotá • Caracas
Lisbon • London • Madrid • Mexico City • Milan • Montreal • New Delhi
San Juan • Singapore • Sydney • Tokyo • Toronto

McGraw-Hill

A Division of The McGraw·Hill Companies

2 3 4 5 6 7 8 9 0   AGM/AGM   0 4 3 2 1 0

P/N 212273-0

Part of ISBN 0-07-134933-2

The sponsoring editor for this book was Simon Yates, and the production supervisor was Clare Stanley. It was set in Sabon by TIPS Technical Publishing.

Printed and bound by Quebecor/Martinsburg.

McGraw-Hill books are available at special quality discounts to use as premiums and sales promotions, or for use in corporate training programs. For more information, please write to the Director of Special Sales, McGraw-Hill, Professional Publishing, Two Penn Plaza, New York, NY 10121-2298. Or contact your local bookstore.

This book is printed on recycled, acid-free paper containing a minimum of 50% recycled, de-inked fiber.

For Penny and Julius—

In memory of Harris

Contents

Quick Reference

Since SSH has a strong following, there are some common problems, questions, or issues that come up with SSH. I've included this list of common questions (not a FAQ[1]) below. Since many of these questions are very broad and cover a variety of topics, they are answered in more than one chapter.

What is SSH? About the SSH Program and Chapter 1

Is there an RFC or IETF draft on SSH? Preface

What makes SSH secure? Chapter 1

What does SSH protect against? Chapter 1

I want to tunnel other applications through SSH. How do I do it? Chapter 9

Are SSH1 and SSH2 compatible? Chapter 2

Is SSH compatible with the .rhosts authentication? Chapters 4 and 6

How can I get SSH to work with TCP Wrappers? Chapter 9

How do I install SSH? Chapter 2

Where does SSH store its public and private keys? Chapters 3, 4, 5, 6, and 7

Can I use SSH without a password? Chapters 3, 5, and 7

How do I use SS H with a firewall? Chapter 8

Can I use SSH as a VPN? Chapters 8 and 9

I don't understand all of this cryptography; where can I get more information about it? Appendix A

What cryptographic algorithms does SSH use? Chapter 1

I'm having problems installing SSH or getting it to work properly. What are some common problems? Chapters 2 and 10

---

1. The most current SSH FAQ is available at http://www.employees.org/~satch/ssh/faq.

List of Figures

List of Tables

Foreword

By Mark S. Kadrich

In the past five years the Internet has exploded and created new markets where once there were none. New opportunities are only limited by the imaginations of those brave enough to try new things and new ways. Millions of people have flocked to the Internet to take advantage of these new opportunities either as consumers or the providers of services and goods for consumers. So, to fill a void, electronic commerce has emerged to become one of the great enabling technologies of the new millennium.

But like the great gold rush of the past century, the "info rush" of the new millennium brings not only great opportunity, but great risk. Like the bandits and claim jumpers of old, hackers and script kiddies are constantly making life difficult for the unwitting and unprepared. In short, threats are everywhere. One minute you have a functioning Web site, the next minute you're wondering where your transaction lists have gone. Doing business over the Net can be a scary thing indeed.

To make the problem worse, the demand for performance has created the requirement for distributed systems and distributed administration techniques. Secure techniques, if you want to keep your job. A security violation predicated on the breakdown of some administrative process can be a hard thing to explain to those that are not technically adept. Like finance managers and CEOs. To them, it's your fault and your responsibility. In any event, you feel like a fool, and quite possibly, an unemployed fool.

As system administrators we have learned that our life is a collection of tools that we use to get the job—whatever it is—done quickly and efficiently. Now we have to add "securely" to that list. This is so that we don't have to face a lot of those annoying hacker-induced process breakdowns. Secure Shell, or SSH, is a tool that can help with the "securely" aspect of our jobs.

Many operating systems have built-in tools that are provided in order to make life easier for the people that use them. Remote logins, file copies, and shells, to name a few. Each has their own implementation and, with it, its own opportunity for exploitation. The most popular, the Berkeley remote command set, has provided system administrators with the basic tools required to manage an entire enterprise from the comfort of their bathrobes for many years.

xvii

Unfortunately, the pitfalls of the Berkeley command set are well known and can be as dangerous as a dark mine shaft. But a tool is a tool, and like any tool the "r" commands are many tools to many people. However, the "r" commands are similar to a set of screw drivers, focused and specific. When you need to drive a screw or pry something, they work fairly well. But too many people try to use them as hammers and pliers. Secure Shell is more like a Swiss Army knife—something the miners of old would have paid dearly for. Like the miners and their tools, here is a way to not only stake your claim, but make sure that it's secure for the long haul.

Anne has done a good job of describing the functionality of Secure Shell and the installation and configuration procedure. You will learn what Secure Shell is, what it will do, and what it won't do. In addition, Anne takes you through the installation and configuration process with examples and detailed listings of actual sessions. Both SSH1 and SSH2 are described, with special detail paid to options and how they interact with host options to create a strong session or a not-so-strong session.

Preface

What This Book Is About

You may have noticed that too many networking applications are unsecure. Fortunately, this book isn't about them—it's about replacing them.

Too many security programs are complicated and make maintenance and administration more of a headache. Secure Shell doesn't give you a headache; in fact, it should minimize them, because not much user re-education is required and administration is minimized.

This book explains to you what Secure Shell is, what Secure Shell isn't, and how to implement it. As a result, this book should be important to you for one reason: securing your network sessions with Secure Shell. Secure Shell is very similar to a Swiss Army knife in that you can use it for many different things that you probably wouldn't expect.

Tatu Ylonen of SSH Communications Security wrote this program back when he was a researcher at the Helsinki University of Technology in July 1995. Tatu created a security application that replaces many of the unsecure UNIX networking applications that are still in use today that don't need to be.

Secure Shell encompasses three major components: UNIX processes,[1] TCP/IP networking, and cryptography. It strengthens a known weakness in UNIX, the Berkeley services, or the "r" commands. The "r" commands provide seamless connections between two systems, but with one major flaw: very poor authentication that can be spoofed from anyone. Secure Shell can also be used as a drop-in replacement for Telnet and FTP, as well as the "r" commands.

In addition, session hijacking and IP spoofing is much more difficult to do with Secure Shell. The encryption used provides for a solid way to authenticate yourself. In a way, it works much like a fingerprint—you can be identified by it, but it's very hard for someone else to steal. Also, the encryption prevents someone from reading your network connections as you type things like personal email messages[2] and your passwords.

---

1. Yes, Secure Shell can run on a variety of platforms including Windows, OS/2, and VMS, as well as many others.
2. Secure Shell is not a substitute for PGP. If you want to encrypt the mail message itself, use PGP, available at http://web.mit.edu/network/pgp.html.

This book will teach you how to get the most out of Secure Shell from an administrative and implementation view. Also, there's a chapter on trouble-shooting Secure Shell to help you work through some common problems that have already been discovered.

There's plenty of additional resources available for Secure Shell to help you. Everything from Web pages to the Usenet group, which is also available through a mailing list, and of course, all the nice people who respond to your questions.

Also, you'll read about what Secure Shell isn't. Secure Shell will not harden your system or network—you will have to do that. Secure Shell does not get rid of the "r" commands or Telnet, you have to do that as well. Secure Shell is a transport—for everything from its own native clients to any other type of net-working clients such as POP, DNS, or even PPP.

And the nice thing is that Secure Shell should work on almost any flavor of UNIX. With the growing popularity of Linux (a freeware flavor of UNIX), Secure Shell is becoming more and more of a critical product for protecting our systems. Secure Shell will not only keep attackers from hijacking your sessions and stealing your passwords, but provide you with a mindset of security when using networking applications.

Audience

This book is designed for UNIX system and network administrators to imple-ment Secure Shell in their environment. This book can also be used by pro-grammers who are looking to use Secure Shell in their scripts or code. However, this book does not go into how to modify the code of Secure Shell—so it's more for administrative purposes than anything.

Also, if you're a network or security consultant, this book should be a great resource for you when working with clients that want to know how to use Secure Shell and what it does. Also, if you need to implement Secure Shell at many sites, this book should help you out.

Basically, if you have basic UNIX system administration and networking skills you should be fine. You are not expected to have a knowledge of how cryptography works—basic cryptography is explained in Appendix A, *"Cryp-tography Basics"* on page 277 and in Appendix B, *"International Cryptogra-phy Laws"* on page 297.

As much as I'd like to please everyone, this book does NOT go into the spe-cifics of how to use Secure Shell for Windows 95, NT, or any other platform.

Sorry, but there are so many different implementations of SSH for Windows and other platforms that this book would have to focus on each implementation of SSH instead of the SSH program itself.

Structure of This Book

This book is divided into four sections: "Getting and Installing Secure Shell (SSH)," "Secure Shell 1 (SSH1)," "Secure Shell 2 (SSH2)," and "Advanced Usage of Secure Shell." These sections will help you install Secure Shell, learn the usage of Secure Shell 1 and Secure Shell 2, and learn some advanced things you can do, including key management, working with firewalls, and port forwarding.

Section I: Getting and Installing Secure Shell

This section covers two chapters, including an introduction to Secure Shell and installing Secure Shell in a UNIX environment. The first two chapters are everything you need to get up and running.

Chapter 1: What Is Secure Shell (SSH)? This chapter goes over what Secure Shell is, what Secure Shell does and doesn't protect against, and the differences between "r" commands and the Secure Shell "s" commands.

Chapter 2: Installing Secure Shell on UNIX. If you haven't installed Secure Shell already on your system, this chapter goes over everything from configuration to compiling to installing the Secure Shell application. It also includes configuration switches and using additional functionality such as SOCKS, TCP wrappers, and RSAREF.

Section II: Secure Shell 1 (SSH1)

This section covers two chapters which involve the first implementation of Secure Shell, Secure Shell 1 (SSH1). This includes usage for both the client and the server. Chapters 3 and 4 will help you tweak your SSH1 environment.

Chapter 3: Secure Shell 1 Server Daemon—sshd. If you're looking for an understanding of how the Secure Shell 1 server daemon (sshd) works and its usage, this chapter should cover the basics. It also covers some basic configuration examples. There are also some examples of the syntax and how you would use the Secure Shell 1 server daemon (sshd) in a real-time environment.

Chapter 4: Secure Shell Clients—ssh and scp. This chapter explains how the Secure Shell 1 clients (ssh and scp) work and their basic usage. It also covers some basic configuration examples and usage examples to get the clients up and working. You'll also find some examples of the syntax and how you would use the Secure Shell 1 clients (ssh and scp) in a real-time environment.

Section III: Secure Shell 2 (SSH2)

This section covers two chapters which involve the second implementation of Secure Shell, Secure Shell 2 (SSH2). This includes usage for both the client and the server. This implementation has an IETF draft available at http://www.ietf.org/ids.by.wg/secsh.html.

Chapter 5: Secure Shell 2 Server Daemon—sshd2 and sftp-server2. If you're looking for an understanding of how the SSH2 server daemon (sshd2 and sftp-server2) works and their usage, this chapter should cover the basics. Some examples of the syntax and how you would use the Secure Shell 2 server daemon (sshd2 and sftp-server2) in a real-time environment are also discussed. It also covers some basic configuration examples.

Chapter 6: Secure Shell 2 Clients—ssh2, scp2, and sftp2. This chapter explains how the SSH2 clients (ssh, sftp, and scp) work and their basic usage. It also covers some basic configuration examples and usage examples to get the clients up and working. Also, look for some examples of the syntax and how you would use the Secure Shell 2 clients (ssh, sftp, and scp) in a real-time environment.

Section IV: Advanced Usage of Secure Shell

After you have an understanding of the basics on how to use the Secure Shell server daemon and clients, this section goes in depth on how to use Secure Shell for various things. This also includes Secure Shell key management, how to get SSH working with firewalls, and some really cool things you can do with SSH.

Chapter 7: Secure Shell Key Management. This chapter covers key management for both SSH1 and SSH2. Host keys, server keys, user keys, key generation, and the authentication agent are covered. Also, configuration files for the keys are covered in this chapter.

Chapter 8: Secure Shell and Firewalls. If you're interested in using Secure Shell in conjunction with or sending it through a firewall, this chapter will help you. It defines what a firewall is, explains how to define rulesets for firewalls for Secure Shell, and explains some uses for Secure Shell and firewalls, such as creating a pseudo-VPN and using SOCKS.

Chapter 9: Other Cool Things You Can Do With Secure Shell. Now that you know the basics for Secure Shell, you can learn how to use some of the cooler things to do with Secure Shell. You can forward different types of TCP applications, including X, POP, FTP, Telnet, DNS, and anything else TCP-based you want. You can also learn how to get Secure Shell working with TCP wrappers for added security, as well as using Secure Shell for remote backups and other authentication methods that Secure Shell doesn't come with by default.

Chapter 10: Troubleshooting Secure Shell. You've tried and tried to get Secure Shell working, but you can't. This chapter is designed to explain how to get Secure Shell working and some of the stranger behaviors and common problems that you might run across.

The Appendices

The appendices provide you with some background information on cryptography, including some basics, terminology, and some of the legal issues you may run into, depending on which country you're in. Also, you'll find a section on obtaining other versions of Secure Shell that are not included on the CD-ROM because of the patent laws involving RSA in the United States. In addition, there is licensing information for both Secure Shell 1 and Secure Shell 2, as well as for the commercial software on the CD-ROM.

Appendix A: Cryptography Basics. This appendix explains the basics of cryptography.

Appendix B: International Cryptography Laws. For those concerned with export issues involving cryptography, this appendix covers some of the legal issues involving cryptography today.

Appendix C: Glossary of Cryptography Terms. This appendix defines those pesky cryptography terms that you may not be familiar with.

Appendix D: What's on the CD-ROM. This appendix tells you what you will find on the CD-ROM.

How to Reach the Author

I'd love to get your feedback about the book because I'm striving to make this better the next go-round. As much as I'd like to help, please do not contact me for technical support—I don't have the time to answer all my email as it is. Please use comp.unix.ssh or the SSH mailing list for support; many cool people on that list will answer your questions. If you're interested in contacting me, you can contact me via snail mail in care of McGraw-Hill Publishing.

Or, if you'd prefer to do this like most computer people do, feel free to contact me via email at stripes@tigerlair.com.

Acknowledgements

Russ Henmi, whose stories and bad jokes have been keeping me going (not to mention the love and support); my family (Mom, Dad, Lane, A.J., Scott, Erika, and Kimmie), who all need to see their names in print (especially Mom); Neil Salkind and all the cool people at Studio B for supporting me through this work; Simon Yates of McGraw-Hill, for letting me work with my own idea and making it live; Tim Mather of VeriSign, for supporting me in my work in information security; Bob Cramer at the University of Florida, who helped me get into the computer field to begin with; and Sue Day of Hewlett-Packard; Brad Lamont and David Kim of International Network Services, for helping me decide which direction I want to go.

Many thanks to Tatu Ylonen, Sami Ahvenniemi, and Jani Hursti of SSH Communications Security for endorsing the use of their software and letting me spend several evenings speaking with them; Pirkka Palomaki and Timo Nultamaki of Datafellows, for letting me use the evaluation copy of their software and reviewing this for sanity; Dan Rask of Van Dyke software, who was willing to take the time so that I could include an evaluation copy of Secure-CRT; and Mark Kadrich, for being an excellent technical editor (and helping me with those definitions)--and a good friend. Also, I have to mention Stephanie Miller (who also gave me lots of help with the definitions), a graduate student at Purdue University, Steve Acheson of CISCO, and Mark Shiozaki of VeriSign, for helping me make sure I know what I'm talking about.

I wouldn't have been able to do this without the help of all the people who wrote cool scripts and programs for Secure Shell:

Cedomir Igaly, Mats Andersson, Peter Gutmann, Robert O'Callahan, Andrew Tridgell, David Mazieres, Neils Möller, Wietse Venema, Jim Barlow, Dave Cinege, Jean Chouanard, Sami Lehtinen, Andy Polyakov, Steve Birnbaum, Noah Friedman, Stephane Bortzmeyer, Per-Erik Martin, David Silfry, Carson Gasper, Sergey Okapkin, Richard Levitte, Takashi Teranishi, Simon Tatham, Charlie Brady, John Saunders, Dave Jones, Cedric Gourio, and Timothy Chen.

Most importantly, I thank the Internet community who has been using Secure Shell and making it become an important part of getting connected.

UNIX Secure Shell

Getting and Installing Secure Shell

What Is Secure Shell (SSH)?

In this chapter:

- What is Secure Shell

- Why use Secure Shell

- How Secure Shell protects

- What Secure Shell doesn't protect against

- The "s" commands versus the "r" commands

In this chapter, you will see the benefits of using Secure Shell and get an overview of how it works, how the Berkeley "r" commands compare to Secure Shell "s" commands, and the improved security you can have with Secure Shell. You will see examples from a UNIX perspective, involving both network and system commands. However, if you want to brush up on cryptography, check out Appendix A, *"Cryptography Basics"* on page 277.

What is Secure Shell ?

When the Berkeley services, or "r" utilities, were introduced, they were some of the most secure programs of their time because they did not send passwords in the clear. With the poor authentication mechanism, however, many people's accounts have been broken into over the years. Because of the lack of security, Tatu Ylonen wrote SSH to replace the insecure network connections that the "r" utilities use.

Secure Shell (SSH) is a secure remote program that can do everything from securing terminal sessions and securing remote file copying to tunneling insecure applications like POP3, SMTP, IMAP, and CVS. SSH builds on the Berkeley services model and makes remote connections even more secure by implementing cryptography for additional authentication mechanisms and using cryptography to make the connection itself secure.

Secure Shell is a drop-in replacement for the Berkeley services, so the syntax is very similar to that of its sister "r" commands. Because many people have found SSH easy to use and implement, SSH is used in a variety of computers today—from UNIX systems to Windows, Macintosh, and VMS.

Why Use Secure Shell?

You probably want to know what's so great about Secure Shell, since you bought this book. *Secure Shell*, also referred to as *SSH*, is a program that started out on UNIX and has proliferated to other platforms as well. This chapter explains how a good application like Secure Shell, when used properly, can close several holes in your network. In addition to the security hole plug, Secure Shell is also cool because:

SSH clients are available for many platforms. Basically, almost any platform of UNIX—including HP-UX, Linux, AIX, Solaris, Digital UNIX, Irix, SCO, and many others—can run Secure Shell. Also, there are clients available, some of them in beta, for platforms other than UNIX, including OS/2, VMS, BeOS, Java, Windows 95, 98, and Windows NT. This enables you to use the SSH client on just about any platform.

It's free for noncommercial use. Many of the releases of SSH are available with open source and are available at no charge for noncommercial use. Also, the UNIX releases have open source, which means that anyone can play with the code and make modifications. However, if you do opt to use SSH in a commercial environment, you need to make sure you meet the licensing agreement of whichever version of SSH you use. Most of the implementations of the SSH client and daemons have some licensing restrictions. The only General Public License (GPL) version of SSH is lsh, and it is currently in beta.

No fear of having your password read over the Internet. This is one of the most recognized benefits of using SSH. If you look at the methods of access to Internet Service Providers (ISPs) or to universities, many are via unsecured means such as Telnet and POP mail clients. So, if every time you access your account, your password is sent in the clear (in other words, unprotected and readable in cyberspace), that's another chance an attacker has to gain access to your account—and you're ultimately responsible.

Support for the application. Because SSH began as an open source application with its source code being publicly available, SSH has gained a lot of acceptance in the UNIX world. *Linux*, another open source application freely available to the public, has gained similar acceptance. This enables developers (and anyone else) to improve the application with patches, bug fixes, and increased functionality. This also means that the application can continue to improve without direct support from the original developers.

SSH replaces unsecure remote applications. SSH was designed to replace the Berkeley services "r" commands; consequently its syntax is identical for similar use. As a result, the user shouldn't notice much difference when using SSH to connect instead of the "r" commands.

You can do cool things with it. You can use SSH to send X traffic securely over an unsecure network and not worry about it being hijacked. You can also tunnel POP and Telnet traffic, and you can even create a Virtual Private Network (VPN) by tunneling PPP traffic through Secure Shell.[1] SSH can also hook in to other authentication methods including Kerberos and SecurID cards. We'll talk about this in more detail in *"Other Cool Things You Can Do With Secure Shell"* on page 239

What SSH Protects Against

SSH provides protection from IP spoofing, source routing attacks, and DNS spoofing attacks. The main method through which SSH provides user authentication is by using public key encryption. This is done using RSA or Diffie-Helman and Digital Signature Standard, depending on the version of SSH you're using. You can use several methods of authentication, including public key authentication, rhosts/shosts authentication, and password authentication, quite easily and securely. Yes, even using .rhosts you can authenticate securely with SSH.

What SSH can provide is a secure method of access to a specific account over a network. Each user, as well as the server, has their own RSA key. A user can verify that the public key the server sends is the same as a previous one by using strict host key checking. This also prevents a user from accessing a host that they don't have the public key for.

Note   For more information on RSA and public key encryption and authentication, please see Appendix A, "Cryptography Basics."

SSH can also secure unsecured connections like X or POP, with a little bit of tinkering. This can help you manage your network connections more securely.

Because SSH provides host authentication, not by IP address but by public key, it makes the network more secure and less susceptible to IP spoofing. This helps you recognize who makes connec-

---

1. Currently only Linux supports this PPP over SSH VPN.

tions to your system so that you can protect yourself from unwanted visitors.

If the user or system is going to use rhosts/shosts style of authentication, the host is challenged to verify using a public and private key message exchange. Otherwise, it uses some other form of authentication. Before any authentication happens, the session is encrypted with a symmetric cipher, such as DES, Triple DES, IDEA, Twofish, or Blowfish. This encrypts the session itself, which prevents anyone from reading your mail as you type it or viewing your online conversation with someone else. It also means any passwords you type cannot be read because they too are encrypted. Basically, the encryption prevents eavesdropping and assures data integrity, meaning it prevents people from tampering with your information, or data. Table 1.1 shows the specific network attack protection that SSH offers.

Table 1.1 *What SSH protects against*

Network attacks	What happens
Packet spoofing	IP packet is not yours, but it is pretending to be
IP/host spoofing	IP address or hostname is yours and someone else is using it
Password Sniffing	Someone reads the network packets which contain your password
Eavesdropping	Someone reads the network packets and sees what you're typing

Of the types of encryption available to use, *IDEA* is the one of the faster ciphers available for SSH. IDEA does have restrictions in Europe because of licensing issues; if you cannot use IDEA, *Blowfish* and *Twofish* are fast ciphers as well. Also, *DES* is more pervasive than IDEA, Blowfish, or Twofish. Even though recent cryptanalysis attacks have been successful against DES in rather short periods of time (mere hours!), the attacks were done with a specially designed computer that cost $250,000.

As stated previously, SSH uses public key encryptionto perform authentication. The two forms used are DSA and RSA. *RSA* is used in the SSH 1.5 protocol for key exchange and for public key authentication. For the SSH 2.0 protocol, *DSA* is used for the public key authentication and *Diffie-Helman* is used for the public key exchange. If you are using the commercial release of the SSH 2.0 protocol, you can also use RSA for authentication.

Now you know what SSH does and how it works. Sounds good. So what *doesn't* it protect against?

What SSH Doesn't Protect Against

Despite how much security SSH offers, it doesn't provide an all-around "lock-down-your-system-while-being-online" service. SSH doesn't plug any holes on any other ports. If someone attacks your network through Telnet, which is port 23, SSH cannot protect against it, because SSH runs on a different port. Another example is Network File System (NFS), which is notorious for having security problems. If someone can mount the root directory via NFS, your machine could be compromised.

To show how to use SSH, let's set up a small network. On one network we have the `tigerlair.com` machines, which for this example include `sherekhan`, `tigger`, `litterbox`, and `hobbes`. Let's say the firewall is `sherekhan`, and for testing, we'll use the `litterbox`. Outside of our trusted network, we have `isp.com`, `work.com`, and `purdue.edu` on the Internet. Figure 1.1 shows our network diagram.

Anatomy of a network attack: Let's say an attacker decides to come in from their ISP account and they want access to `tigger.tigerlair.com`, our mail server. If `sherekhan.tigerlair.com` is misconfigured or Telnet traffic is allowed through, then the attacker has the ability to brute-force access to `tigger`. Now I'm really in trouble, because someone has gained access to my mail server and they're now using it to bounce spam (unwanted advertisements via email) from.

Now I need to secure it. If I want someone to get into my systems from the Internet, I would want to use SSH to allow people inside. If I allow other protocols for someone to access my systems, then I'm more susceptible to someone gaining root access through other means.

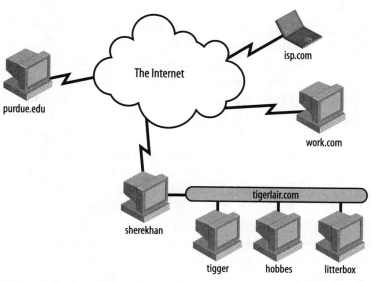

Figure 1.1 *Our network.*

If someone malicious gets access to root on your UNIX system, SSH provides no protection for you, because the intruder can replace SSH with his own version that will mail him clear text of everything you do. The SSH executables and private keys can now be bypassed or replaced. Make sure you plug any holes that may make your system easy to compromise before trusting any application completely. Also, SSH does not provide protection against Trojan horses or denial-of-service attacks (DoS). Table 1.2 shows what SSH doesn't protect against.

Table 1.2 *What SSH doesn't protect against*

Vulnerability	What it allows
NFS mounting	Mount filesystems over a network
Local attacks	Host compromises
Internet attacks	Host compromises
Denial of service	Disruption of services and accessibility

How SSH Works

SSH has two parts—a client and a server. The server is a *daemon*, which means it runs in the background without any type of constant administration, and it accepts connections into the system from the client. The client is the interface for the user.

The Server. The server consists of one file, the `sshd` program. This is usually placed in the `/usr/local/sbin` directory. The server provides the processing for remote connections, including public key authentication and key exchange, symmetric key encryption, and the unsecure connection itself. For SSH2, a `sftp-server` manages the secure file transfer connection.

The Client. The client consists of several different files. These files include `ssh`, which lets you run programs on a remote machine without logging in, remote copying (`scp`), and remote logons (`slogin`). SSH 2 now has a secure file transfer client (`sftp`) which is used for secure file transfer to replace the File Transfer Protocol (FTP). Because FTP is unsecure, SSH replaces it with its own client. In addition to using the `sftp` client, you also have to use the `sftp-server`. See Figure 1.2 on page 11 for an illustration of how the client/server connection works.

The "s" Commands Versus the "r" Commands

So now I can show you examples of how SSH provides you with the security that you need by comparing it to its unsecure predecessors, the Berkeley "r" commands. The Berkeley "r" commands and the SSH "s" commands share the same overall functionality; however, SSH provides improved security over the "r" commands.

The Berkeley "r" Commands

The Berkeley "r" commands[1] are an integral part of UNIX. Because UNIX is an open system, many people feel the need to secure their systems because of sensitive data. However, with the increasing paranoia and interest in network security, administrators and users are starting to realize the problems with using the Berkeley "r" commands.

---

1. Berkeley "r" commands are cleverly named, because the commands begin with the letter "r"—`rsp`, `rcp`, and `rlogin`.

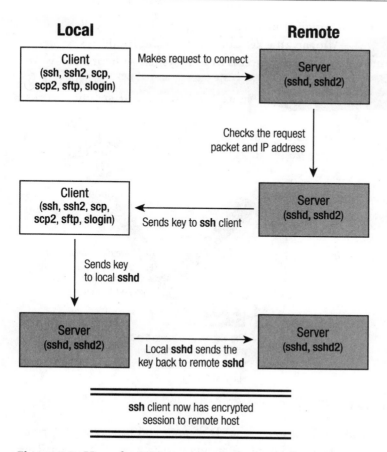

Figure 1.2 *How the SSH server and clients work.*

The "r" commands were originally developed as a security improvement over Telnet, making it so that you didn't have to type your password over the network in the clear (at that time it was a big win). The "r" services also provided authentication by hostname or IP address, which Telnet doesn't provide. The "r" commands authenticate by hostname and username, which made the Berkeley services a significant step in secure network connections.

Unfortunately, the hostname and IP address became an unreliable way to secure connections. Attackers began to use IP addresses that were already issued to someone else to bypass the "r" commands authentication scheme. This allows an attacker to send packets from his host and pretend to be you, but no packets are actually originating from your system, in what's called *IP spoofing*. Also, an attacker can take the valid IP address or username and use it to gain access to your system without a password. All someone has to do is reconfigure their machine to use your hostname or IP address. Figure 1.3 shows how IP spoofing works.

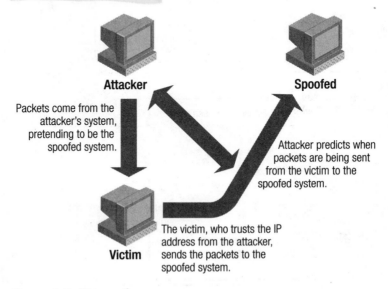

Attacker

Spoofed

Packets come from the attacker's system, pretending to be the spoofed system.

Attacker predicts when packets are being sent from the victim to the spoofed system.

The victim, who trusts the IP address from the attacker, sends the packets to the spoofed system.

Victim

Figure 1.3 *IP spoofing.*

Attackers can also use your DNS and send you wrong information from their DNS server pretending to be your DNS server. This is called *DNS spoofing*, which can also affect the "r" services authentication. SSH builds on what the "r" commands do, but with stronger authentication methods.

The Berkeley "r" commands refer to a family of files that can allow seamless remote access to another host. These commands include remote logon (`rlogin`), remote shell (`rsh`), and remote copy (`rcp`). Table 1.3 lists the currently available Berkeley services.

Three of these services have their own ports assigned to them. Check the `/etc/services` file on your system to check for the actual ports. The most common ports are port 512 for `rsh`, port 513 for `login`, and port 514 for `rexec`. The rest of the commands use various ports usually through the remote procedure calls (RPC services).

Table 1.3 *Currently available Berkeley services*

Command	What it does
rlogin	Remote login
rsh	Remote shell
rcp	Remote copy

Many of these client programs have daemons that control them, like the remote shell daemon `rshd`, the remote execution daemon `in.rexecd`, and the remote who command `in.rwhod`. Many of these daemons are run by the `inetd` superdaemon. Table 1.4 lists the Berkeley services daemons.

Table 1.4 *Berkeley services daemons*

Daemon	What it does
in.rlogind	Remote login
in.rshd	Remote shell
in.rexecd	Remote execute of a program or script
in.rwhod	Display who is logged on remote machines
rusersd	Display who is logged on remote machines

The Files

To understand how "r" command security holes occur, you need to have an understanding of the files themselves. The problem isn't the actual files—the problem is when they're misconfigured. And it doesn't take much to misconfigure these files and leave your system wide open.

hosts.equiv. This file contains hosts that have equivalent access to your host via the account name and hostname. This file applies system-wide to any account on the system and affects more users than the `.rhosts` file. The `hosts.equiv` file is located in the `/etc` directory.

.rhosts This file can be found in user directories such as `/home/me` and `/home/root`. It sets the user's preference to trusted hostnames, which overrides the system-wide file `/etc/hosts.equiv`.

The Dangers

What's so unsecure about the Berkeley "r" commands? The first thing to consider is that the traffic is not encrypted. This enables anyone with a packet sniffer to see exactly what you are typing, word for word.

The next thing to consider is that the Berkeley services authenticate based on IP address and the DNS name of the remote host. The authentication comes from the information in the `/etc/hosts.equiv` and `.rhosts`. In these files, you can have a variety of entries that authorize a user from various hosts. All of these files use the same basic format. You are also not vulnerable to IP source routing, which is when an attacker's host can disguise itself as a trusted host or client.

The format of the authentication files is the current hostname followed by the username. You can provide comments by preceding each line with a "#".

```
# This is where the user and the host go
hostname username
```

So, for example, you have a `/etc/hosts.equiv` file; the contents of the `litterbox` host on my private network may look something like this:

```
work.com russ
purdue.edu stephanie
isp.com brad
```

Now anyone who sets up their system to have the hostname `work.com`, `purdue.edu`, or `isp.com` through IP spoofing can pretend to have that hostname or IP address. All the attacker has to do is pick the correct username to gain access to your system.

In this case, the accounts `russ@work.com`, `stephanie@purdue.edu`, and `brad@isp.com` can log in to this machine, have remote shell access, and remote copy into this machine just by having those accounts. This is unsecure because

this information can easily be spoofed by an attacker. So, here's the
first thing the attacker may try:

```
nuke~# rlogin litterbox
Password:
```

In this case, root is enabled on the source system.[1] As you can
see, root is not enabled in the /etc/hosts.equiv file on the remote
system. However, if the intruder finds a way to obtain the
/etc/hosts.equiv remotely, he can have immediate user access to
the system. To make matters even worse, you can use wildcards in
the host or username fields. If you want to allow any host or any
user, just replace the username or the host with a "+".

The following is an example of how an authentication file can
be used with wildcards:

```
anyone.com +
+ stephanie
```

So now we trust anyone coming from the anyone.com hostname
or any user account stephanie. The user account stephanie can be
from any host on the Internet. Let's go back to our attacker: He's
got root access to his system and finds out that the user stephanie
on any system can get into your host. So, he creates an account
called stephanie on his host.

```
nuke~# adduser stephanie
nuke~# su - stephanie
% rlogin litterbox
Welcome to the litterbox.
stephanie~>
```

This means that the attacker now has access to your system and
can do whatever he wants to disguised as the user stephanie. He
can also try to gain access to other accounts on the system, even
root. If your machine doesn't have the latest patches installed, it's
possible for the attacker to exploit a security vulnerability in one or
more of the programs on your system to gain access to root.

The attacker doesn't even have to log on to the system to do
damage or access sensitive files:

---

1. From now on, any prompt you see with the "#" represents a prompt for the
   root account. Other prompts represent user accounts.

```
nuke~# su - stephanie
nuke~stephanie> rcp litterbox:/etc/passwd
```

If you haven't shadowed your passwords, the intruder now has a copy of your passwords and needs only to run one of the many available password crackers out there to get the clear text versions of the passwords.

Another dangerous thing to do:

```
+ root
```

In this scenario, the attacker doesn't even need to create a user account to break in. According to your `/etc/hosts.equiv`, you are trusting anyone with the root account on any host. With the growing popularity of operating systems like Linux and FreeBSD, anyone with a PC can have root access. All they have to do is test `rlogin` with the hostname.

```
nuke~# rlogin litterbox
Welcome to the litterbox.
litterbox:/#
```

Now the attacker has the root account. Maybe not the password, but that can be easily changed with minimal effort. If you have shadowed passwords, your attacker can obtain your passwords and crack them:

```
nuke~# rcp /etc/shadow
```

This is the most dangerous of all:

```
+ +
```

Now, anyone with any account from any host can access your system. What's really frightening is to see this on a production system in use today. Please, do not do this if you value your system or any information on it. Needless to say, all the examples above work with the "+ +" entry in the `/etc/host.equiv` file.

The "s" (secure) Commands

The SSH "s" commands were designed to be drop-in replacements for the "r" commands. The writers of SSH made the commands identical in use and nomenclature so they could be drop-in replacements for the Berkeley "r" commands. Most of the security features that are provided by the "s" commands are transparent to the user when SSH is installed and configured properly.

Unlike the Berkeley services, the SSH commands use only one daemon, `sshd`, and a single TCP port, 22. With only one daemon to manage the services, this makes SSH easy to monitor and configure. Table 1.5 lists all the client commands available with SSH.

Table 1.5 *The clients available in SSH*

Command	What it does
ssh	Secure remote shell
scp	Secure remote copying
slogin	Secure remote login
sftp	Secure file transfer[1]

With SSH, you are still vulnerable to misconfigured `.rhosts` and `/etc/hosts.equiv` files; however, you are not vulnerable to IP spoofing, IP source routing, or DNS spoofing. This is because the packets that can be viewed or changed through these types of network attacks are protected by encryption. Not only is the data itself protected, but the packet information, including sequence numbers and other critical information, is not spoofable.

Summary

SSH provides a UNIX administrator with the ability to run secure sessions through an untrusted network. Because of the way SSH is written, it is designed to be a drop-in replacement for remote connections like the Berkeley services, such as `rlogin`, `rsh`, and `rcp`.

SSH protects the session by using public key encryption to do user and host authentication. This gives much greater protection from network attacks than authentication by password and by hostname alone can offer. This includes protection from packet sniffers, which grab passwords and packet information. In addition to authenticating, SSH provides an encrypted session to protect against spoofed packets and password sniffing. This enables

---

1. The `sftp` client is only available with SSH2.

you to use your account over an unsecure channel and still not pass data in the clear.

Despite the benefits SSH provides, it does not protect against every type of attack. If your host is compromised through local or remote means, SSH is compromised as well. This includes NFS filesystem mounting, poor password choices, Trojan horses, and denial-of-service attacks.

Even though the Berkeley "r" commands provide a seamless means to access a remote system, they do not provide a strong form of authentication, and IP addresses and hostnames can easily be spoofed. SSH is not affected by spoofing because it establishes a connection to the remote system and encrypts the packets. However, SSH is still susceptible to the same .rhosts and /etc/hosts.equiv misconfiguration problems.

Installing Secure Shell on UNIX

In this chapter:

- Requirements

- Installation process

- Running both SSH1 and SSH2

- Testing the application

Now that you've had some background information on Secure Shell (SSH), you're ready to install SSH. Keep in mind that there are differences between configuring the client and the server. Also, you'll see some differences in where files are installed for Secure Shell 1 (SSH1) and Secure Shell 2 (SSH2), but more on that in upcoming chapters.

Which One Do I Install?

You probably want a straightforward answer, but it depends. SSH1 and SSH2 are different implementations of the same program, but they use different protocols. Therefore, they're not compatible.

The version of SSH to install depends on whether you already have SSH1 or SSH2 installed on the system you're connecting to, you're starting from scratch, or you're having systems connect to yours. If you're installing SSH from scratch and you know each system that is going to connect with SSH, then take your pick on which version.

If you're going to have other systems connect to you and you know the version they use, install that one. If you don't know which versions of SSH are connecting to you or that you're connecting to, install both. However, with the SSH2 currently in IETF draft, it is being pushed as the standard for SSH. Even if you run SSH1, you may want to install SSH2, because it is being used more as it increases in functionality. Table 2.1 shows which version you may want to install.

As you can see from this, SSH1 and SSH2 are not compatible. In order to have backward compatibility for SSH2, you need to install both SSH1 and SSH2.

Requirements

It's important to meet the requirements necessary to set up the software. Different operating systems have varied requirements for SSH, especially if you're going to be running on other non-UNIX operating systems, including Windows and Macintosh. Keep in mind that the requirements cover every version of UNIX that SSH runs on.

Table 2.1 *Which version of SSH to install*

What I know	Which SSH version to install
The system I'm connecting to runs SSH1	SSH1
The system I'm connecting to runs SSH2	SSH2
The system I'm connecting to runs SSH1 and SSH2	SSH1, SSH2
The systems connecting to me run SSH1	SSH1
The systems connecting to me run SSH2	SSH2
The systems connecting to me run SSH1 and SSH2	SSH1, SSH2
I'm not sure which version of SSH is connecting to me	SSH1, SSH2
I'm not sure which version of SSH I'm connecting to	SSH1, SSH2

The ingredients you need to set up the software are an ANSI C compiler, either cc or gcc (depending on which flavor you're using), and at least 400 to 500 kilobytes of disk space. The GNU compiler, gcc, is available for free and is included with some implementations of UNIX. If you are using gcc, make sure you have version 2.7.2.3 or higher.

To find out which version of gcc you have, type the following:

```
tigerlair:/home/stripes- gcc -v
gcc version 2.7.2.3
```

If you're also concerned about disk space, you can check with the df command:

```
tigerlair:/home/stripes- df -k
Filesystem  1K-blocks     Used    Avail Capacity  Mounted
/dev/hda1      127151    27634    89345    24%    /
/dev/hda2      127151     3219   113760     3%    /var
/dev/hda3      508655   352447   115516    75%    /home
procfs              4        4        0   100%    /proc
```

You can install and even run SSH as a user other than root; however, you won't be able to use Berkeley services rhosts authentication with SSH. As for memory, for each instance of SSH you create, SSH consumes 200 kilobytes of memory. If you plan on doing X forwarding, you'll want to have more memory available.

Getting SSH

Before installing SSH, you need to get a copy of the code. To get a copy of the code, you can either obtain it from the CD-ROM that comes with this book for U.S. distributions, or you can download it from the SSH download site. Also, you have the option of getting pre-compiled binaries and installing those instead.

Note   The official SSH download site is `ftp://ftp.cs.hut.fi/pub/ssh`

To Get the Source

When you get the source code to SSH, it will be in a gzipped tar file. The format to the file is `ssh-version.tar.gz`. For example, if you're getting SSH 2.0.12, the file you will get is `ssh-2.0.12.tar.gz`. Make sure you also get the file `ssh-version.tar.gz.sig`, which is the Pretty Good Privacy (PGP) signature to the code. The PGP signature makes sure no one has replaced the code with a Trojan horse or back door.

Note   PGP is commonly used for email and file encryption. PGP gained popularity for email encryption without having to worry about having your keys escrowed by any government.

To get the tar ball off the CD-ROM:[1]

```
# cp /cdrom/implementations/ssh-1.2.26.tar.gz
/usr/local/src
```

You can also download the code from `ftp.cs.hut.fi` in the `/pub/ssh` directory.

---

1. Depending on which version number of SSH you're getting, this file will vary but will be in the implementations directory on the CD-ROM. Also, where you copy the file to is up to you. `/usr/local/src` is used for example purposes, but is recommended.

To Get Pre-Compiled Binaries

For those of you who don't want to have any fun with the installation process, you can download pre-compiled binaries of SSH from several sites. Table 2.2 shows where you can get some of the available pre-compiled binaries.

Table 2.2 *Pre-compiled binaries and their locations*

Pre-compiled binary	Where to get it from
NetBSD package	`ftp://ftp.cdrom.com/.3/NetBSD/NetBSD-current/pkgsrc/security/ssh/`
Redhat RPMs	`ftp://ftp.replay.com/pub/replay/linux/redhat/i386/`
Stackguard[2]	`http://www.cse.ogi.edu/DISC/projects/immunix/StackGuard/ssh.html`

Installation Process

Installation should not be problematic—keep in mind, the key word is "should." I've had no problems on some systems and others give you weird compiling errors. This section covers a smooth installation, that is, one without any problems. If you are having problems, please see *"Troubleshooting Secure Shell"* on page 263. You may need to compile the code on your system. For either the code or pre-compiled binaries with PGP signatures available, you should check the integrity of the signature of the file. You can do this with the Pretty Good Privacy key and the signature file (usually noted by `ssh-version.tar.gz.sig`, as in `ssh-2.0.12.tar.gz.sig`). To check the integrity of the file, simply run PGP against the signature of the file. It displays as:

```
$ pgp ssh-2.0.12.tar.gz.sig
File has signature. Public key is required to check
signature.
File 'ssh-2.0.12.tar.gz.sig' has signature, but with no
text.
Please enter filename of material that signature applies
to: ssh-2.0.12.tar.gz
```

2. Stackguard prevents about buffer overflows and is available at
   `http://www.cse.ogi.edu/DISC/projects/immunix/StackGuard`.

Then you should find out if the file is the correct one or not. Do not use the file if the signature does not come up valid.

Note   In the United States, the PGP 2.6.2 will not check the signature, because of the limitations with RSAREF. You need to use a later version of PGP.

Compiling the code should be straightforward. When you run the configure script, it guesses information about your system's environment and sets files in SSH to know where they are. If you do need to set some switches, the switches are covered in detail later in this chapter. The basic steps for installation are:

1. `cd /usr/local/src`
2. `gzip -dc ssh-xx.xx.xx.tar.gz | tar -xvf -`
3. `cd ssh-xx.xx.xx`
4. `./configure`
5. `make`
6. `make install`

The `xx.xx.xx` should be replaced with the real version number (that is, 1.2.27 or 2.0.13).

This should be all you have to do for a vanilla install. The source code and configuration files are in a tar archive that has been GNU zipped (`gzip`). Unzip the tar file and unarchive. However, you may want to turn some options on, compile with RSAREF, or enable third-party security support for SecurID or proxies.

Note   Secure Shell can be unzipped and unarchived in any directory you want. A sources directory (`/usr/local/src`) may be a good place to store source code.

Installing SSH1

The first thing you want to run is the configure script:

```
# cd ssh-1.2.26
# ./configure
```

The configure script checks your host for its hardware, location of key files, compiler, and its operating system. The first part of the

configure script checks for the compiler and what the compiler
understands. This configure script was done on a Slackware Linux
system. If you turn on the quiet option, you will not see this output. Your output should look something like this:

```
# ./configure
creating cache ./config.cache
checking host system type... i386-unknown-linux 2.0.35
checking cached information... ok
checking for gcc... gcc
checking whether the C compiler (gcc ) works... yes
checking whether the C compiler (gcc ) is a cross-
compiler... no
checking whether we are using GNU C... yes
checking whether gcc accepts -g... yes
checking for POSIXized ISC... no
checking that the compiler works... yes
checking if the compiler understands -pipe... yes
checking whether to enable -Wall... no
checking return type of signal handlers... void
checking how to run the C preprocessor... gcc -pipe -E
```

The next thing the configure script checks for is some header
files and settings for variable sizes. These include ANSI header files
and the byte ordering, as well as the size of the int, both long and
short. Then it makes sure that it has checked the locations of the
ANSI C headers, which are necessary for compiling Secure Shell.
Here's what displays:

```
checking for ANSI C header files... yes
checking for size_t... yes
checking for uid_t in sys/types.h... yes
checking for off_t... yes
checking for mode_t... yes
checking for st_blksize in struct stat... yes
checking for working const... yes
checking for inline... inline
checking whether byte ordering is bigendian... no
checking size of long... 4
checking size of int... 4
checking size of short... 2
checking for termios.h... yes
checking for utmpx.h... no
checking whether utmpx have ut_syslen field... no
checking for ANSI C header files... (cached) yes
```

The next check is for the POSIX header files. These include
things like the utmp, the shadow passwords, and system clocks. In
addition, the networking header files for TCP/IP are included,
which are also crucial for compiling Secure Shell. It should like this:

```
checking for sys/wait.h that is POSIX.1 compatible... yes
checking for unistd.h... yes
checking for rusage.h... no
checking for sys/time.h... yes
checking for lastlog.h... no
checking for utmp.h... yes
checking for shadow.h... no
checking for sgtty.h... yes
checking for sys/select.h... yes
checking for sys/ioctl.h... yes
checking for machine/endian.h... yes
checking for paths.h... yes
checking for usersec.h... no
checking for utime.h... yes
checking for netinet/in_systm.h... yes
checking for netinet/in_system.h... no
checking for netinet/ip.h... yes
checking for netinet/tcp.h... yes
checking for ulimit.h... no
checking for sys/resource.h... yes
checking for login_cap.h... yes
checking whether time.h and sys/time.h may both be
included... yes
checking for dirent.h that defines DIR... yes
```

The next checks are for various system functions, in addition to
login and getting the statistics of the file modes and processes. Certain fields in utmp, such as ut_name and ut_host, are found. These
may vary as to where they are found on your system, because different UNIX operating systems have libraries and the functions stored
in different directories on different systems. It should display as:

```
checking for opendir in -ldir... no
checking whether stat file-mode macros are broken... no
checking whether sys/types.h defines makedev... yes
checking whether utmp have ut_pid field... no
checking whether utmp have ut_name field... yes
checking whether utmp have ut_id field... no
checking whether utmp have ut_host field... yes
checking whether utmp have ut_addr field... no
checking whether you have incompatible SIGINFO macro... no
```

```
checking for crypt in -lc... no
checking for crypt in -lcrypt... yes
checking for getspnam in -lsec... no
checking for get_process_stats in -lseq... no
checking for bcopy in -lbsd... no
checking for main in -lnsl... no
checking for socket in -lsocket... no
checking for getpwnam in -lsun... no
checking for openpty in -lbsd... no
checking for login in -lutil... yes
```

Listed below are various C functions that are system- and networking-specific. The umask and fchmod are used for setting file permissions. Some networking functions such as gethostname and socketpair are also checked here. Some of these may not be found on your system; however, they may not be critical to compiling or installing Secure Shell. Look for:

```
checking for vhangup... no
checking for setsid... yes
checking for gettimeofday... yes
checking for times... yes
checking for getrusage... yes
checking for ftruncate... yes
checking for revoke... yes
checking for makeutx... no
checking for strchr... yes
checking for memcpy... yes
checking for setlogin... yes
checking for openpty... yes
checking for _getpty... no
checking for clock... yes
checking for fchmod... yes
checking for ulimit... no
checking for gethostname... yes
checking for getdtablesize... yes
checking for umask... yes
checking for innetgr... yes
checking for initgroups... yes
checking for setpgrp... yes
checking for setpgid... yes
checking for daemon... yes
checking for waitpid... yes
checking for ttyslot... yes
checking for authenticate... no
checking for strerror... yes
checking for memmove... yes
```

```
checking for remove... yes
checking for random... yes
checking for putenv... yes
checking for crypt... yes
checking for socketpair... yes
```

Some options checked are related to the functionality of Secure Shell. This includes optimizing and various features like X and system-specific linking. Some executables such as passwd, perl5, and xauth are checked for in this listing. X functionality may be disabled by passing options to the configure script, which is discussed later in the chapter. It looks like:

```
checking whether ln -s works... yes
checking for a BSD compatible install... /usr/bin/install -c
checking for ar... ar
checking for ranlib... ranlib
checking for makedepend... makedepend
checking for X... libraries /usr/X11R6/lib, headers /usr/X11R6/include
checking for dnet_ntoa in -ldnet... no
checking for dnet_ntoa in -ldnet_stub... no
checking for gethostbyname... yes
checking for connect... yes
checking for remove... (cached) yes
checking for shmat... yes
checking for IceConnectionNumber in -lICE... yes
checking for passwd... /usr/bin/passwd
checking for xauth... /usr/X11R6/bin/xauth
checking for X11 unix domain socket directory... /tmp/.X11-unix
checking for perl5... /usr/bin/perl5
checking for getpseudotty... no
checking for pseudo ttys... bsd-style ptys
```

System files and their location are important in the installation and configuration process. Whether or not your system uses shadow passwords, the location of the login files (/etc/default/login, utmp, wtmp, and lastlog) and the mail spool are system-specific, but knowledge of these files is important to the Secure Shell client and daemon. Here's what displays:

```
checking for /etc/default/login... no
checking for shadow passwords... no
checking location of mail spool files... /var/mail
checking location of utmp... /var/run/utmp
checking location of wtmp... /var/log/wtmp
```

```
checking location of lastlog... /var/log/lastlog
checking whether /var/log/lastlog is a directory... no
```

Encryption is one of the main reasons for running Secure Shell. You can define which ciphers to include and you can even turn off encryption with the options listed later in the chapter, but *don't*. Running SSH without encryption is not recommended unless you are testing the connection. If you decide to turn off encryption, you'll see:

```
checking whether to include the IDEA encryption algorithm... yes
checking whether to include the Blowfish encryption algorithm... yes
checking whether to include the DES encryption algorithm... no
checking whether to include the ARCFOUR encryption algorithm... no
checking whether to include the none encryption algorithm... no
```

The next set of options decides which programs SSH is going to use for logging in to remote systems, which include `login` or `rsh`, programs that are used for logging in to remote systems. Additionally, configure checks the location of `rsh`. The configure script also checks for `remsh` and `resh`, which are remote execution programs like `rsh`. It looks like:

```
checking whether to use login... no
checking whether to use rsh... yes
checking for remsh... no
checking for resh... no
checking for rsh... /usr/bin/rsh
```

The location of the system configuration files and paths are important. The `/etc` directory is the default location for the configuration files for Secure Shell, as well as the networking configuration and other system files. SSH has a "feature" that allows only people in the `nologin.allow` file to log in via `ssh` even if the `nologin` file exists (for administration purposes and the like). Look for:

```
checking default path... use system default
checking etcdir... /etc
checking whether to use nologin.allow file to override
nologin... no
```

The next checks are for third-party support. This includes SecurID, which is a hardware password-challenge device about the size of a credit card; TIS authentication server and Kerberos, each of which has a separate authentication mechanism; TCP wrappers, which allow or deny access to TCP services based on the rules files; and SOCKS, which is an application proxy. You will see:

```
checking whether to support SecurID... no
checking whether to support TIS authentication server... no
checking whether to use Kerberos... no
checking whether to enable passing the Kerberos TGT... no
checking whether to use libwrap... no
checking whether to support SOCKS... no
checking whether to support SOCKS5... no
checking whether to support SOCKS4... no
```

RSAREF is an encryption toolkit that contains the RSA algorithm as well as other ciphers. To be legal in the United States, you have two options: compile Secure Shell with RSAREF or purchase F-Secure SSH from Datafellows. However, you can compile it without RSAREF, but this creates problems if you're trying to keep your system kosher. You can get the RSAREF from `http://www.spinnaker.com/crypt/rsaref/`. Look for:

```
checking whether to use rsaref... yes
checking whether to allow group writeability... no
```

You can use SSH to forward specific ports to other computers. If you want to send them to local privileged ports, you need to have Secure Shell running as root. You can forward a specific port to any destination port. You can disable forwarding from both the server and client, or only one of the two. The client and server forwarding options define everything except the forwarding of X traffic, which is defined in a separate option. The following displays:

```
checking whether to disable forwardings in server... no
checking whether to disable forwardings in client... no
checking whether to disable X11 forwarding in server... no
checking whether to disable X11 forwarding in client... no
```

You can set specific Secure Shell options in the configure script as well. SSH is installed as a root program, but is run from a user account. You can disable running Secure Shell as root and change the settings for the Secure Copy, `scp`, statistics. You can also define where the Secure Shell daemon process ID file is placed as well. You'll see:

```
checking whether to install ssh as suid root... yes
checking whether to enable TCP_NODELAY... yes
checking whether to enable SO_LINGER... no
checking whether to include scp statistics at all... yes
checking whether to enable scp statistics... yes
checking whether to enable scp statistics for all files... yes
checking where to put sshd.pid... /var/run
```

Files are created after the configuration is set, including updating `config.cache`, which confirms whether or not a configuration setting has been checked. Also, several other files are created: the `Makefile`, the man pages (`sshd.9`, `ssh.1`, and `make-ssh-known-hosts.1`), the `zlib Makefile`, and `config.h`. The `Makefile` is the most critical because that's what controls the compilation and installation. Look for:

```
updating cache ./config.cache
creating ./config.status
creating Makefile
creating sshd.8
creating ssh.1
creating make-ssh-known-hosts.1
creating zlib-1.0.4/Makefile
creating config.h
```

A modified version of GNU MP—a portable C library for arbitrary precision arithmetic on integers, rational numbers, and floating-point numbers—is included with the Secure Shell distribution. This library is used for a set of arithmetic functions optimized to be as fast as possible. This includes the ASM code, which links some of the functions to assembly code—thus increasing the speed of the computations.

Many of these messages resemble what happens in the checks for the Secure Shell application itself, so I won't include them. You can see here, though, that the asm code is checked to make sure everything is there. This can be bypassed in the options. It looks like:

```
configuring in gmp-2.0.2-ssh-2
running /bin/sh ./configure --cache-file=../.config.cache --srcdir=.
loading cache ../.config.cache
checking for a BSD compatible install... (cached) /usr/bin/install -c
checking whether build environment is sane... yes
checking whether make sets ${MAKE}... yes
..................
```

```
checking asm code... ok
checking asm links... done
checking asm sources... done
checking asm objects... done
checking asm syntax... BSD_SYNTAX
checking asm syntax header... ../../mpn/x86/syntax.h
checking for gmp-mparam.h... ../../mpn/generic/gmp-mparam.h
checking other objs... done
checking other sources... done
checking other links... done
checking links to mpz sources in mpbsd... done
```

After the GNU MP configuration, the config.cache is updated, and additional Makefiles are created. This enables the main Makefile to run the compiler to install the other libraries that are included. You'll see:

```
updating cache ../../config.cache
creating ./config.status
creating Makefile
creating demos/Makefile
creating mpbsd/Makefile
creating mpf/Makefile
creating mpf/tests/Makefile
creating mpn/Makefile
creating mpn/tests/Makefile
creating mpq/Makefile
creating mpq/tests/Makefile
creating mpz/Makefile
creating mpz/tests/Makefile
```

This checks for the system defaults. However, you can add compiling options if you'd like. The configure script will also generate a Makefile and the configuration files, including config.cache and config.status. If you want to keep several different configurations, you'll want to save these files in a separate directory with different names so that you know what they are and they don't accidentally get overwritten on a new configure of Secure Shell.

Setting the Configure Options

The usage for configure looks like this:

```
# ./configure options host
```

All options begin with a double dash (--). These options can set output type or redirect it, set directories and filenames, set the host type, or enable certain packages and features such as Kerberos or TCP Wrappers. This section goes over the general options; more specific options are covered a bit later. All of these options should look very similar to the "Checking" descriptions listed earlier in the chapter.

These options do not affect the results of the `configure` script. They display certain version numbers or define where the output goes or the type of output. These can help with debugging, figuring out compatibility issues, and getting some basic help and usage information. Table 2.3 shows the verbosity options.

Table 2.3 *Verbosity options for configure script*

Option	What it does
`--cache-file=FILE`	Puts the results in filename FILE, defaults to config.cache
`--help`	Prints a list of options and configure script usage
`--no-create`	No output files created, more to see what would happen
`--quiet, --silent`	Will not print the messages that show what configure is checking for
`--version`	Shows autoconf version that generated configure (helpful for debugging)

The directory and filename options can set where the executables are, install certain files like program executables and system-dependent files in specified directories, define locations of C include and object files, the location of man pages, and X include and library files. You can also configure your program names to have a suffix prepended or appended to the end of the filename. Table 2.4 on page 34 shows filename and directory options for the configure script.

Table 2.4 *Filename and directory options for configure script*

Option	Directory and filenames that can be set
`--prefix=PREFIX`	Set `PREFIX` directory for installing system-independent files
`--exec-prefix=EPREFIX`	Set `EPREFIX` directory for installing system-dependent files
`--bindir=DIR`	Define the location of user executables in `DIR` (e.g. `ls`, `cd`)
`--sbindir=DIR`	Define the system admin executables in `DIR` (e.g. `/sbin`, `/usr/local/sbin`)
`--libexecdir=DIR`	Install the program executables in the `DIR` directory
`--datadir=DIR`	Set `DIR` directory for read-only architecture-independent data
`--sysconfdir=DIR`	The system configuration files go in this `DIR` directory
`--sharedstatedir=DIR`	Set modifiable system-independent data in the `DIR` directory
`--localstatedir=DIR`	Set the modifiable system-dependent data in the `DIR` directory
`--libdir=DIR`	Location of the object code libraries in `DIR` directory
`--includedir=DIR`	Location of the C header files in `DIR` directory
`--oldincludedir=DIR`	Location of the C header files for non-`gcc` in `DIR` directory
`--infodir=DIR`	Location of the info documentation in `DIR` directory
`--mandir=DIR`	Location of the man documentation in `DIR` directory

Table 2.4 *Filename and directory options for configure script (cont'd)*

Option	Directory and filenames that can be set
`--srcdir=DIR`	Find the sources in `DIR` directory
`--program-prefix=PREFIX`	Add `PREFIX` to installed program names (e.g. `fw-`)
`--program-suffix=SUFFIX`	Append `SUFFIX` to installed program names (e.g. `exe`)
`--program-transform-name=SCRIPT`	Run `sed` script on installed program names
`--x-includes=DIR`	X include files are in `DIR` directory
`--x-libraries=DIR`	X library files are in `DIR` directory

The three options `BUILD`, `HOST`, and `TARGET` define which host gets configured for Secure Shell. The host is usually guessed by the configure script, so you may simply let the script do that. Usually it can figure this out; if not, use one of the options below to define your host. Table 2.5 shows host options for the configure script.

Table 2.5 *Host options for configure script*

Option	Setting the host type
`--build=BUILD`	Configure for building on `BUILD`, `BUILD = HOST`
`--host=HOST`	Configure for `HOST`, which is usually guessed by `configure` script
`--target=TARGET`	Configure for `TARGET`, `TARGET = HOST`

The next set of options define which type of features and packages get compiled into your build of Secure Shell. These options begin with `--enable` or `--disable` for a feature such as SUID bits and assembly language. The `--with` or `--without` is used for most packages including ciphers, SecurID support, and TCP wrappers. For the ARG variable, you can use yes or no, depending on whether or not you want to turn on or off a specific option. Table 2.6 shows syntax for enabling or including features and packages for the configure script.

Table 2.6 *Syntax for enabling or including features and packages for configure script*

Setting a feature or package	What it does
`--disable-FEATURE`	Does not use `FEATURE`, the same as `--enable-FEATURE=no`
`--enable-FEATURE[=ARG]`	Includes this `FEATURE`, where `ARG=yes`
`--with-PACKAGE[=ARG]`	Uses this `PACKAGE`, where `ARG=yes`
`--without-PACKAGE`	Does not use this `PACKAGE`, the same as `--with-PACKAGE=no`
`--enable-deprecated-linux-pw-encrypt`	Enables using of deprecated linux `pw_encrypt` function.
`--enable-warnings`	Enables `-Wall` if using `gcc`, turns on compiling warnings

Certain ciphers can be set as well. The default ciphers are IDEA, Blowfish, and Triple DES. You can enable single DES and arcfour, but neither are recommended, because they are not strong enough ciphers and are easily cracked. It is also NOT recommended to include `--with-none`, because that means that you can send packets over a network or the Internet unsecurely. See Table 2.7 for cipher options for the configure script.

You can enable or disable certain login features to Secure Shell. You can define the default path that will be passed to the user's shell at login, and you can enable `login -f` to complete the login connection. This lets a user into a remote account without having to specify a password because the proper authentication has already been done. You can also define Secure Shell not to use `rsh` for any reason, and I recommend that you do so if you want to

Table 2.7 *Cipher options for configure script*

Option	Ciphers included or not included
`--with-idea`	Use IDEA (default)
`--without-idea`	Don't use IDEA: avoids patent problems in commercial use
`--with-blowfish`	Include blowfish (default)
`--without-blowfish`	Don't include blowfish
`--with-des`	Include DES support
`--without-des`	Don't allow DES (default)
`--with-arcfour`	Include arcfour
`--without-arcfour`	Don't include arcfour (default)
`--with-none`	Include support for unencrypted connections
`--without-none`	Don't allow unencrypted connections (default)
`--with-rsaref=PATH`	Use RSAREF (try to avoid patent problems in U.S.)
`--without-rsaref`	Use normal RSA routines (default)

have completely secure connections. Otherwise, if SSH cannot connect for some reason, SSH falls back and connects via `rsh`. Table 2.8 shows login options for the configure script.

Table 2.8 *Login options for configure script*

Option	Login specification
`--with-login[=PATH]`	Use `login -f` to finish login connections
`--with-rsh=PATH`	Specify where to find `rsh`
`--without-rsh`	Do not use `rsh` under any conditions
`--with-path=PATH`	Default path passed to user shell by `sshd`

You can define where the Secure Shell system files go. The
default is the `/etc` directory; however, you can define another
directory if you feel more comfortable with that. You can also
define whether or not to use the SSH "feature" of the
`nologin.allow` file. Table 2.9 shows system file options for the configure script.

Table 2.9 *System file options for configure script*

Option	System files
`--with-etcdir=PATH`	Directory containing `ssh` system files (default `/etc`)
`--with-nologin-allow[=PATH]`	If a `nologin.allow` override should be used (default `/etc/nologin.allow`)

You can enable support for third-party authentication or applications with options, including support for SecurID cards, TIS
authentication servers, Kerberos and Kerberos tickets, TCP wrappers, and SOCKS proxy. With additional authentication through
Kerberos, SecurID, or TIS, you enable support for your current
applications that already use these. Sockifying Secure Shell enables
you to use Secure Shell through the SOCKS firewall proxy. See
Table 2.10 for third-party support options for the configure script.

Table 2.10 *Third-party support options for configure script*

Option	Third-party support
`--with-securid[=PATH]`	Enable support for Security Dynamics SecurID card
`--with-tis[=DIR]`	Enable support for TIS authentication server
`--with-kerberos5=[KRB_PREFIX]`	Compile in Kerberos5 support
`--enable-kerberos-tgt-passing`	Pass Kerberos ticket-granting-ticket
`--with-libwrap[=PATH]`	Compile in libwrap (tcp_wrappers) support

Table 2.10 *Third-party support options for configure script (cont'd)*

Option	Third-party support
`--with-socks`	Compile with SOCKS firewall traversal support
`--with-socks5[=PATH]`	Compile with SOCKS5 firewall traversal support
`--with-socks4[=PATH]`	Compile with SOCKS4 firewall traversal support

Special options in Secure Shell can be set, including port forwarding for both the client and the server, so that you can forward certain ports through the Secure Shell application, such as POP, HTTP, and Telnet. You can also disable or enable Secure Shell to run as SUID root, or even turn off the assembly language optimizations that are run from GNU MP. The `--disable-asm` option can fix a compilation problem in the GNU MP libraries. Table 2.11 shows special options for Secure Shell in the configure script.

Table 2.11 *Special options for Secure Shell in configure script*

Option	What it does
`--enable-group-writeability`	Turns on group writability
`--disable-server-port-forwardings`	Disables all port forwardings in the server
`--disable-client-port-forwardings`	Disables all port forwardings in the client
`--enable-suid-ssh`	Installs `ssh` as suid root
`--disable-suid-ssh`	Installs `ssh` without suid bit
`--disable-tcp-nodelay`	Disables `TCP_NODELAY` socket option
`--enable-so-linger`	Enables setting `SO_LINGER` socket option
`--without-scp-stats`	Turns off the `scp` statistics

Table 2.11 *Special options for Secure Shell in configure script (cont'd)*

Option	What it does
`--disable-scp-stats`	Disables `scp` statistics display
`--disable-all-scp-stats`	Disables all files `scp` statistics display
`--disable-asm`	Disables assembly language optimizations.

X settings are defined separately from the other settings. Port forwarding for X is done with a different set of options than port forwarding for TCP ports. You can even tell Secure Shell that you don't want to run any X through Secure Shell. However, if you are going to be using X over a remote connection, you'll want to run it through an encrypted connection like Secure Shell. Table 2.12 shows X settings for the configure script.

Table 2.12 *X settings for configure script*

Option	X settings
`--without-x`	without X11 support
`--with-x`	use the X Window System
`--disable-server-x11-forwarding`	Disable X11 forwarding in server
`--disable-client-x11-forwarding`	Disable X11 forwarding in client

After configure is run without any problems, the `Makefile` is created from the `Makefile.in`. The `Makefile` is large, and you have lots of variables to play with. However, from a non-programmer standpoint, it's necessary to understand which options the `make` command takes.

Even though this is not a book on Makefiles, you should be aware of some key variables. You can define which compiler to use, which is usually `gcc` or `cc`, or you may want to define the location of the compiler (for example, `/usr/local/bin/gcc`). If your compiler does weird things or needs special variables, you can also define specific flags to the compiler (for creating objects or executables, for instance) or the linker. Table 2.13 shows compiler settings for the Makefile.

Table 2.13 *Compiler settings for the Makefile*

Compiler setting	What it does
CC=compiler	specifies name (and sometimes location) of C compiler (default: gcc or cc)
CFLAGS=flags	specifies flags to C compiler (default: -0 -g or just -0)
PERL=PATH	location of Perl program
X_EXTRA_LIBS	Extra X libraries you may want to include
LDFLAGS=flags	specifies flags to linker, default: none, and system-dependent

According to the next step, you run make without any options. This creates the object files and then the executables. It displays as:

```
# make
gcc -pipe -c -I. -I./gmp-2.0.2-ssh-2 -I./zlib-1.0.4 -
DHAVE_CONFIG_H  -DHOST_KEY_FILE=\"/etc/ssh_host_key\" -
DHOST_CONFIG_FILE=\"/etc/ssh_config\" -
DSERVER_CONFIG_FILE=\"/etc/sshd_config\" -
DSSH_PROGRAM=\"/usr/local/bin/ssh1\" -DETCDIR=\"/etc\" -
DPIDDIR=\"/var/run\" -DSSH_BINDIR=\"/usr/local/bin\" -
DTIS_MAP_FILE=\"/etc/sshd_tis.map\" -g -02 -
I/usr/X11R6/include ssh.c
gcc -pipe -c -I. -I./gmp-2.0.2-ssh-2 -I./zlib-1.0.4 -
DHAVE_CONFIG_H  -DHOST_KEY_FILE=\"/etc/ssh_host_key\" -
DHOST_CONFIG_FILE=\"/etc/ssh_config\" -
DSERVER_CONFIG_FILE=\"/etc/sshd_config\" -
DSSH_PROGRAM=\"/usr/local/bin/ssh1\" -DETCDIR=\"/etc\" -
DPIDDIR=\"/var/run\" -DSSH_BINDIR=\"/usr/local/bin\" -
DTIS_MAP_FILE=\"/etc/sshd_tis.map\" -g -02 -
I/usr/X11R6/include sshconnect.c
gcc -pipe -c -I. -I./gmp-2.0.2-ssh-2 -I./zlib-1.0.4 -
DHAVE_CONFIG_H  -DHOST_KEY_FILE=\"/etc/ssh_host_key\" -
DHOST_CONFIG_FILE=\"/etc/ssh_config\" -
DSERVER_CONFIG_FILE=\"/etc/sshd_config\" -
DSSH_PROGRAM=\"/usr/local/bin/ssh1\" -DETCDIR=\"/etc\" -
DPIDDIR=\"/var/run\" -DSSH_BINDIR=\"/usr/local/bin\" -
```

```
DTIS_MAP_FILE=\"/etc/sshd_tis.map\" -g -O2 -
I/usr/X11R6/include log-client.c
gcc -pipe -c -I. -I./gmp-2.0.2-ssh-2 -I./zlib-1.0.4 -
DHAVE_CONFIG_H  -DHOST_KEY_FILE=\"/etc/ssh_host_key\" -
DHOST_CONFIG_FILE=\"/etc/ssh_config\" -
DSERVER_CONFIG_FILE=\"/etc/sshd_config\" -
DSSH_PROGRAM=\"/usr/local/bin/ssh1\" -DETCDIR=\"/etc\" -
DPIDDIR=\"/var/run\" -DSSH_BINDIR=\"/usr/local/bin\" -
DTIS_MAP_FILE=\"/etc/sshd_tis.map\" -g -O2 -
I/usr/X11R6/include readconf.c
gcc -pipe -c -I. -I./gmp-2.0.2-ssh-2 -I./zlib-1.0.4 -
DHAVE_CONFIG_H  -DHOST_KEY_FILE=\"/etc/ssh_host_key\" -
DHOST_CONFIG_FILE=\"/etc/ssh_config\" -
DSERVER_CONFIG_FILE=\"/etc/sshd_config\" -
DSSH_PROGRAM=\"/usr/local/bin/ssh1\" -DETCDIR=\"/etc\" -
DPIDDIR=\"/var/run\" -DSSH_BINDIR=\"/usr/local/bin\" -
DTIS_MAP_FILE=\"/etc/sshd_tis.map\" -g -O2 -
I/usr/X11R6/include hostfile.c
gcc -pipe -c -I. -I./gmp-2.0.2-ssh-2 -I./zlib-1.0.4 -
DHAVE_CONFIG_H  -DHOST_KEY_FILE=\"/etc/ssh_host_key\" -
DHOST_CONFIG_FILE=\"/etc/ssh_config\" -
DSERVER_CONFIG_FILE=\"/etc/sshd_config\" -
DSSH_PROGRAM=\"/usr/local/bin/ssh1\" -DETCDIR=\"/etc\" -
DPIDDIR=\"/var/run\" -DSSH_BINDIR=\"/usr/local/bin\" -
DTIS_MAP_FILE=\"/etc/sshd_tis.map\" -g -O2 -
I/usr/X11R6/include readpass.c
gcc -pipe -c -I. -I./gmp-2.0.2-ssh-2 -I./zlib-1.0.4 -
DHAVE_CONFIG_H  -DHOST_KEY_FILE=\"/etc/ssh_host_key\" -
DHOST_CONFIG_FILE=\"/etc/ssh_config\" -
DSERVER_CONFIG_FILE=\"/etc/sshd_config\" -
DSSH_PROGRAM=\"/usr/local/bin/ssh1\" -DETCDIR=\"/etc\" -
DPIDDIR=\"/var/run\" -DSSH_BINDIR=\"/usr/local/bin\" -
DTIS_MAP_FILE=\"/etc/sshd_tis.map\" -g -O2 -
I/usr/X11R6/include tildexpand.c
.........
sed "s#&PERL&#/usr/bin/perl5#" <./make-ssh-known-hosts.pl
>make-ssh-known-hosts
chmod +x make-ssh-known-hosts
gcc -pipe -c -I. -I./gmp-2.0.2-ssh-2 -I./zlib-1.0.4 -
DHAVE_CONFIG_H  -DHOST_KEY_FILE=\"/etc/ssh_host_key\" -
DHOST_CONFIG_FILE=\"/etc/ssh_config\" -
DSERVER_CONFIG_FILE=\"/etc/sshd_config\" -
DSSH_PROGRAM=\"/usr/local/bin/ssh1\" -DETCDIR=\"/etc\" -
DPIDDIR=\"/var/run\" -DSSH_BINDIR=\"/usr/local/bin\" -
DTIS_MAP_FILE=\"/etc/sshd_tis.map\" -g -O2 -
I/usr/X11R6/include ssh-askpass.c
rm -f ssh-askpass
gcc -pipe  -o ssh-askpass ssh-askpass.o xmalloc.o -
```

```
L/usr/X11R6/lib -lSM -lICE -lX11  -lcrypt -L/usr/local/lib
-lutil
```

After the program compiles properly and creates the executables, you can run them in the /usr/local/src/ssh-1.2.26 directory. However, you probably want to put them in a directory that users have a PATH defined for and have the proper permissions set on the executables; to do that, run make with the install option.

First, you'll want to verify things with the -n option:

```
# make -n install
```

If everything looks good, install SSH:

```
# make install
```

After you have created the executables, make install removes any old version of Secure Shell (any Secure Shell executable that has the appendage .old as in ssh1.old), sets the permissions for ssh and ssh1 to 755, and moves older versions of Secure Shell (usually SSH1) to ssh1.old. When it does install Secure Shell, the owner is root. This also creates the necessary directories, generates the host key, and installs the configuration files and man pages. You'll see:

```
install: $(PROGRAMS) make-dirs generate-host-key install-
configs
-rm -f $(install_prefix)$(bindir)/ssh1.old
-chmod 755 $(install_prefix)$(bindir)/ssh1
-chmod 755 $(install_prefix)$(bindir)/ssh
-mv $(install_prefix)$(bindir)/ssh1
$(install_prefix)$(bindir)/ssh1.old
$(INSTALL_PROGRAM) -o root -m $(SSH_INSTALL_MODE) ssh
```

The Makefile is very powerful and it allows you to do other things, such as generate the proposed RFC for Secure Shell with make RFC. This runs the nroff and sed commands, text formatting applications that take the text and format it properly. This snippet of the Makefile shows you what is actually done. Notice that none of the code itself is touched or compiled.

```
RFC: RFC.nroff rfc-pg
tbl $(srcdir)/RFC.nroff | nroff -ms | sed
's/FORMFEED\[Page/
[Page/' | ./rfc-pg -n5 >RFC
```

You can use the Makefile to create each program separately. If you simply want to create sshd, ssh, ssh-keygen, ssh-agent, ssh-add, or scp; all you have to do is tell the Makefile which one you want. For example, if you want to create only the daemon, you would type make sshd. The portion of the Makefile below shows how each program is compiled separately and the compiler options it takes:

```
sshd: $(SSHD_OBJS) $(GMPDEP) $(RSAREFDEP) $(ZLIBDEP)
 -rm -f sshd
 $(CC) $(LDFLAGS) -o sshd $(SSHD_OBJS) \
       $(GMPLIBS) $(ZLIBLIBS) $(WRAPLIBS) $(LIBS) \
       $(KERBEROS_LIBS)

ssh: $(SSH_OBJS) $(GMPDEP) $(RSAREFDEP) $(ZLIBDEP)
 -rm -f ssh
 $(CC) $(LDFLAGS) -o ssh $(SSH_OBJS) \
       $(GMPLIBS) $(ZLIBLIBS) $(WRAPLIBS) $(LIBS) \
       $(KERBEROS_LIBS)

ssh-keygen: $(KEYGEN_OBJS) $(GMPDEP) $(RSAREFDEP)
 -rm -f ssh-keygen
 $(CC) $(LDFLAGS) -o ssh-keygen $(KEYGEN_OBJS) $(GMPLIBS) \
       $(LIBS)

ssh-agent: $(AGENT_OBJS) $(GMPDEP) $(RSAREFDEP)
 -rm -f ssh-agent
 $(CC) $(LDFLAGS) -o ssh-agent $(AGENT_OBJS) $(GMPLIBS) \
       $(LIBS) $(KERBEROS_LIBS)

ssh-add: $(ADD_OBJS) $(GMPDEP) $(RSAREFDEP)
 -rm -f ssh-add
 $(CC) $(LDFLAGS) -o ssh-add $(ADD_OBJS) $(GMPLIBS) $(LIBS)

scp: $(SCP_OBJS) $(LIBOBJS) $(RSAREFDEP)
 -rm -f scp
 $(CC) $(LDFLAGS) -o scp $(SCP_OBJS) $(LIBOBJS) $(LIBS)

ssh-askpass: $(SSH_ASKPASS_OBJS)
 -rm -f ssh-askpass
 $(CC) $(LDFLAGS) -o ssh-askpass $(SSH_ASKPASS_OBJS) \
       $(XLIBS)
```

```
make-ssh-known-hosts: make-ssh-known-hosts.pl
 -rm -f make-ssh-known-hosts
 sed "s#&PERL&#$(PERL)#" \
<$(srcdir)/make-ssh-known-hosts.pl >make-ssh-known-hosts
 chmod +x make-ssh-known-hosts
```

If you want, you can create your own host key separately. Your host key is a 1024-bit RSA key that SSH uses to recognize your host. This file is stored in the /etc/ssh_host_key and is created during the installation, so unless you're using the executables from the temporary directory, you shouldn't have to run this separately. If you already have a host key, it will not be re-created. You'll see:

```
generate-host-key:
   -@if test -f $(install_prefix)$(HOST_KEY_FILE); \
        then echo "You already have a host key in
$(install_prefix)$(HOST_KEY_FILE)."; \
    else \
       umask 022; echo "Generating 1024 bit host key."; \
       ./ssh-keygen -b 1024 -f
$(install_prefix)$(HOST_KEY_FILE) -N ''; \
    fi
```

During the installation, the necessary directories are created. It also checks to see if the directory exists first; if it is found, the script skips it and checks the next directory. If you want, you can run this yourself without creating any of the program or configuration files. This includes the directories for the man pages as well as the configurations. It displays as:

```
make-dirs:
   -umask 022; if test '!' -d $(install_prefix)$(prefix); then \
    mkdir $(install_prefix)$(prefix); fi; \
   if test '!' -d $(install_prefix)$(exec_prefix); then \
    mkdir $(install_prefix)$(exec_prefix); fi; \
   if test '!' -d $(install_prefix)$(etcdir); then \
    mkdir $(install_prefix)$(etcdir); fi; \
   if test '!' -d $(install_prefix)$(bindir); then \
    mkdir $(install_prefix)$(bindir); fi; \
   if test '!' -d $(install_prefix)$(sbindir); then \
    mkdir $(install_prefix)$(sbindir); fi; \
   if test '!' -d $(install_prefix)$(mandir); then \
    mkdir $(install_prefix)$(mandir); fi; \
   if test '!' -d $(install_prefix)$(man1dir); then \
    mkdir $(install_prefix)$(man1dir); fi; \
   if test '!' -d $(install_prefix)$(man8dir); then \
    mkdir $(install_prefix)$(man8dir); fi
```

You can install the configuration files as well. First, you want to create the configuration directories before installing the files. Or, you can use the `install-configs` option to re-install your configuration files. Look for:

```
install-configs:
    -if test '!' -f $(install_prefix)$(HOST_CONFIG_FILE);
then \
      $(INSTALL_DATA) -m 0644 $(srcdir)/host_config.sample \
       $(install_prefix)$(HOST_CONFIG_FILE); fi
    -if test '!' -f $(install_prefix)$(SERVER_CONFIG_FILE);
then \
      cat $(srcdir)/server_config.sample | \
      sed "s#_ETCDIR_#$(etcdir)#g" >/tmp/ssh_inst.$$$$; \
      $(INSTALL_DATA) -m 0644 /tmp/ssh_inst.$$$$ \
       $(install_prefix)$(SERVER_CONFIG_FILE); \
      rm -f /tmp/ssh_inst.$$$$; fi
```

If you need to uninstall the executables, you can run `make uninstall`. This removes any installed files, including the configuration files and man pages from your system. This is not what you want to do if you just want to get rid of your old object and configuration files. You'll see:

```
uninstall:
    for p in ssh $(NORMAL_PROGRAMS) $(X_PROGRAMS) $(OTHER_PROGRAMS)
$(SCRIPT_PROGRAMS); do \
      rm -f $(install_prefix)$(bindir)/$$p; \
      rm -f $(install_prefix)$(bindir)/$$p.old; \
      rm -f $(install_prefix)$(bindir)/$${p}1; \
      rm -f $(install_prefix)$(bindir)/$${p}1.old; \
      rm -f $(install_prefix)$(bindir)/`echo $$p | sed '$(transform)'`; \
    done
    for p in $(SBIN_PROGRAMS); do \
      rm -f $(install_prefix)$(sbindir)/$$p; \
      rm -f $(install_prefix)$(sbindir)/$$p.old; \
      rm -f $(install_prefix)$(sbindir)/$${p}1; \
      rm -f $(install_prefix)$(sbindir)/$${p}1.old; \
      rm -f $(install_prefix)$(sbindir)/`echo $$p | sed '$(transform)'`; \
    done
    rm -f $(install_prefix)$(bindir)/slogin
    rm -f $(install_prefix)$(bindir)/slogin1
    rm -f $(install_prefix)$(bindir)/`echo slogin | sed '$(transform)'`
    for p in $(MAN1PAGES) $(MAN1GENERATED); do \
      rm -f $(install_prefix)$(man1dir)/$$p.1; \
      rm -f $(install_prefix)$(man1dir)/$${p}1.1; \
```

```
      rm -f $(install_prefix)$(man1dir)/`echo $$p | sed '$(transform)'`.1; \
   done
   rm -f $(install_prefix)$(man1dir)/slogin.1
   rm -f $(install_prefix)$(man1dir)/slogin1.1
   rm -f $(install_prefix)$(man1dir)/`echo slogin.1 | sed '$(transform)'`
   for p in $(MAN8GENERATED); do \
     rm -f $(install_prefix)$(man8dir)/$$p.8; \
     rm -f $(install_prefix)$(man8dir)/$${p}1.8; \
     rm -f $(install_prefix)$(man8dir)/`echo $$p | sed '$(transform)'`.8; \
   done
```

If you want to get rid of your old object, assembly, and core files; you use make clean. This does not do anything to the executables, but removes any of the object and core files you might need to recompile, or just cleans up the directory a bit. If you want to remove and re-create the Makefile and other configuration files for Secure Shell and GNU MP compiling, use make distclean. This also removes any man pages in the temporary directory as well. Look for:

```
clean:
    -rm -f *.o gmon.out *core $(PROGRAMS) rfc-pg
    cd $(GMPDIR); $(MAKE) clean
#   cd $(RSAREFSRCDIR); rm -f *.o *.a
    cd $(ZLIBDIR); $(MAKE) clean
distclean: clean
    -rm -f Makefile config.status config.cache config.log
config.h
    -rm -f ssh.1 sshd.8 make-ssh-known-hosts.1
    cd $(GMPDIR); $(MAKE) distclean
    cd $(ZLIBDIR); $(MAKE) distclean
```

Installing SSH2

The installation steps for installing SSH2 are the same as those for installing SSH1:

1. cd /usr/local/src

2. gzip -dc ssh-x.xx.xx.tar.gz | tar -xvf -

3. cd ssh-xx.xx.xx

4. ./configure

5. make

6. make install

The xx.xx.xx should be replaced with the real version number (2.0.11, for example). The compiling options are very similar as well. Because the key files for SSH1 and SSH2 have different names, they do not conflict with each other. SSH1 keys do not work with the non-commercial release of SSH2, either the official release from SSH Communications Security or Ish: it only supports DSA keys. The Data Fellows UNIX commercial release supports both DSA and RSA keys.

Keep in mind that if you want to keep both versions of Secure Shell compatible, make sure you have the latest release of SSH1, either 1.2.26 or greater. Earlier versions *will not* work, and you will get errors because a configure option that was originally found in SSH1 (`--disable-crypt-asm`) is no longer available in SSH2.

A new option included with the `Makefile` is the ability to remove all the `*.old` files in the directory where Secure Shell, both 1 and 2, is installed. To do this, type:

```
# make clean-up-old
```

Note   Keep in mind that SSH2 has a stricter license than SSH1. Please read the licensing in the appendices for both SSH1 and SSH2 before installing on your system(s).

Running Both SSH1 and SSH2

Because many ISPs and other entities are still running SSH1, you need to be aware of backward-compatibility issues with SSH1 and SSH2. In order to make both versions of Secure Shell work well together, you've got some important things to remember.

First, you need to get the SSH2 clients to be compatible with the SSH1 server. Keep in mind that they are not automatically compatible—you'll need to change the configuration files to get them to work with each other.

Note   You can get a good copy of SSH2 and SSH1 from the CD-ROM that is included with this book. The latest copy of SSH1 and SSH2 is available from `http://www.cs.hut.fi/pub/ssh`.

Here's a laundry list of things you'll need to do:

- Unpack and install the SSH1 sources, version 1.2.26 or higher

- Unpack and install the SSH2 sources

- Configure the system

Note that the Secure Shell binaries in /usr/local/bin now point to the SSH2 versions of the program. This happened during the installation, so this should be transparent to you.

```
# ls -l /usr/local/bin/s*
lrwxrwxrwx 1 root root 4 Jul 30 9:02 /usr/local/bin/ssh ->
ssh2
lrwxrwxrwx 1 root root 4 Jul 30 9:02 /usr/local/bin/scp ->
scp2
```

The SSH1 executables did not go away—instead they are renamed to ssh1, scp1, sshd1, and so on. This means if you want to use the older Secure Shell clients explicitly, you can without having to worry about affecting the newer Secure Shell release.

Note SSH2 is not backward-compatible with any version of SSH1 earlier than 1.2.26. If you do try to get it to work, you will come up with weird errors, such as packet length too long.

To configure the system properly, you need to edit the configuration files for SSH2 only, not SSH1. The files you need to edit are in the /etc/ssh2. To create backward-compatibility with SSH1, edit the /etc/ssh2/sshd2_config, which is the SSH2 server daemon configuration file.

You need to add the following lines to the /etc/ssh2/config file (keep in mind that the lines that begin with the # are comments):

```
# Turn on SSH1 compatibility
Ssh1Compatibility yes
# Tell SSH2 where it can find the SSH1 client
Ssh1Path /usr/local/bin/ssh1
```

The SSH2 server configuration files are covered more in depth in *"Secure Shell 2 Server Daemon—*sshd2 *and* sftp-server2*"* on page 123.

This forwards any SSH2 connection that finds a SSH1 server but no SSH2 server to its older counterpart. If you want to connect to a SSH1 server by default, simply use the SSH1 commands,

which also include the key management commands for SSH1. SSH
key management commands and usage are covered in *"Secure
Shell Key Management"* on page 191.

Testing the Application

SSH is not without its bugs. For example, you may find some problems getting complete C2 characteristics with the C2 security package. The secure copy, scp, for both SSH1 and SSH2 has its share of
problems and compatibility problems.

Now that you've installed it, you want to know if it really
works. Keep in mind that you won't be seeing the cryptographic
portion of SSH, because the encryption is invisible to the user.
What you're looking at is the connectivity, to see if you can open a
socket to a remote computer. Don't worry about speed of the
application—all you're looking for is the network connectivity.

A successful login should look something like a rsh login. Even
though you do not see it, your connection is secured and being
encrypted. Your password is used to protect your authentication
key, not to authenticate you directly, unless you are using password
authentication. The example below shows how you *don't* see the
encryption happening. If the following displays, your Secure Shell
connecting is working fine:

```
tigerlair:/home/stripes- ssh hobbes.tigerlair.com
password:
Welcome to Hobbes' Tiger Lair
Unauthorized user beware: Tigers byte! Be 8 bit careful!
hobbes:/home/stripes-
```

However, if your connection to SSH can connect, but you cannot encrypt, you'll see a warning before you're prompted for your
password. This is the case when no SSH daemon is running on the
remote system or if SSH is blocked on the router or firewall. If you
do not want to continue via rsh, you can press control+c to exit.
Even if SSH warns you, it's easy to forget that rsh is not SSH. Look
for:

```
tigerlair:/home/stripes- ssh litterbox.tigerlair.com
Using rsh. WARNING: Connection will not be encrypted.
password:
```

> If you want to keep secure connections, do not use `rsh` even if Secure Shell cannot encrypt.

Note

SSH2 will drop to SSH1 if a compatible daemon (SSH 1.2.26 or higher) of SSH1 is on the same host. This is a normal occurrence, and it simply means that the host you are trying to connect to does not have SSH2 installed on it. In this case, you'll get a message saying that SSH1 is being executed for compatibility. Your connection is still being encrypted; however, the authentication is RSA and not DSA. Again, this is transparent to you. You'll see:

```
tigerlair:/home/stripes- ssh tigger.tigerlair.com
Executing /usr/local/bin/ssh1 for ssh1 compatibility.
password:
Welcome to Tigger's Tiger Lair
Unauthorized user beware: Tigers byte! Be 8 bit careful!
tigger:/home/stripes-
```

Summary

SSH requires a system to have the necessary environment to install and run. This includes the right operating system, enough memory and CPU power, and of course, disk space. Depending on the type of operating system, you may need to have a compiler and/or the appropriate libraries.

The UNIX platform is the most intensive installation because it is compiled and configured directly from the code. However, it is the most configurable installation. Because most other operating systems have compressed files in an archive, they only have to install the appropriate file or run the installation program.

Running both versions of SSH is not unheard of, and this chapter covered some tips on how to get them both working. After you've got your version of SSH installed on your favorite UNIX flavor, you'll want to test the application. Some known problems may occur, and some possible solutions are covered in *"Troubleshooting Secure Shell"* on page 263.

SECTION

II

Secure Shell 1 (SSH1)

Secure Shell 1 Server Daemon—sshd

In this chapter:

- SSH 1.5 Protocol

- The nuts and bolts

- Usage

- Files

Now that you've installed and configured Secure Shell on your UNIX system, you'll want to know how to use the Secure Shell server daemon, sshd. This is the part of Secure Shell that maintains and accepts connections on the remote side, but you only need the client for your local system.

SSH 1.5 Protocol

The first release of Secure Shell is based on the SSH 1.5 protocol. This protocol defines how it works, how the packet is assembled, and what the protocol provides. Secure Shell has two different protocols—SSH 1.5 is used in Secure Shell releases 1.2.26 and earlier, and SSH 2.0 is used in version 2.0.0 and higher. SSH 1.5 is covered in this chapter, and SSH 2.0 is covered in Chapter 5, "Secure Shell 2 Server Daemon - sshd2 and sftp-server2."

How It Works

Before ATMs were so popular at banks, people frequently used drive-through tellers for all their transactions. When the customer drove up to a window, he or she spoke with a bank teller inside, who then sent a plastic canister through a tube that went from their desk to the car. In this tube, the customer placed checks to deposit, along with the deposit slip, or they requested to withdraw money from an account.

So, after sending the canister through the tube back to the teller, the customer waited in their car. Then the teller would send the canister back through the tube with the requested amount of cash or receipt for the check. As you can see, the money could only be removed from the secure container in two ways—by opening it in the proper manner or by physically breaking the tube.

The two people—the customer and the teller—communicate through the tube with the canister. Because the customer can identify that the teller is indeed a bank employee and the teller can verify who the customer is, each is confident about the other's identity.

Secure Shell works in a similar fashion. You can consider the tube as a connection to the two systems, and the canister is an encrypted data packet, with the data itself being the actual banking transaction. Because the bank has what the customer wants, the bank would be considered the server, and the customer would be considered the client.

Let's take a look at the "bank" of Secure Shell: the Secure Shell server daemon. The daemon on the remote side handles the connections from the client. The Secure Shell daemon is also responsible for executing shell commands or logins on the remote host and sending the information securely to the remote site from the client and vice versa. Other things that the Secure Shell server secures is X11 and port forwarding, as well as the Secure Shell Agent, ssh-agent, connections.

The encryption cipher is decided on by the Secure Shell server daemon, which is on the remote side. This controls the host key checks and makes sure they work properly. If you have problems with your host key, you'll probably want to run the remote SSH server in debug mode as well as the client. Other critical encryption functions that the server handles is error-checking with encryption, to not allow sensitive information outside.

Unlike other TCP/IP applications, Secure Shell is designed to work on its own instead of with wrappers or through the Internet daemon inetd. Nonetheless, many people do want to run the Secure Shell daemon through TCP wrappers. Although you can run it through inetd for the TCP wrappers (tcpd), which is run from inetd, this is not necessary. Using TCP wrappers is covered in *"Other Cool Things You Can Do With Secure Shell"* on page 239.

The Connection

The SSH 1.5 protocol handles connection establishment, key exchange, user and server authentication, and TCP connections such as forwarding, pty allocation for interactive sessions, X11, and the Secure Shell agent. This is handled all in one "layer" instead of a multitude of layers like TCP/IP handles things.

The packet itself is a TCP packet and contains the following: the packet length, random padding, the packet type, the data itself, and the check bytes. Out of all of this, everything is encrypted except for the packet length. If this packet is compressed, it becomes about half the size. Figure 3.1 on page 58 shows how the Secure Shell packet looks.

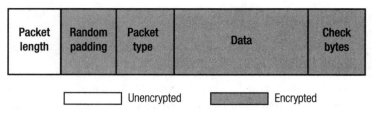

Packet length	Random padding	Packet type	Data	Check bytes

☐ Unencrypted   ▧ Encrypted

Figure 3.1 *SSH 1.5 packet.*

The Nuts and Bolts

After you start the Secure Shell server, the sshd is executed and starts listening on port 22 by default. You'll find this out through a port scan on a host to see where the Secure Shell daemon is listening. You can also see if the process is running on your ps command.

Note

Since you don't want to type **sshd** every time you boot your system (which shouldn't be that often anyway), you'll want to start this daemon at boot, and this is covered later in the chapter.

To start the Secure Shell daemon, simply type:

```
# sshd
```

This does not display anything and brings you back to your prompt. If you want to make sure that sshd is running, you can check your processes:[1]

```
bash# ps -aux | grep sshd
root 52 0.0 1.9 1488 588 ? S Dec 8 0:00 /usr/local/sbin/sshd
```

After the Secure Shell daemon has started, it starts listening on a port for a socket. The default port that the Secure Shell daemon runs on is port 22. This can be changed; however, make sure that other TCP/IP daemons are not using or listening on those ports.

Usually the Secure Shell daemon does listen for a socket, unless it is started from the Internet daemon inetd, which listens for the socket instead. For now, let's assume you're not going to run Secure Shell through inetd. After the Secure Shell daemon starts

---

1. Depending on your UNIX system, you may have to use different options for the ps command. The option -eaf usually works if -aux doesn't. Anyway, check your man pages to be on the safe side.

listening for a socket, it waits until it connects. When it connects,
the Secure Shell daemon spawns a child process, which in turn generates an RSA host key. After the key is generated, the Secure Shell
daemon is ready for the local client to connect to another Secure
Shell daemon or waits for a connection from a remote client. See
Figure 3.2 for an illustration of how this works.

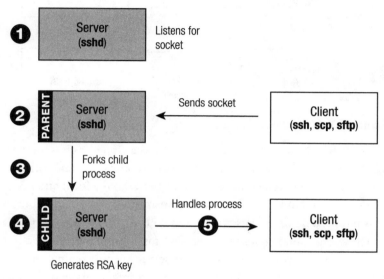

Figure 3.2 *Secure Shell daemon connection handling.*

At this point the Secure Shell daemon is sitting around and listening for a socket. When it hears a connection, the socket is
bound to a particular port. Usually the socket comes in on a non-
privileged port (1023 or higher) and is bound to port 22. Before
the port is bound, Secure Shell needs to get the IP address of the client. This is used for the log, but if the connection is not coming
from a known network address, the IP address 0.0.0.0 is assigned.

Now that the connection is made, the servers exchange public
host keys. After the keys are validated, the servers exchange the
supported cipher information. The local server may support Triple
DES and IDEA, and the remote server may only support DES and
IDEA. Usually the stronger cipher is chosen, and the remote server
sends back whichever cipher it has chosen. See Figure 3.3 on
page 60 for an illustration of how this works.

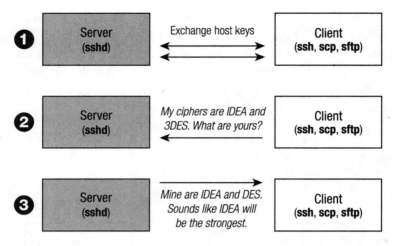

Figure 3.3 *How the cipher is chosen.*

Now that the host keys are validated and a cipher is chosen, the local server recognizes that it has gotten the connection and forks a child process to manage the connection between the local and remote server. Now the client starts transmitting encrypted data. This happens before the user is prompted for a passphrase.

The connection between the two systems continues until the client has ended its connection. Then the server keeps listening for connections until the daemon is killed, either intentionally or through a system crash. Then if a socket is heard, the connection process repeats itself. If Secure Shell exits with an error, it does not dump the core which prevents leaking the private information. Take a look at Figure 3.4 to see what happens at the end of a connection.

So, the overall connectivity looks like this:

- connection request on port 22 from client
- server forks a child process
- servers exchange host keys
- session key and local host key exchanged from client
- supported cipher decided on by servers
- encrypted data transferred
- connection broken down

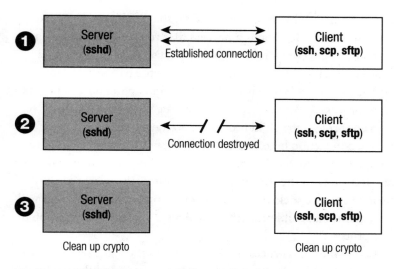

Figure 3.4 *When a Secure Shell connection ends.*

Secure Shell Daemon Processes

After you understand how the daemon functions, you'll want to know how to handle the processes. Usually after a connection is negotiated, a child process is spawned from the parent to handle the interaction between the client and the remote server. Keep in mind that the client can be started on either end, the local host or the remote host.

After the Secure Shell daemon is started, the process identification number (PID) is stored in /etc/sshd_pid. This makes it easier to kill the appropriate daemon. If a child process is running, you don't want to accidentally kill that, especially while it's binding to a socket.

One way the Secure Shell daemon handles processes is that it works like inetd. You can send it a SIGHUP signal (which is a kill -HUP signal), and the sshd executes itself. As a result, it rereads its configuration file and regenerates its server key. Remember that inetd handles the SIGHUP signal the same way.

The Parent Process

As in all implementations that are UNIX-based, you have files and you have processes. Because sshd is the Secure Shell daemon file that runs the Secure Shell daemon processes, we have two processes from sshd to be concerned with: the parent and the child processes. So, a daemon is a process that runs in the background on its own and controls the application it's running. The initial process that is started from the daemon is the parent process.

The parent's job is to listen (unlike human parents) and to fork child processes. And that's all it does. The connections themselves are run through the child processes. So the parent says, "Aha! We have a connection here!" and then it spawns the child process to complete the session. The parent tells the child process to make the connection with the socket. In the meantime, the parent keeps listening for more sockets. If more connections occur, the parent will fork additional child processes. See Figure 3.5 for an illustration of this process.

Before the child process makes the connection, the session key is given to the child process to encrypt the session, and the parent process marks that key as "used." At this point, the host key is cleared.

Naturally, we don't want to listen endlessly, waiting for an authentication from the remote server. The daemon has a built-in "alert" that causes the server to exit when the authentication is made or the alert times out. The alert is turned off during debugging mode to help detect problems with authentication.

The Child Process

With the parent process actively listening for sockets and forking child processes, the child process makes the connection with the client. When the child process starts, it starts running with the user (the person who started the client) UID, not root. This keeps someone from running processes as root on your system.

To start the session, the child process closes the listening socket and starts using the accepted socket to make the session. Next, the logging is restarted because the process identification number has changed. The child process then authenticates the user. If the session is not interactive, the session is connected and then torn down. Otherwise, the child process allocates for an interactive session things like pseudo terminals, X11 connections, TCP/IP protocols, and the authentication agent, ssh-agent.

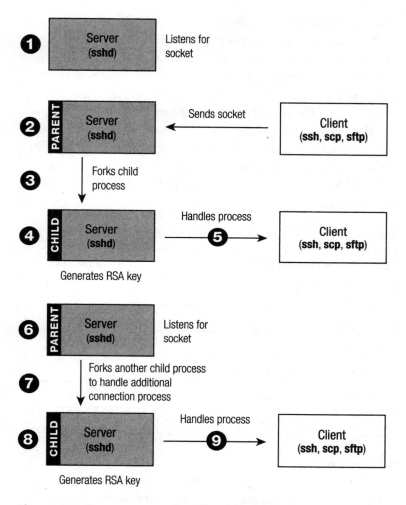

Figure 3.5 *How processes handle additional connections.*

Now that the connection is made, the client needs to know that we are the local server and that the client can request a connection to any port they want to. The client starts from port 22, and the server side connects to any port (usually port 1021 or higher). If the user wants to define which port they are connected to without letting the client know, they can, especially since the client decides what is permitted. When the connection is done, the connection is torn down and the encryption is cleared up.

The Encryption of Secure Shell

The encryption with Secure Shell is a major part of the functionality of the server. The Secure Shell daemon does a few checks on things like key lengths, public keys, check bytes, and authentication. Some of the encryption is split between the child and the parent processes. The parent process generates the host key and gives it to the child process to negotiate with the client. The child process also handles the session itself, which consists of the user authentication and the symmetric key encryption for the data transfer. Table 3.1 breaks down the encryption task to either the parent or child process.

Table 3.1 *Encryption task by parent or child process*

Encryption-related task	Process
Generates host key	Parent
Keeps list of keys	Parent
Key exchange	Child
Handles session encryption	Child
Handles session authentication	Child
Handles destruction of keys	Child

Key Exchange

After the connection is identified by the parent, the child process makes the incoming connection. At this point, version identifiers for Secure Shell have been exchanged by the client and server. After the appropriate version identification is made by the server, it is ready to send the sever key and do the key exchange with the client.

You'll find two keys on the local system: a RSA 1024-bit host key, which is used to recognize the host and that it's not being spoofed, and a RSA 768-bit server key, which is regenerated every hour if it has been used. The reason the server key is regenerated every hour is that this is enough time to keep the key alive without being cracked. Also, the server key is not stored on the disk but in memory. Checks are made to make sure that both keys are significantly different. The host key is stored locally on the disk, which defaults to /etc/ssh_host_key for the private key and /etc/ssh_host_key.pub for the public key.

After the keys are exchanged and validated, the keys are not needed for any other encryption functions. If additional Secure Shell connections need to be made, additional keys will be generated. The next thing the Secure Shell daemon does is really cool—it generates a series of check bytes that the client sends to the remote server through a user packet.

These check bytes—a packet that includes 64 bits of random data—must be matched by the remote host. This is how Secure Shell protects against IP spoofing attacks. However, it only protects against a remote host *outside* your local network, but not against someone sniffing your network and obtaining the check bytes that way. For password-protected accounts, this is not an issue. For authentication using Berkeley services (using the .rhosts or /etc/hosts.equiv for authentication), the check bytes can be picked up and someone can log in to your host. This still makes Berkeley services somewhat dangerous for authentication. Secure Shell is a replacement for the Berkeley services, so do not use them. You may want to remove them completely.

When we send out our public key, we include our check bytes. They must be included in the encrypted reply to establish a secure connection. The next packet we receive should be encrypted using our host and server public keys, and we decrypt it. At the end of this packet, there should be a set of check bytes. These check bytes should match those we sent earlier with our public key. This is used to verify the remote host has properly received our connection.

After the exchange is complete, the RSA public and private server keys are then destroyed.

Encrypting the Session

We receive a couple of things in this packet: our check bytes and the session key. Our check bytes verify this is the remote server that we sent it to, and the session key is in the decrypted integer from the check bytes. After the session key is extracted, the connection between the remote and local host is now encrypted with a supported symmetric key cipher. This is the way that the secret key is sent to the server without divulging it publicly.

So the encryption steps work like this:

1. Generate check bytes.

2. Attach check bytes to local public key and send to remote server.

3. Receive encrypted packet including remote public key and check bytes.

4. Verify the check bytes are what we originally sent.

5. Extract session key from the decrypted integer from the encrypted packet.

6. Start the session key and encrypt the session from now on.

7. Send an encrypted acknowledgement packet.

8. Established connection sends only the encrypted packets.

9. Connection is torn down; session keys are destroyed.

Next we send our acknowledgement packet. This packet is now encrypted with the session key, along with any other packets we send to the remote server from this point on. After the connection is broken down and the socket connections are destroyed, the session key is destroyed.

Authenticating the Users

Now that we are sending everything over an encrypted channel, it shouldn't bother you to be typing your password over the network (unless you are using a weak form of encryption), because it is now sent encrypted through the tunnel. The session to you will look like any other client session like telnet or rsh; however, we'll go over this in the next chapter. In the meantime, let's see how the actual authentication works.

First, the Secure Shell client (be it ssh, scp, slogin) checks for the /etc/nologin message, in case the remote system is shutting down or rebooting. If this is not the case, the login process kicks in and the client sends the appropriate username to the remote server. When the username is accepted, the authentication type is checked.

The purpose of using Secure Shell is to have strong security—it is highly recommended that you use some form of RSA authentication with Secure Shell. You can also use it in conjunction with rhosts authentication and password authentication. When you are authenticating with RSA public keys, the passphrase protects the private key. This passphrase is different than what you type in to log in to your account—this passphrase is what you entered when your keypair was generated. If you are authenticating by password, make sure you type your account password—not your private key password.

If the Secure Shell client is coming from a privileged port, it is checked for rhosts authentication (which includes `$HOME/.rhosts` and `/etc/hosts.equiv`). If there is no rhosts authentication (and there shouldn't be if you want this to be really secure), you are then prompted for your login password.

Next, the password is read. You can also authenticate with rhosts (which includes using an RSA key), RSA host authentication, RSA challenge-response authentication, Security Dynamics SecurID cards, the TIS challenge-response authentication, or password-based authentication. You can use password-based authentication with the RSA host authentication (and this is recommended).

> You can authenticate to Secure Shell without your login password; however, this can minimize security.   **Note**

A Word on Not Using Passwords to Protect Your Secure Shell Keys

On the Secure Shell mailing list, this is a popular question: How do I use Secure Shell without a password?

Think of the reason you're using Secure Shell, and you'll realize why this is a bad thing to do. Secure Shell is designed to prevent someone from hijacking a session and obtaining access to your host remotely through poor methods of authentication (bad passwords, Berkeley services, NFS, NIS, and the like).

So, why would you not want to use password authentication? Many people want to do this for convenience, especially for script writing. You do have one easy way around this: run the Secure Shell authentication agent. After starting the agent, all you need to do is add the keys into memory. This makes it so you don't have to worry about passwords while the daemon is running. If the system gets rebooted or the daemon crashes, then you'll have to re-enter the passwords.

If this seems too much of a bother for you, you should be aware of the risks that can very likely happen if you are not using password authentication:

- If someone accesses your computer, they have instant access to your keys even if the Secure Shell authentication agent is not running.

- Someone can hijack your private and public host keys and spoof your host.

- If you are doing this with rhosts authentication enabled, you are vulnerable to several rhosts authentication attacks. If you must use a host authentication file along with the RSA keys, you have to use the shosts files ($HOME/.shosts or /etc/shosts.equiv) for Secure Shell only. This will protect only against rsh attacks, not the private keys being hijacked.

The following are some recommendations for increasing your security with passwords:

- Use strong passwords for all keys and account access. This includes not using dictionary or well-known words and using a combination of upper and lowercase letters, numbers, and special characters (!@#$%^&*).

- Do not embed passwords in a script. Especially with the growing popularity of Expect, putting passwords in remote access scripts is becoming a common practice. This is really bad because you are storing your password in a cleartext file.

- Realize that on a multi-user machine, you are risking the root account by not password-protecting your keys. If you are not password-protecting your keys, always password-protect the keys in the root account!

Basically, this falls under the rationale for using strong passwords in the first place. Make sure you password-protect every key with strong passwords. If you do not, be aware of the risks you are taking and know that you are seriously putting the security of your system at risk.

Usage of the Secure Shell Daemon

Now that you understand how the Secure Shell daemon works, you have several options when running the daemon. Like most UNIX networking daemons, you can set the debugging mode, change the location of key files, and set the verbosity. You can also change the key sizes and the port that the daemon is listening on.

-b bits You can specify the number of bits in the server key. This defaults to 768 bits; however, you can make this larger or smaller, depending on whether or not you are running from `inetd` or want stronger security.

-d This puts the server in debug mode. The SSH daemon is started, but does not run in the background nor does it fork any child processes. The Secure Shell daemon will only process one connection at a time. The debugging output goes to the system log, and the "alert" mechanism is turned off. This option should only be used for debugging the server, not for increasing logging messages.

-f config_file You can specify a specific configuration file. The default is `/etc/sshd_config`, but if you're running SSH without root privileges, you will need to define this file elsewhere.

-g login_grace_time This is what sets the "alert" mechanism in the Secure Shell daemon. It gives the client a certain grace time to authenticate with the server, which defaults to 600 seconds (10 minutes). If the client does not authenticate, the server process disconnects from that socket. You can set this to zero, which means you have no limit on authentication time. If you put the Secure Shell daemon in debug mode, this will be set to zero automatically.

-h host_key_file This specifies which file you are using for the private host key. You have to use this option if you are not running the Secure Shell daemon as root. Normally, the private host key file is not readable by anyone but the root account; however, this is not the case if you are running it from a user account. Also, if you are using an alternative file, make sure you set the permissions to something like 400.

-i You can specify whether or not to run Secure Shell from inetd. This depends on whether or not you're running the Secure Shell daemon with TCP wrappers or if you want to run Secure Shell from inetd. Running Secure Shell from inetd causes its own problems, and this can be a latency issue. Clients would have to wait too long for a normal length or stronger server key for when the keys are regenerated. However, you could use a smaller server key to increase performance; but be aware that the weaker the key, the easier it is to crack.

-k key_gen_time You can specify how frequently the server key is regenerated. The host key should not be regenerated unless you need to change the password or if the host key was compromised or corrupted (use ssh-keygen for the host key). The default for this is an hour, or 3,600 seconds. After regenerating the key, it gets more difficult to recover for decrypting the encrypted packets even if the host is compromised. If you set this to zero, it means that the server key will not get regenerated, and I strongly recommend against it.

-p port You can specify which port the server listens for sockets on. The default is port 22, which is reserved for Secure Shell. Keep in mind that this is also the port defined in the /etc/services file, unless you change it. You may want to define an alternate port if port 22 is already being used for another application or if you are running the Secure Shell daemon from another user besides root.

-q This is the quiet mode, which means that nothing is sent to the system log. The stuff that is usually sent is the start of a connection, the authentication of the user, and the termination of the connection. You may not want to enable this option unless your logs fill up quite quickly. Audit trails are always good for checking to see if someone has illegally gained access to your system.

-V This prints the version number that is read from the client. It also checks for Secure Shell version 2 compatibility.

What is the difference between a server key and a host key? The server key is used to constantly verify the server to the client to prevent spoofing. The host key is used to verify the host itself.

Note

Some Examples

The default setting for the Secure Shell daemon is using a 768-bit server key that regenerates every hour, an authentication time-out of 10 minutes, listens on port 22 for connections, and finds its configuration files in the /etc directory. So the default Secure Shell daemon runs like this:

```
# sshd
```

Or you can pass it these options and it does the same thing as the default:

```
# sshd -b 768 -f /etc/sshd_config -k 3600 -g 600 -h /etc/
ssh_host_key -p 22
```

You can define the Secure Shell port as something greater than 1024 for a non-privileged Secure Shell daemon:

```
# sshd -p 2022
```

Using a different configuration file for a different port? No problem!

```
# sshd -p 2022 -f /etc/sshd_config_weird_port
```

And if you want to run Secure Shell through inetd, you can do that too. Don't forget to shrink the server keys. Keep in mind that you really don't want to run this on the command line—you'll want to run it from a script which in turn runs it from inetd:

```
# sshd -i -b 512
```

You should edit /etc/inetd.conf before running sshd from it.   **Note**

Initiating Secure Shell from the Startup Scripts

Most administrators who are running Secure Shell want it running all the time and probably want to have it run without having to start it all the time. To solve this, simply put it in a startup script.

Table 3.2 shows by operating system some locations to start the Secure Shell daemon from.

Table 3.2 *Location of startup scripts per operating system*

Operating system	Startup script[2]
Slackware Linux	/etc/rc.d
Redhat Linux	/etc/rc*.d
Solaris	/etc/rc*.d
HP-UX	/etc/rc*.d
Irix	/etc/rc*.d
AIX	/etc
DEC UNIX	/etc/rc*.d

I found that in Linux installations the script installs it automatically. However, if you find you need to edit your scripts to add it, you can include the following script snippet to your startup script.

My UNIX system is a Slackware Linux system, and the networking initialization script is /etc/rc.d/inet2. In this script, you will see that the Secure Shell daemon is started here. If you need to, you can edit your startup script to put Secure Shell daemon in the correct path and specify the options you want. You'll see:

```
#!/bin/sh
#
# rc.inet2   This shell script boots up the entire INET system.
#            Note, that when this script is used to also fire
#            up any important remote NFS disks (like the /usr
#            distribution), care must be taken to actually
#            have all the needed binaries online _now_ ...
#
# Author:    Fred N. van Kempen, <waltje@uwalt.nl.mugnet.org>
#
# Constants.
NET="/usr/sbin"
```

---

2. * represents any number, since many of the start-up scripts allow you to start applications wherever you want, depending on the run level. However, you may want to put your start-up script for SSH in the same place where inetd starts up.

```
IN_SERV="lpd"
LPSPOOL="/var/spool/lpd"
# At this point, we are ready to talk to The World...
# echo "Mounting remote file systems..."
# /sbin/mount -a -t nfs    # This may be our /usr runtime!!!
echo -n "Starting daemons:"
# Start the SYSLOGD/Klogd daemons. These must come first.
if [ -f ${NET}/syslogd ]; then
  echo -n " syslogd"
  ${NET}/syslogd
  sleep 1 # prevent syslogd/klogd race condition on SMP kernels
  echo -n " klogd"
  ${NET}/klogd
fi
# Start the SUN RPC Portmapper.
if [ -f ${NET}/rpc.portmap ]; then
  echo -n " portmap"
  ${NET}/rpc.portmap
fi
# Start the INET SuperServer
if [ -f ${NET}/inetd ]; then
  echo -n " inetd"
  ${NET}/inetd
else
  echo "no INETD found. INET cancelled!"
  exit 1
fi
# Look for sshd in the two most common locations
# (compiled with --prefix=/usr or with --prefix=/usr/local)
# and if we find it, start it up
if [ -x /usr/local/sbin/sshd ]; then
  echo -n " sshd"
  /usr/local/sbin/sshd
elif [ -x /usr/sbin/sshd ]; then
  echo -n " sshd"
  /usr/sbin/sshd
fi
# Start the various INET servers.
for server in ${IN_SERV} ; do
  if [ -f ${NET}/${server} ]; then
    echo -n " ${server}"
    ${NET}/${server}
  fi
done
# # Start the various SUN RPC servers.
if [ -f ${NET}/rpc.portmap ]; then
  # Start the NFS server daemons.
  if [ -f ${NET}/rpc.mountd ]; then
```

```
     echo -n " mountd"
     ${NET}/rpc.mountd
   fi
   if [ -f ${NET}/rpc.nfsd ]; then
     echo -n " nfsd"
     ${NET}/rpc.nfsd
   fi
fi # Done starting various SUN RPC servers.
# The 'echo' below will put a carriage return at the end
# of the list of started servers.
echo
# Done!
```

Note   Remember to include whatever options you need to run the Secure
               Shell daemon for your environment. Also, your script may not look
               like this—this is specific to Slackware Linux.

Logging Your Connections

The Secure Shell daemon, by default, logs the initial request for
a connection, the authentication, and the closing of the connection.
Because this code is free, you are more than welcome to edit it to
make more information logged. The following is from the /var/
adm/messages log file on Slackware Linux. An example log section
with a Secure Shell connection is shown below:

```
Jun 23 14:40:28 tigerlair sshd[60]:
log: Server listening on port 22.
Jun 23 14:40:28 tigerlair sshd[60]:
log: Generating 768 bit RSA key.
Jun 23 14:40:29 tigerlair sshd[60]:
log: RSA key generation complete.
```

This shows what happens when the Secure Shell daemon is first
started. When a connection is made, your log files may look something like this:

```
Jul  9 08:19:25 tigerlair sshd[1880]:
log: Connection from 206.184.139.144 port 926
Jul  9 08:19:34 tigerlair sshd[1880]:
log: Password authentication for stripes accepted.
Jul  9 08:19:42 tigerlair sshd[1880]:
log: Closing connection to 206.184.139.144
```

You can also turn on verbose logging or turn logging off completely with the quiet option.

Also, you can use TCP wrappers with the `-D PARANOID` option to log each socket. This may duplicate some of the efforts of the Secure Shell daemon, or you can configure it to provide you with more information.

Keep in mind that where your logs go is system-dependent. Linux distributions may put the information in the system log, located in `/var/adm/syslog`, and HP-UX or AIX may put the logging information in a completely different location. Check your operating system manuals for log file locations.

Configuring Secure Shell

Secure Shell has a configuration file where you can define options. Some of these options are not definable by the command-line options, but you can configure extra stuff to work with Secure Shell. Like most configuration files and shell scripts, empty lines and lines starting with the "#" are not read. The default configuration file for Secure Shell is `/etc/sshd_config`.

Below are the options that you can set in the `sshd_config` file for Secure Shell. The format for defining these options in the `/etc/sshd_config` file is:

```
OptionType Argument
```

If you have multiple arguments, they are separated by a space. This format applies to all the options listed below.

Note   Some of these options depend on whether or not an option has been enabled while running the configure script.

Allowing by Username

You can filter on usernames and groups for allowing access via Secure Shell. Also, you have the ability to set account expiration information. The options below help you monitor user account and provide filters for allowing (or not allowing) users through your host:

AllowGroups/DenyGroups You can define any user group to have access or to not have access. For example, you can say that all groups are allowed in with a wildcard "*" or not define either of these values at all, which will also allow all groups in (this is the default). You can also define wildcards on a per-character basis

with the "?" wildcard. You can define that you only want the
group "sales" to not login through Secure Shell, and if you do this,
make sure you have Telnet and the Berkeley services turned off as
well. If you want to list multiple groups, use a space to separate.
Keep in mind that this still requires you to authenticate.

Usage:

```
AllowGroups user
DenyGroups  bin root
```

AccountExpireWarningDays If an account is going to expire,
you can specify when to start sending warning messages. This
value is a number, which represents the number of days before the
expiration. The default is 14, which is 14 days (or 2 weeks). If
warning messages are disabled, the default is set to zero.

Usage:

```
AccountExpireWarningDays 7
```

AllowUsers/DenyUsers If you want to define allowing or denying users by their username (and host, if you need to), you can with
this option. If you need to define the host, you can use the hostname itself or the IP address. You can also use wildcards to define a
range or usernames or host addresses. This defaults to allowing all
users in. Even if a user can log in, they still have to authenticate.

Usage:

```
AllowUsers stripes hobbes tiger riffer
DenyUsers  hacker@evilhost.com root
```

Allowing by Hostname

In addition to filtering by username or groups, you can filter
access to Secure Shell by host as well. Filtering by host also gives
you the ability to filter on IP addresses. With wildcards, you can filter a range of addresses or by entire domains.

AllowHosts/DenyHosts This works in a similar fashion to the
`AllowGroups/DenyGroups` option. Instead of filtering on user
groups, this filters per host. The default is all hosts are allowed to
connect. However, you can deny or allow certain hosts; for
instance, if you know that `bad.com` is a host that is known to spon-
sor hackers, you may want to deny access from that host. You can
also use wildcards like "*" or "?" to not allow or allow specific

hosts or domains like `DenyHosts *.uk` This would prevent anyone from a host in the United Kingdom from logging in. You can also use IP addresses or define an address range instead of the hostnames. If you want to list multiple hosts or ranges, use a space to separate them. Keep in mind that you still have to authenticate even if your host is allowed to connect.

Usage:

```
AllowHosts *.example.com
DenyHosts  *.example.org
```

AllowSHosts/DenySHosts You can filter the hostnames or IP addresses even further. You can use the `.rhosts` or `/etc/hosts.equiv` to define which hosts you allow by using the `AllowSHosts` or `DenySHosts` option. The format for these options is the same as `AllowHosts/DenyHosts`. However, these options work a little differently. If you use the `AllowSHosts` option, the `.shosts` (or the `/etc/shosts.equiv`, or even the `.rhosts` and `/etc/hosts.equiv`) are checked to make sure they match the hostnames listed by this option. If `DenySHosts` is used, then any name that matches the pattern listed that is found in the `.shosts` (or the `/etc/shosts.equiv`, or even the `.rhosts` and `/etc/hosts.equiv`) is ignored.

Usage:

```
AllowSHosts tigerlair.com
DenySHosts  *.anyoneelse.com
```

IgnoreRhosts This defines whether or not `.rhosts` and `.shosts` is used for authentication. This does not have any effect on the system-wide files, `/etc/hosts.equiv` and `/etc/shosts.equiv`. The default for this option is "no." If you do want to use this, please use `.shosts` instead of `.rhosts` for improved security.

Usage:

```
IgnoreRhosts yes
```

IgnoreRootRhosts This defines whether or not to use a trusted host file (`.shosts` or `.rhosts`) for authentication for the root account. The default value is the same as `IgnoreRHosts`, but it should always be "yes" to keep people from remotely logging in to a tty for the root account.

Usage:

```
IgnoreRootRhosts yes
```

Authentication

Secure Shell provides different authentication methods: passwords, rhosts, RSA keys, and TIS authentication mechanisms. You can either use one or a combination of any of the above for accessing accounts via Secure Shell. However, be aware that rhosts authentication is the weakest, and any combination along with the RSA key is going to be your strongest form of authentication

ForcedEmptyPasswdChange If you have an empty password on a user account, you can define whether or not it should be changed when someone logs in to the account via Secure Shell. This helps keep your system secure by not allowing non-password-protected accounts from accessing your host. For security reasons, you'll want to set ForceEmptyPasswdChange to "yes", even though the default is "no."

Usage:

```
ForcedEmptyPasswdChange yes
```

ForcedPasswdChange If a password has expired, you can force a change at the next login. This argument has two choices: yes or no. The default is "yes," and you'll be fine leaving it that way.

Usage:

```
ForcedPasswdChange yes
```

PasswordAuthentication You can define whether or not you want to use passwords to access accounts via Secure Shell. The default is "yes," and what the passwords do is protect the RSA key, not the account itself, by more conventional means. You may opt to turn off password authentication, but it's better to leave it on, because it helps to have an additional method of authentication.

Usage:

```
PasswdAuthentication yes
```

PasswordExpireWarningDays This is very similar to the AccountExpireWarningDays option, but it applies to passwords instead. If a password is going to expire, you can specify when to start sending warning messages. This value is a number, which represents the number of days before the expiration. The default is 14, which is 14 days (or 2 weeks). The warning messages are disabled

if the value is left at the default of zero. This setting also affects the
ForcedPasswdChange option.

Usage:

PasswordExpireWarningDays 21

PermitEmptyPasswords This defines whether or not you want
to use passwords to help authenticate. You can allow null passwords; however, I strongly recommend that you don't. If someone
accesses your host (desktop, laptop, server, and so on), it's one less
thing that they need a password to have access to. The default is
"yes," but ignore that. Always use strong passwords and set this to
"no."

Usage:

PermitEmptyPasswords no

RhostsAuthentication This option sets your authentication to
be based on the .rhosts or /etc/hosts.equiv alone. This doesn't
require a password or an RSA key. This opens your system up to
Berkeley services attacks that are well known and the reason you
are using Secure Shell in the first place. The default is "no," and
you're best leaving it that way. If you do want to use rhosts authentication, use it in conjunction with the RSA authentication in
RhostsRSAAuthentication.

Usage:

RhostsAuthentication no

RhostsRSAAuthentication This option sets your authentication
to be based on the .rhosts or /etc/hosts.equiv with the RSA key.
This doesn't require a password, but it does require that the remote
side has an RSA key and .rhosts or /etc/hosts.equiv file to
authenticate against. This opens your system up to Berkeley services attacks, but the threat is minimized because of the required
RSA key.

Usage:

RhostsRSAAuthentication no

RSAAuthentication You can use a myriad of authentication
types; or as you can see, you can use a sole type as well. If you want

to define only RSA authentication to be accepted, you can. This does not require rhosts or passwords to help authenticate. The default is "yes" and this is fine to leave as is.

Usage:

```
RSAAuthentication yes
```

TISAuthentication Secure Shell also supports alternative authentication mechanisms like TIS Authentication Server, authsrv. If you configure Secure Shell to support TIS, you'll want to set this to "yes" (the default is "no"). In order to use this option, you need to run the configure script witht the option --with-tis=/path/to/tis.

Usage:

```
TISAuthentication no
```

Kerberos Options

Kerberos is a third-party UNIX authentication system that uses "tickets" to authenticate. Also, for Kerberos to work, applications that use it have to be "kerberized." However, Secure Shell acknowledges this and provides Kerberos support without having to kerberize it. This is currently only supported in SSH1. In order to use these options, make sure you run the configure script with the --with-kerberos5=KRB_PREFIX option.

KerberosAuthentication This specifies whether or not to support Kerberos tickets for authentication or to let passwords be validated through the Kerberos KDC or DCE Security Server. The default is "yes," but if you don't have a kerberized environment, you can turn this off.

Usage:

```
KerberosAuthentication no
```

KerberosOrLocalPasswd If you have Kerberos authentication turned on and the password fails, you can have the password checked through a secondary mechanism like the /etc/passwd or /etc/shadow or even through SecurID. If you are using Kerberos, you probably want to leave it as your only authentication mechanism, depending on your setup. The default setting is "no."

Usage:

```
KerberosOrLocalPasswd no
```

KerberosTgtPassing If you want to be able to forward a Kerberos ticket to the server, turn this option on. The default is "yes." This option is important only if you have turned on Kerberos authentication. In order to use this option, you need to run the configure script with the option `--enable-kerberos-tgt-passing`.
Usage:

```
KerberosTgtPassing no
```

Server Options

These options are specific to how the Secure Shell daemon functions. This includes TCP forwarding, listening on specific addresses and ports, sending keepalive messages, and server key settings.

AllowTcpForwarding This option specifies whether or not you can forward TCP traffic through Secure Shell. This does not include X traffic, and we'll cover that in another section. However, if you want to forward POP3, SMTP, IMAP4, Telnet, or other TCP connections through Secure Shell, you could. The default for this is "yes." This does not stop users from forwarding whatever type of traffic they want through Secure Shell, because users can create their own forwarders that do not honor the Secure Shell specific setting. What happens is SSH trusts the connection from the remote port, no matter what type of network traffic you are sending through. You would need to start a new server, and if you don't have root privileges, remember that only non-privileged ports are allowed.
Usage:

```
AllowTcpForwarding yes
```

KeepAlive The Secure Shell daemon can be set to send keepalive messages or to not send them. Keepalive messages let the remote server know whether or not the connection has died; and as a result, kills the active process. However, if the route temporarily goes away, it can get frustrating to see a message like this:

```
Connection down; disconnecting.
```

OK, so that's annoying. But if you don't send keepalives, you may have hanging sessions that leave ghost processes and eat your server's resources. The default setting is "yes," which means that the server sends keepalives. If you want to disable keepalive messages, you'll have to disable both the server and client configuration files. If you decide to turn them off, be aware that this may leave you with hanging processes.

Usage:

```
KeepAlive yes
```

KeyRegenerationInterval You can specify how frequently the server key is regenerated. The host key should not be regenerated unless you need to change the password or the host key was compromised or corrupted (use ssh-keygen for the host key). The default for this is an hour, or 3,600 seconds. After regenerating the key, it gets more difficult to recover for decrypting the encrypted packets even if the host is compromised. Setting this to zero means that the server key will not be regenerated and is strongly advised against. This is the same as the -k option.

Usage:

```
KeyRegenerationInterval 4000
```

ListenAddress If you are running a multi-homed host, you can specify which address you want the server to listen on. This defaults to your main IP interface, if you don't have more than one (and if you have only one, you don't have to set this).

Usage:

```
ListenAddress 1.2.3.4
```

Port You can specify a port for the Secure Shell daemon to listen on. The default port is 22; however, you may want to define another port when port 22 is in use or for application purposes. This is the same as the -p option. Remember that you need to use a non-privileged port if you don't have root privileges.

Usage:

```
Port 2022
```

ServerKeyBits You can specify the number of bits in the server key. This defaults to 768 bits; however, you can make this larger or smaller, depending on whether or not you are running from inetd or want stronger security. The smallest value is 512, and you can make this larger; however, be aware of performance issues. This is the same as the -b option.

Usage:

```
ServerKeyBits 512
```

StrictModes You can have the server check the file modes (permissions) and ownership of the user's home directory (and rhosts, if applicable) before making the login connection. This is a good idea because a user may have accidentally left their directory and files world-writable. If they did, make sure you shoot them. The default setting for StrictModes is "yes."

Usage:

```
StrictModes yes
```

Umask This sets the default umask for the Secure Shell daemon and its child process. The default is not to set the umask because many user account initialization scripts like .tcshrc have it in them. If you want to set a default in case someone has not, you can set this option. Make sure you check out the man page on umask before setting this variable.

Usage:

```
Umask 022
```

File Locations

The following options define where the Secure Shell daemons key files are located. This includes the key files, the random seed, and the process identification file.

HostKey This specifies which file you are using for the private host key. You have to use this option if you are not running the Secure Shell daemon as root. Normally, the private host key file is not readable by anyone but the root account; however, this is not the case if you are running it from a user account. The default file is /etc/ssh_host_key. Also, if you are using an alternative file, make sure you set the permissions to something like 400. This is the same as the -h option.

Usage:

```
HostKey /usr/local/etc/ssh_host_key
```

PidFile This defines the location of the process identification file for the parent sshd process. This default is either /etc/sshd.pid or /var/run/sshd.pid and is system-dependent.

Usage:

```
PidFile /usr/local/etc/sshd.pid
```

RandomSeed This defines the location of the random seed file used to generate server keys. The default location is /etc/ssh_random_seed.

Usage:

```
RandomSeed /usr/local/etc/ssh_random_seed
```

Account Activity Options

These options define what affects a remote account's environmental settings when you log in via Secure Shell. Most of these settings are set during login using environmental settings like .profile or .cshrc. However, you can make sure they take effect by setting them in the Secure Shell daemon configuration file.

LoginGraceTime This is what sets the "alert" mechanism in the Secure Shell daemon. It gives the client a certain grace time to authenticate with the server, which defaults to 600 seconds (10 minutes). If the client does not authenticate, then the server process disconnects from that socket. You can set this to zero, which means there is no limit on authentication time. Keep in mind that this can be the basis of a denial of service attack, so be careful. If you put the Secure Shell daemon in debug mode, then this is set to zero automatically. This is the same as the -g option.

Usage:

```
LoginGraceTime 660
```

CheckMail This sets whether or not the Secure Shell daemon should print if a user has new mail or not at login. This can be set in a user environmental startup script like .tcshrc or a system equivalent like /etc/profile for Korn Shell. The default setting for this is "yes," and this is a preference setting.

Usage:

```
CheckMail yes
```

IdleTimeout If you want to make sure someone is not maintaining a long-term idle connection to your host, you can set this variable. For example, if someone has logged in to your host via Secure Shell, and you know this person has a habit of walking away from their terminal without locking it, you may want to set this option. This sends the child process that has the connection a SIGHUP signal, which cleanly disconnects. The default to this is not set. To set it, you can use seconds (s), minutes (m), hours (h), days (d), or weeks (w). If you set a number without a letter, it defaults to seconds.

Usage:

```
IdleTimeout 5m
```

PrintMotd This defines whether or not the user account prints the system message of the day located in /etc/motd. This is only for interactive logins (not scp or ssh with a command after it). The default setting is "yes." This can also be set in the user's environmental initialization file.

Usage:

```
PrintMotd no
```

Logging Options

These options affect the output that is sent to the log files. You can either increase the logging, which might violate users' privacy, or turn it off completely—minus a few error messages.

FascistLogging If you have a need to log every little thing your users do (on a firewall, for instance), you can turn this on. However, if it is not a critical system such as a firewall or a server, don't use this. Fascist logging may violate personal privacy and is definitely *not* recommended if you don't need to know every little detail. The default is "no," and unless you have really good reason, don't turn this on. Also, if you do turn this on, notify your users.

Usage:

```
FascistLogging no
```

QuietMode This is the quiet mode, which means that nothing is sent to the system log. The stuff that is usually sent is the start of a connection, the authentication of the user, and the termination of the connection. You may not want to enable this option unless your logs fill up quite quickly. Audit trails are always good for checking to see if someone has illegally gained access to your system. The default is "no." This is the same as the -q option.

Usage:

```
QuietMode no
```

SilentDeny This specifies whether or not to deny a connection without logging. If not, the connection attempt is logged and an error message is sent to the user. The default for this is "no."

Usage:

```
SilentDeny no
```

SyslogFacility There are various methods for logging Secure Shell daemon messages. These include DAEMON, USER, AUTH, LOCAL0, LOCAL1, LOCAL2, LOCAL3, LOCAL4, LOCAL5, LOCAL6, and LOCAL7. The default is DAEMON, being the logging daemons. If you don't do anything funky with your logging, you're best leaving this with the default.

Usage:

```
SyslogFacility DAEMON
```

X11 Connections

One set of options is devoted to X11 traffic. This has to do with the X forwarding (not including other TCP traffic, which is covered in another set of options), the X display offset, and the location of the xauth program.

X11Forwarding This option defines whether or not X forwarding is allowed through the Secure Shell daemon. Like other TCP traffic, this can be overridden by user-defined forwarders. It's up to you whether to allow X traffic through. However, if you are going to let X traffic through remotely, you'll want to forward it through Secure Shell. The default setting is "yes."

Usage:

```
X11Forwarding yes
```

X11DisplayOffset This option defines the first display number available for the Secure Shell daemon's X11 forwarding. Usually, you have a display defined something like:

```
setenv DISPLAY "localhost:0.0"
```

You can define the display as "1" or whatever you want. This keeps the Secure Shell daemon from conflicting with the actual X servers. The default is 10.

Usage:

```
X11DisplayOffset 2
```

X11AuthLocation This defines the location of the xauth program for X authentication. There is no default for this, just set it if xauth or X binaries are not found during the configuration.

Usage:

```
X11AuthLocation /usr/local/X11/bin
```

A Sample Server Configuration File

Now that you know what your options are, here is an example of a Secure Shell daemon configuration file sshd_config. You can set yours how you like; this is just for illustration purposes:

```
# This is ssh server systemwide configuration file.
# These are some settings that we set through the TCP
# wrappers
# (commented for notes, we don't need to define them here)
# Date created - 11 Nov 98
# AllowHosts *.myhost.com goodguys.atotherhosts.com
# DenyHosts lowsecurity.knownhosts.com evilhosts.com
Port 22
ListenAddress 0.0.0.0
HostKey /etc/ssh_host_key
RandomSeed /etc/ssh_random_seed
ServerKeyBits 768
LoginGraceTime 600
KeyRegenerationInterval 3600
IgnoreRhosts no
StrictModes yes
QuietMode no
X11Forwarding yes
X11DisplayOffset 10
FascistLogging no
PrintMotd no
```

```
KeepAlive yes
SyslogFacility AUTH
RhostsAuthentication no
RhostsRSAAuthentication yes
RSAAuthentication yes
PasswordAuthentication yes
PermitEmptyPasswords no
UseLogin no
KerberosOrLocalPasswd yes
CheckMail no
```

Summary

The Secure Shell server daemon, sshd, is the controlling feature of Secure Shell. Secure Shell is unique because it uses various forms of authentication, including RSA public key, passwords, and rhosts. It also uses various symmetric key ciphers to encrypt the messages, including DES, 3DES, and IDEA. This is unlike most TCP applications like Telnet and FTP, which send information in the clear.

Secure Shell server daemon listens on port 22, which is a well-known port for Secure Shell. After the daemon hears a socket, it forks a child process that handles the host and server key authentication and client connections. When the connection is torn down, the child process goes away and the parent process remains listening for other Secure Shell connections.

The Secure Shell daemon has many options; some can be taken at the command line, whereas others are passed through a configuration file. The default configuration file is /etc/sshd_config. The options you can define include the types of authentication, X and other TCP network traffic, logging features, and filtering by hostname or username.

Secure Shell Clients—
ssh **and** scp

In this chapter:

- How it works

- The nuts and bolts

- Usage

- Files

Now that you know how the server works, you'll need to understand how the client works as well. As you have seen, most of the communication is handled by the server, including authentication and encryption.

How It Works

If you read Chapter 3 on how the Secure Shell 1 daemon works, you'll remember the drive-through bank teller analogy used for Secure Shell. If we go back to that analogy, the Secure Shell daemon would be the teller, the Secure Shell client would be the driver, the established connection the tube, and the data it passes between the two is the transaction inside the canister.

The Secure Shell client negotiates the encryption type, the type of connection (interactive or command line), compression if desired, the information passed between the remote and local servers, and forwarding. The forwarding includes the TCP/IP forwarding and X11 traffic. The client is what the user sees as SSH, but to the administrator, it defines what the user uses for authentication files, passwords, hostname, and username.

The client portion of Secure Shell provides the user with an interface; it's what most people are familiar with when they talk about Secure Shell. To most users, this will look like a remote login like telnet, rsh, or rlogin, or even a remote copy such as rcp.

Most of the actual connection is handled on the Secure Shell daemon side, which is covered in Chapter 3. The client does provide the user with an interface and a set of options that allow a user to login, send commands to a remote server, or copy files securely. The client is also what requests the connection from the local host to a remote host.

In addition, the client initiates the connection with the server and usually cuts the connection with a user command. The client also provides the user authentication via password or via .rhosts. The user public keys, which are stored in the user's home directory, are what the client uses so the user can log in remotely.

Secure Shell 1 uses two clients: ssh and scp. The ssh client allows secure remote logins and commands to be issued from a remote server, and the scp client allows secure file copying over networks. There is also slogin, which is simply an alias for ssh.

The Nuts and Bolts

Before any connection from the client takes place, the Secure Shell daemon needs to create a server key and a host key. A connection is always initiated by the client side. This includes both clients, ssh and scp. The server listens on a specific port, usually port 22, waiting for connections. The clients usually connect from port 1023 or higher.

The basic syntax for the Secure Shell client is:

```
$ ssh <options> <hostname> [command]
```

Without the command parameter, the Secure Shell client goes into interactive mode. Otherwise, Secure Shell executes the command on the remote server, then exits. You can also do this:

```
$ ssh <hostname>
```

This puts you into interactive mode using the defaults in the configuration files. You can also forward TCP/IP traffic like POP, NNTP, and X. This is covered in *"Other Cool Things You Can Do With Secure Shell"* on page 239.

Connecting

The client does not have to connect to a remote server; it may connect to the same server machine that the client is located on. This would happen on the local host, so it is through a TCP/IP socket connection. Other types of sockets can be used for Secure Shell, but they aren't currently implemented. See Figure 4.1 on page 92 for how TCP/IP connects.

> Be aware of security issues of connecting to root directly with
> Secure Shell. You probably want to log in as a user account with
> Secure Shell first, then su to root. You can also disable direct root
> logins.

Note

After the server daemon makes the connection to the socket, the client handles the interaction between the user and the remote host.

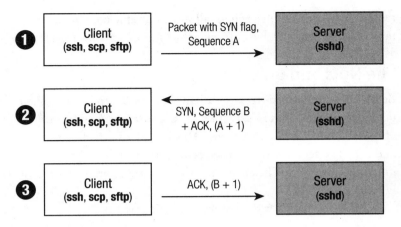

Figure 4.1 *The TCP handshake.*

The SSH client will fall back on rsh or rcp if no compatible SSH daemon is found on the remote server (the remote server is not accepting Secure Shell connections, port 22 is blocked by the firewall, and the like). Because Secure Shell always connects 8-bits clean, it will not connect this way unless defined by rlogin (rlogin uses the -8 to define the connection as 8-bit instead of 7-bit). However, you probably don't want to fall back on rlogin or rsh if you want to keep secure connections.

The basic steps for the client connection are the following:

1. Negotiates connection

2. Reads user and system configuration files

3. Authenticates user account (against RSA key, password, .rhosts or any combination thereof)

4. Forks process (if being run in the background)

5. Runs on a tty or standard input, depending on the type of connection

6. Close connection

Before Establishing the Connection

The Secure Shell client needs to do several tasks before running the connection on a remote host. One is to set a default umask of

022 which makes the files writable by the owner only, but world-readable. Because the modes are not set explicitly, this provides for a basic default set of permissions for the files.

Next, the Secure Shell client reads the configuration files. The first configuration files it reads are the user configuration files, which are located in the $HOME/.ssh directory. If the user does not specify any files such as known hosts, the Secure Shell client looks toward the system-wide configuration settings, which are stored in /etc/ssh_config.

If that does not exist, some defaults are set up by the client itself, such as the username, which defaults to the username running the Secure Shell client locally. Hostnames and usernames are limited to 255 characters maximum.

After a connection is opened to the remote host, the only time that the Secure Shell client needs root privileges is for rhosts authentication. However, it does run as root. Even though this is necessary for .rhosts authentication, the SUID bit is not set for scp. It looks like:

```
tigerlair:/home/stripes- ls -l /usr/local/bin/ssh /usr/local/bin/scp
-rws--x--x 1 root other 1383412 Sep 11 11:29 /usr/local/bin/ssh*
-rwxr-xr-x 1 root other 1383412 Sep 11 11:29 /usr/local/bin/ssh*
```

If the connection fails, the Secure Shell client will try to run rsh if allowed in your configuration of Secure Shell. If it succeeds, the host private key is loaded for RSA authentication. This is usually done before the Secure Shell client is no longer running as root because the host private key is only readable by root.

```
tigerlair:/home/stripes- ls -l /etc/ssh_host_key
-r-------- 1 root other 1383412 Sep 11 11:29 /etc/ssh_host_key*
```

During the Connection

As the connection is being established, the $HOME/.ssh directory is created if it doesn't already exist on the local host. This creates several files for the user, including the user private and public identity files (which is an RSA keypair), known hosts, and the random seed for that user. After the keypair is exchanged successfully between the host and the user accounts, a connection is estab-

lished. Figure 4.2 shows how the client functions during an interactive and non-interactive connection to the remote server.

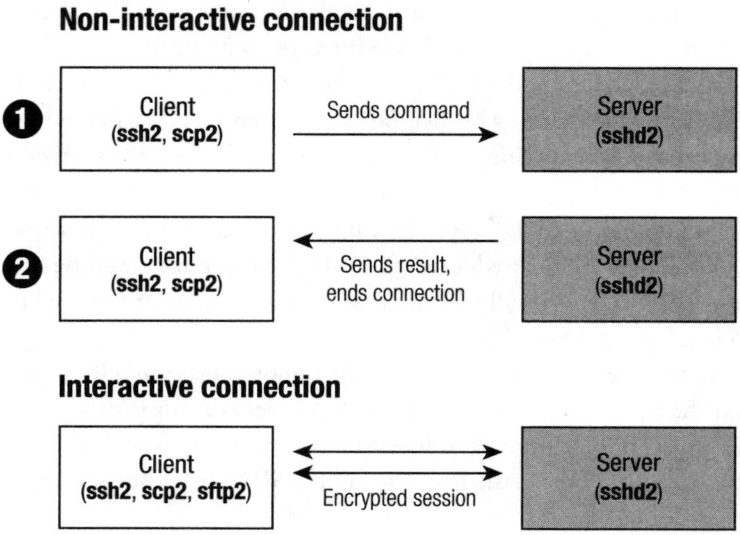

Non-interactive connection

Figure 4.2 *The interactive and non-interactive connections.*

The session is established on a tty if it is an interactive connection. Also, if compression is enabled, it's enabled after the successful key exchange. When the connection is established, the host
private key is cleared from memory. This prevents it from staying
in memory in case of a core dump.

If a tty is located, the Secure Shell client creates the packet and
stores the TERM information inside. Like the commands, there's no
limit on the string length, just on the packet size. This packet also
includes the window size of the terminal and the tty modes. It then
sends it to the remote server and awaits a response.

To execute a command on the remote host, it has to be specified.
For example, let's say you are going to use ssh with a command.
You need to specify it at the end of the command line. If you are
going to use a terminal, a tty will be allocated so you can execute
the remote commands interactively. This does not store any commands in the buffer because they are executed real-time.

Otherwise, if you do provide a command, the Secure Shell client will assume anything after the hostname is a command and store it in the buffer. It can be any length, because no limit is placed on the length of the command itself—only the packet that sends it. This prevents buffer overflow.

As the client is sending output, it does not actually get logged. Instead, all the output goes directly to the terminal on the local host. This includes the status line for scp, as well as any active terminal for the Secure Shell client—interactive or not.

Closing the Connection

When the user has decided to end the session, either because the command has been completed or logged out of an interactive session, the connection must be closed. The client must receive a signal and trap it, and the signal must be something that signals an exit. When the session is closed, the connection to the remote server is severed. Before the client exits, it returns a status.

Secure Copying—scp

Another nice functionality that the Secure Shell client does is allow you to copy remotely through Secure Shell. It uses the same ports as the ssh client for copying. As a matter of fact, the scp client is a modified version of the Berkeley services rcp that uses ssh as a transport. Because the Berkeley services rcp uses rcmd to execute the command remotely, it's not very secure. Using ssh allows scp to copy files using the same security that ssh does: RSA authentication, symmetric key encryption, and anti-spoofing mechanisms. See Figure 4.3 for how scp uses ssh for making connections.

Figure 4.3 *Secure Copy using* ssh *as a transport.*

The syntax is a little more complicated than ssh. It looks like this:

```
$ scp user@source:/directory/file user@destination:/directory/file
```

We'll review the syntax for scp later in this chapter.

Unlike the ssh client, scp does not run as SUID root. This is because it uses ssh to manage the connection, and that already runs as SUID root. Before connecting, scp establishes its functionality: verbose, statistics, compression, batch, cipher type, and non-privileged ports. The verbosity is how much information scp presents, statistics show you the status line on how much has downloaded, compression is used for increasing performance, batch mode is whether or not scp prompts for a password, and nonprivileged ports is used for using scp for any ports above 1023. The cipher type is the type of symmetric encryption used during the connection.

Before the connection is made, scp creates a socket pair for communicating with ssh. When the connection is made, the key-pairs are exchanged and the remote copy command is executed on the remote system. After the remote copy command is executed as the user on the host, the function returns a value before it closes: zero or higher if it succeeds and less than zero if it fails.

Usage of the Secure Shell Clients

Now that you have some understanding of how the Secure Shell clients work, it's important to know the options you can pass them. This includes the agents, the ciphers, the escape characters, how to send the client into the background, the verbosity, ports and port forwarding, and compression. This section covers usage on both ssh and scp clients.

Usage for ssh

Both Secure Shell clients, ssh and scp, use different syntax for the command options. The ssh client has many more options because it is has more functionality than just copying files. Also, it must provide some functionality for scp as well because scp uses ssh as a transport.

For all intents and purposes, ssh has a very simple syntax:

```
$ ssh [options] hostname [command]
```

Command-Line Options

You can set certain configuration settings with SSH on the command line. These options must be listed before the hostname. They include disabling the authentication agent, choosing the cipher, compressing the data, using a specified escape character, specifying file locations, port forwarding, using a certain level of verbosity, and setting SSH as a background process.

-a With this option, you can disable forwarding for the authentication agent. This prevents the passphrase that was loaded into memory from being used for this issuance of the Secure Shell client. If you want, you can specify this in the configuration file per host instead of globally.

-c cipher You can choose which symmetric key cipher you want to encrypt the network traffic with. This does not affect the authentication, which uses RSA public key. Your choices for ciphers are IDEA, DES, 3DES, and Blowfish. You can also choose "none," but this disables any encryption and renders the Secure Shell client unsecure. The "none" choice should only be used for debugging and testing purposes only, not for actual use. Arcfour has a security vulnerability associated with SSH, so don't use it. Your best bet is to use 3DES, IDEA, or Blowfish. Blowfish is the fastest supported algorithm for SSH1. For the best security, use IDEA. If IDEA is not supported for both Secure Shell servers, use 3DES. What's also cool about enabling 3DES is it works with DES connections as well.

> Be aware that DES is not secure. It's better than no encryption, but you can use other options to make your connection more secure.   **Note**

-C Compresses all the data being sent through the Secure Shell client, including input, output, error messages, and forwarded data. This uses the gzip algorithm, and the compression level can be defined through the configuration file option `CompressionLevel`. This works great for slow lines like modems, but it doesn't help much on an already fast network. Also using the configuration file, you can configure this option on a per host basis.

-e escape_character This defines the escape character. The default is "~" but can be set to any character or control character. You can also define the escape character to "none." This will make the session transparent, but you'll be unable to do anything if you want to suspend or run the session in the background. To use the escape character, type the escape character followed by a period and this closes the connection. If you type the escape character followed by **control+Z**, the connection gets suspended. The control character is only recognized after a carriage return.

  -f Sends the ssh connection to the background. This happens after authentication has been completed and forwarding for TCP/IP has been established. This is really great for starting X programs at the remote host. What happens here is the user is prompted for a password (provided the authentication agent isn't running), and then the connection is sent to the background.

  -g This allows the remote host to connect to a local port via port forwarding. Usually this is only allowed by the localhost.

  -i identity_file This defines the RSA private key, or identity file, through which authentication is read. The default file is $HOME/.ssh/identity. You can define multiple files for different hosts. If you do define different files, you may want to name them per host (identity.thishost, identity.thathost, for example).

  -k This option disables Kerberos ticket forwarding. This is another option you may want to define per host in the configuration file. Some hosts may want to use Kerberos, and others may not.

  -l login_name This specifies the username that you log in with on the remote host. The default is the same username as the one on the local host. This may also be defined on a per-host basis in the configuration file. This is a very practical option because in today's world many people have access to different hosts with different accounts.

  -L port:host:hostport This forwards any connection to the local host on the specified port to the hostport on the remote host. Basically, the socket listens to the port on the local host, and whenever a connection is made to this port (say, port 110 POP, for example), the connection is forwarded to the secure channel and the connection is made to the remote host on the hostport. Port forwarding can also be defined on a per-host basis via the configuration file. For privileged ports, only root can forward them.

  -n This option works similarly to the -f option; however, it will not work if you need to type a password. Standard input is redirected from `/dev/null`, and it must be used when the Secure Shell client is being sent to the background. This is commonly used for scripts and to send X traffic that's being run on the remote host. It's good to use this option with the authentication agent.

-o option This is used for passing options in the configuration file when no command-line option is defined. This includes `StrictHost-KeyChecking` and `UseRsh`, which do not have their own command-line option. These options and others are covered later in this chapter. This option has the same format as if it were in the configuration file.

-p port You can specify which port the client connects to the server on. The default is port 22, which is reserved for Secure Shell. Keep in mind that this port is defined in the `/etc/services` file for the server, unless otherwise specified. This may be specified on a per-host basis in the configuration file.

-P Use a port above 1023, a non-privileged port. You cannot use this for rhosts authentication (either combined with RSA or by itself).

-q This is the quiet mode, which means that nothing is displayed, including warning and diagnostic messages. You'll want to turn this option off if you're running into authentication or connection problems.

-R port:host:hostport This forwards any connection from the remote host on the specified port to the hostport on the local host. This works in the reverse way that the `-L` option does. A socket listens to a port on the remote host, and whenever a connection is made to this port, it is forwarded to the local host and the hostport. This port forwarding can be specified on a per-host basis in the configuration. Privileged ports can only be forwarded when logging in as root on the remote host.

-t This option forces the Secure Shell client to work in interactive mode by forcing a pseudo tty, even when a command is given. This can be used for executing screen-based programs on a remote host.

-V This prints the clients version number and exits.

-v Verbose mode. Causes `ssh` to print debugging messages about its progress. This is helpful in debugging connection, authentication, and configuration problems.

-x Disables forwarding for X traffic. Because X is known to be unsecure to begin with, paranoid sites may want to use this option. This option can be defined on a per-host basis via the configuration file.

Some Examples

These options are not set by default. The default setting for the Secure Shell client is to run in the foreground (if no command is passed) and start at terminal. Also, the traffic is not compressed by default. When compressing data, the process may slow down traffic and only waste CPU cycles since you may not get any increased bandwidth out of it. X traffic is automatically forwarded, but if it causes errors to send it, you can turn it off.

So, to log in to a remote account using Secure Shell, you can use:

```
$ ssh host.com
```

Or you can use slogin (which is a hard link to ssh):

```
$ slogin host.com
```

Let's say you want to log in with a different username; for example, the local host I'm on has the username "anne." The account I have on the remote host is "ahc." To log in with "ahc," I use the following:

```
$ ssh -l ahc host.com
```

Because I'm using a modem line and want to log in with the same account on my local system, I need to turn on compression. I also want to use the IDEA cipher:

```
$ ssh -C -c idea host.com
```

If you want to connect to the remote host and run the process in the background, you can do that very easily. This is usually used in conjunction with X programs or in shell scripts. Keep in mind this will prompt for authentication. You'll also want to turn off the escape character.

```
$ ssh -f -e host.com xload
```

If you want to redirect input from /dev/null and run the remote program in the background, use the -f option's related option: -n. This does not prompt for passwords, so make sure you use this with .shosts or the authentication agent. Again, you'll probably want to turn off the escape character.

```
$ ssh -n -e host.com xclock &
```

If you want to connect to the remote server on a different port besides port 22, usually a non-standard port, use the `-p` option.

```
$ ssh -p 2022 host.com
```

Usage for `scp`

As stated previously in the chapter, the syntax for `scp` is a little more complicated than `ssh`. It looks like this:

```
$ scp user@source:/directory/file user@destination:/directory/file
```

The nice thing about `scp` is you can copy to the remote host or the local host. So, depending on where the file you are sending is located (either the remote or local host), you need to specify the username, the hostname, the directory, and the file. This may sound complicated and like a lot to remember, but if you are doing this right, you should be OK. I use `scp` to copy files to and from my Linux host at home and my ISP account.

Command-Line Options

If you need to toggle between displaying statistics, setting the cipher, defining the identity files, preserving file attributes, setting up the ports, enabling compression, setting batch mode, and defining options for `ssh` (since `scp` uses `ssh` as a transport), these options will help you establish some of the functionality you want for ssh.

-a This turns on the statistics display for each file. The statistics display shows the progress on the copying of each file. If you want to turn this on globally, you can use the `-Q` option.

-A This option turns off statistics display for each file. If you are using `scp` in a script, you may want to turn this off completely using the `-q` option.

-B Batch mode. Batch mode prevents asking for passphrases so you can use `scp` in scripts.

-c cipher This is the same option that is defined in `ssh`, since it is passed directly to `ssh`. You can choose which symmetric key cipher you want to encrypt the network traffic with. This does not affect the authentication, which uses RSA public key. Your choices for ciphers are IDEA, DES, 3DES, Blowfish, and Arcfour. You can also choose "none," but this disables any encryption and renders the Secure Shell client unsecure. The "none" choice should only be used for debugging and testing purposes only, not for actual use. DES and Arcfour are both known to be cryptanalyzed ciphers, so don't use them. Your best bet is to use 3DES, IDEA, or Blowfish. Blowfish is the fastest supported algorithm for SSH1. For the best security, use IDEA. If IDEA is not supported for both Secure Shell servers, use 3DES.

-C This is the same option that is defined in ssh, since it is passed directly to ssh. It compresses all the data being sent through the Secure Shell client, including input, output, error messages, and forwarded data. This uses the gzip algorithm, and the compression level can be defined through the configuration file option CompressionLevel. This works great for slow lines like modems, but it doesn't help much on an already fast network. Also, using the configuration file, you can configure this option on a per-host basis.

-i identity_file This is the same option that is defined in ssh, since it is passed directly to ssh. It defines the RSA private key, or identity file, through which authentication is read. The default file is $HOME/.ssh/identity. You can define multiple files for different hosts. If you do define different files, you may want to name them per host (identity.thishost, identity.thathost, for example).

-L Use a port above 1023, a non-privileged port. You cannot use this for rhosts authentication (either combined with RSA or by itself). However, this is very helpful for connecting through some firewalls that do not have configurations for it. This is the same as the -P option for ssh. You can also say UsePriviledgePort=no in the configuration file or "-o UsePriviledgePort=no" on the command line. There's no logical reason for using -L for defining a non-privileged port, except that the author was running out of letters.

-o ssh_option This specifies options to be passed to ssh. Because ssh is the transport and the options that can be passed to scp are limited, this enables the user to specify more options for scp. These options are listed under the ssh usage section previously in this chapter.

-p Preserves the file attributes from the source host. This includes modification times, access times, and modes from the original file. This option is taken directly from rcp and is very useful if you are backing up files and want to ensure file integrity.

-P port You can specify which port the client connects to the server on. The default is port 22, which is reserved for Secure Shell. Keep in mind that this port is defined in the /etc/services file for the server, unless otherwise specified. It may be specified on a per-host basis in the configuration file, which is different than ssh because rcp uses -p to preserve file attributes.

-q This option turns off the statistics display. This is not on an individual file basis, but for all files. This can be very useful in shell scripts. If you want to turn this off on a per-file basis, use the -A option.

-Q This option turns on the statistics display. This is not on an individual file basis, but for all files. This is also very useful in shell scripts. If you want to turn this off on a per-file basis, use the -a option.

-r Recursively copies entire directories and the files inside. This option copies files and directories in every directory below the current one defined.

-S path_to_ssh This option specifies the path to ssh. This is used if you've installed ssh in a non-standard directory.

-v Verbose mode. Causes ssh and scp to print debugging messages about its progress. This is helpful in debugging connection, authentication, and configuration problems.

> For turning on and off the statistics display options, you can define on a file or global basis. Just remember that -a and -Q are similar and -A and -q are similar, not -a and -q and -A and -Q. Don't mix the upper- and lowercase options.
>
> **Note**

Some Examples

The following options are not set by default. The default setting for the scp is to run in the foreground and display the statistics. Also, the traffic is not compressed by default as well because this may slow down traffic and only waste CPU cycles. Also, batch mode is not set and port 22 is used by default. We'll assume that the local host account name is "anne" and the remote host account name is "ahc."

So, to copy a file from my local host to my remote host:

```
$ scp filename ahc@host:/home/ahc/
```

To copy a file from the remote host to the current directory on the local host, I use the same command. However, it looks a little different:

```
$ scp ahc@host:/home/ahc/filename
```

If you want to see statistics, they look something like this:

```
$ scp ahc@host:/home/ahc/filename
SHOW OUTPUT
```

If you've got the authentication agent running and you want to use scp in batch mode:

```
$ scp -B ahc@host:/home/ahc/filename
```

You can copy an entire directory structure when you're backing up a Web site, for instance, and compress it because you're doing it over a modem line:

```
$ scp -r -C ahc@host:/home/ahc/tools
```

Configuring the Secure Shell Client

Secure Shell has a configuration file where you can define options by default. This sets options for both the ssh and the scp clients. Some of these options are not definable except for the command-line option, but you can configure them from the configuration file. Like most configuration files and shell scripts, empty lines and lines starting with the "#" are not read. The default configuration file for Secure Shell is /etc/ssh_config. This sets the options for both the ssh and scp clients.

With the client, the user can have their own specified settings in the $HOME/.ssh/config file, which has the same format as the /etc/ssh_config file. The order in which options are applied to the client works like this:

1. Command-line options

2. The user's configuration file

3. The system-wide configuration file

The following are the options that you can set in the `ssh_config` file for Secure Shell. The format for defining these options in the `/etc/ssh_config` file is:

```
OptionType Argument
```

If you have multiple arguments, they are separated by a space. This format applies to each of the following options.

Hostname Options

You can define some options affecting the remote host you connect to with some configuration options. All of them also apply to IP addresses as well as network hostnames. With wildcards, you can filter by entire domains or a range of addresses.

Host This defines which host is affected by the options configured in the configuration file. You can use wildcards ('*' for multiple characters and '?' for single characters). This is the same as the hostname that is given on the command line.

Usage:

```
Host tigerlair.com
```

HostName This can be used like an `/etc/hosts` file. It can define aliases for real hostnames. The default is the hostname that is given on the command line. You can use IP addresses as well as domain names.

Usage:

```
HostName tigerlair.com
```

StrictHostKeyChecking This can be used to configure the client on whether or not to automatically add host keys to the `$HOME/.ssh/known_hosts` file or to ask for them. If you frequently connect to different hosts (for instance, you are using a shell account from an ISP and your connection gets a dynamically allocated IP address), this may not be a good idea and could become quite irritating. If you are setting up Secure Shell to run on a production environment where the hosts should not be changing, you'll probably want to set this to "no." Your options are "no," "yes," and "ask." The "ask" option prompts you if you want to add a host to your `known_hosts` file. The idea here is that you need to manually

import the host's public key over a secure medium, like a trusted
person with the key on a floppy.

Usage:

```
StrictHostKeyChecking ask
```

Authentication

Secure Shell provides different authentication methods: passwords, rhosts, RSA keys, and TIS authentication mechanisms. You
can either use one or a combination of any of the above for accessing accounts via Secure Shell. However, be aware that rhosts
authentication is the weakest, whereas any combination with the
RSA key is going to be your strongest form of authentication.

BatchMode This turns off prompting for passwords when
turned on. This is great if you're using Secure Shell in scripts or
running cron or batch jobs. Remember, it does help to have the
authentication agent going instead of using rhosts for this. The
default is "no," and your choices are "yes" and "no."

Usage:

```
BatchMode no
```

NumberOfPasswordPrompts This specifies the amount of password prompts before exiting. This must be an integer less than 5.
The server puts a limit on the number of attempts at 5, so the client
can only restrict it further, which prevents someone from running
the client on a remote host and getting as many password attempts
they want and brute forcing the password. The default value is one.

Usage:

```
NumberOfPasswordPrompts 3
```

PasswordAuthentication You can define whether or not you
want to use passwords to access accounts via Secure Shell. The
default is "yes," and what the passwords do is protect the RSA key,
not the account itself by more conventional means. You may opt to
turn off password authentication, but leaving it on is better because
it provides an additional means of authentication. This is similar to
the PasswordAuthentication for the Secure Shell daemon.

Usage:

```
PasswordAuthentication yes
```

PasswordPromptHost This specifies whether or not to include the remote hostname in the password prompt. This only has an effect on what the user sees, not on what the program actually does.

Usage:

```
PasswordPromptHost yes
```

PasswordPromptLogin This specifies whether or not to include the remote username in the password prompt. This only has an effect on what the user sees, not on what the program actually does.

Usage:

```
PasswordPromptLogin yes
```

RhostsAuthentication This option sets your authentication to be based on the .rhosts or /etc/hosts.equiv alone. This doesn't require a password or an RSA key and opens your system to Berkeley services attacks that are well known by the public and the reason you are using Secure Shell in the first place. The default is "no," and you're best leaving it that way. If you do want to use Rhosts authentication, use it in conjunction with the RSA authentication in RhostsRSAAuthentication. This is similar to the Secure Shell server daemon setting RhostsAuthentication. However, it does not have the same significant effect on security in the way that the server-side configuration does.

Usage:

```
RhostsAuthentication no
```

RhostsRSAAuthentication This option sets your authentication to be based on the .rhosts or /etc/hosts.equiv with the RSA key. This doesn't require a password, but it does require that the remote side have an RSA key to authenticate against. This opens your system up to Berkeley services attacks, but the threat is minimized because of the required RSA key. If you do leave this option at "yes" (the default), you may want to set some stricter login requirements for hosts. Again, if you want to lean on the more secure side of things, turn off any type of rhosts authentication.

This is similar to the Secure Shell server daemon configuration option RhostsRSAAuthentication.

Usage:

```
RhostsRSAAuthentication no
```

RSAAuthentication You can use a myriad of authentication types; or as you can see, you can use a sole type as well. If you want to define only RSA authentication to be accepted, you can. This does not require rhosts or passwords to help authenticate. The default is "yes" and this is fine to leave as is. This is similar to the Secure Shell server daemon configuration option RSAAuthentication.

Usage:

```
RSAAuthentication yes
```

TISAuthentication Secure Shell also supports alternative authentication mechanisms like TIS Authentication Server, authsrv. If you configure Secure Shell to support TIS, you'll want to set this to "yes" (the default is "no"). This is similar to the Secure Shell server daemon option TISAuthentication.

Usage:

```
TISAuthentication no
```

Kerberos Options

Kerberos is a third-party UNIX authentication system that uses "tickets" to authenticate. Also, for Kerberos to work, applications that use it have to be "kerberized." However, Secure Shell acknowledges this and provides Kerberos support without having to kerberize it.

KerberosAuthentication This specifies whether or not to support Kerberos tickets for authentication or to let passwords be validated through the Kerberos KDC or DCE Security Server. The default is "yes," but if you don't have a kerberized environment, you can turn this off. This is similar to the Secure Shell server daemon option KerberosAuthentication.

Usage:

```
KerberosAuthentication no
```

KerberosTgtPassing If you want to be able to forward a Kerberos ticket to the server, turn this option on. The default is "yes." This option is important only if you have turned on Kerberos ticketing. This is similar to the Secure Shell server daemon option `KerberosTgtPassing`.

Usage:

```
KerberosTgtPassing no
```

Client Options

These options are specific to how the Secure Shell client functions overall. These general settings include things like the username on the remote host, connection attempts, proxy commands (if used), the cipher, forwardings, the escape character, and using `rsh`.

Cipher This option lets you choose the cipher you connect with. You can use IDEA, 3DES, Blowfish, DES, and Arcfour. You can also pick "none," but don't do this unless you are debugging. Your best bets are to pick either IDEA, 3DES, or Blowfish. Because IDEA is not supported by all servers, if you pick IDEA and it's not supported, it will fall back to 3DES.

Usage:

```
Cipher IDEA
```

ClearAllForwardings This option clears all forwardings (including X11) after taking in all command-line options and the options defined in the user and system-wide configuration files. This is useful if you are making multiple connections. The `scp` client sets this by default so it will not fail even if you do have some forwardings defined in the configuration files.

Usage:

```
ClearAllForwardingsyes
```

ConnectionAttempts Here you can specify the amount of times that the Secure Shell client tries to connect to the remote server before exiting (or falling back on `rsh` if you decide). If you have some unstable connections, you may want to set this to a low number (make sure you use integers).

Usage:

```
ConnectionAttempts 3
```

EscapeChar This defines the escape character. The default is the tilde (~). This is the same as the -e option you can pass on the command line. The argument should only be a single character, or a single character followed by a carat (^) to indicate a control character, or "none" to disable the escape character (which makes the connection transparent).

Usage:

```
EscapeChar z^
```

FallBackToRsh You can define the Secure Shell client so that if it fails to connect (usually because there is no daemon running on the remote or local side), it will try to connect to the remote client via rsh. Before running rsh, you will get a warning that the session is not encrypted. It will look something like this:

```
tigerlair:/home/ahc: ssh www.trusting.host.com
Secure connection to www.trusting.host.com refused;
reverting to insecure method.
Using rsh. WARNING: Connection will not be encrypted.
```

Usage:

```
FallBackToRsh no
```

ForwardAgent This option can be configured to forward the connection to the authentication agent on the remote host. This helps when you are not using passwords and want to use Secure Shell for things like shell scripts.

Usage:

```
ForwardAgent yes
```

KeepAlive The Secure Shell daemon can be set to send keep-alive messages or not to send them. Keepalive messages let the remote server know whether or not the connection has died; and as a result, kills the active process. However, if the route temporarily goes away, it can get frustrating to see a message like this:

```
Connection down; disconnecting.
```

OK, so it is annoying. But if you don't send keepalives, you may have hanging sessions that leave ghost processes and eat your server's resources. The default setting is "yes," which means that the server sends keepalives. If you want to disable keepalive messages, you have to disable both the server and client configuration files. Be aware that this may leave you with hanging processes if you decide to turn them off. This is similar to the Secure Shell server daemon configuration setting KeepAlive.

Usage:

```
KeepAlive yes
```

ProxyCommand This specifies which command to execute to connect to the proxy server. This command can only be as long as the end of the line and is executed with the /bin/sh. Two substitutions you can use are %h and %p for host and port, respectively. At some point in the command, the connection should be to an inetd superdaemon running the Secure Shell daemon (sshd -i) or should call sshd running on some host. Keep in mind that SOCKS support can be compiled during the installation, which is covered in Chapter 2, "Installing Secure Shell on UNIX."

Usage:

```
ProxyCommand ssh %h 2> ssh_connection_error_log
```

User This lets you specify a username for logging in on the remote host. You may want to define this if you are constantly logging on a remote host with a different username than you have on your local host. This way you don't have to constantly type it on the command line with the -l option.

Usage:

```
User ahc
```

UseRsh This option specifies whether or not rsh should be used for this host. If the host does not support the ssh protocol, then rsh or rlogin is automatically executed. If this option is specified, all the other options are ignored. So, aside from the inherent security issues with rsh, you may not want to use this.

Usage:

```
UseRsh no
```

File Locations

These options define where the Secure Shell client files are located. This includes the user's identity file and the known host files for the system and the user.

GlobalKnownHostsFile This defines the location of the system's known hosts file. The default location is /etc/ssh_known_hosts.

Usage:

```
GlobalKnownHostsFile /usr/local/etc/ssh_known_hosts
```

IdentityFile This specifies where the user's RSA private key is located. The default is $HOME/.ssh/identity. You can define various identity files that can be used by the authentication agent. You can also define an identity file for each host that you are going to connect to. You can use the tilde (~) instead of $HOME to represent the user's home directory.

Usage:

```
IdentityFile ~/.ssh/identity.thishost
```

UserKnownHostsFile This specifies the known_hosts file to use for this particular user. The default is $HOME/.ssh/known_hosts. Like the IdentityFile option, you can use the tilde (~) instead of $HOME to represent the user's home directory.

Usage:

```
UserKnownHostsFile ~/.ssh/my_known_hosts
```

X11 Connections

The following is a set of options devoted to X11 traffic; they apply specifically to X forwarding, but not other TCP traffic or the location of the xauth program.

ForwardX11 This option defines whether or not X forwarding is automatically sent through the Secure Shell channel and is where the DISPLAY environmental variable gets set. Like other TCP traffic, this can be overridden by user-defined forwarders. It is up to you to allow X traffic through. However, if you are going to let X traffic through remotely, you'll want to forward it through Secure Shell. This is similar to the X11Forwarding option on the Secure Shell daemon.

Usage:

```
ForwardX11 yes
```

X11AuthLocation This is similar to the XAuthLocation for the Secure Shell daemon. This defines the location of the xauth program for X authentication. There is no default for this, just set it if xauth or X binaries were not found during the configuration.

Usage:

```
X11AuthLocation /usr/local/X11/bin
```

Compression

Compression is used to shrink the amount of data that will eventually be pumped into the packets. The packet size is a kernel setting, MTU, and is typically about 1700 bytes. If you are using a slow connection like a modem or passing large applications like X through a slow network, you'll probably want to turn compression on. Not only can you decide whether or not you want compression, but you can also define what level of compression you want.

Compression This defines whether or not you use compression. This is the same algorithm that the gzip application uses. You have two obvious choices: yes or no. Keep in mind if you're on a fast network, you don't want to bother turning compression on because it will actually slow things down as opposed to speed them up.

Usage:

```
Compression yes
```

CompressionLevel You can define how much compression you want. You can only set this if compression has been turned on. The highest level you can have is 9, and the lowest you can have is 1. The default is 6, which works just fine for most slow connections like a modem line. However, if you are trying to push X traffic through a modem line, you probably want to use 8 or 9.

Usage:

```
CompressionLevel 9
```

Ports

With Secure Shell, you can do a lot of things with the ports. This includes defining ports for forwarding both locally and remotely, the actual port that the Secure Shell client connects on, and whether or not privileged ports are used.

GatewayPorts This option specifies whether or not remote hosts may or may not connect to a locally forwarded port. Usually, only the local host is allowed to do this. This is the same as the -g command-line option.

Usage:

```
GatewayPorts no
```

LocalForward This forwards any connection to the local host on the specified port to the hostport on the remote host. This allows the socket to listen to the port on the local host, and whenever a connection is made to this port (say port 110 for POP, for example), the connection is forwarded to the secure channel and the connection is made to the remote host on the hostport. For privileged ports, only root can forward them. This is the same as the -L option for the ssh client.

Usage:

```
LocalForward 1025:remotehost:110
```

Port You can specify a port for the Secure Shell client to connect to. The default port is 22; however, you may want to define another port when port 22 is in use or for application purposes. This is the same as the -p option. This is also similar to the Port option for the Secure Shell server daemon configuration file.

Usage:

```
Port 2022
```

RemoteForward This forwards any connection from the remote host on the specified port to be forwarded to the hostport on the local host. This works in the reverse way the -L option does. A socket listens to a port on the remote host, and whenever a connection is made to this port, it is forwarded to the local host and the hostport. Privileged ports can only be forwarded when logging in as root on the remote host. This is the same as the -R option for the ssh client.

Usage:

```
RemoteForward 110:remotehost:1025
```

UsePrivilegedPort Use a port above 1023, a non-privileged port. You cannot use this for rhosts authentication (either combined with RSA or by itself). However, this is very helpful for connecting through some firewalls that do not have configurations for it. This is the same as the -P option.

Usage:

```
UsePrivilegedPort yes
```

A Sample Client Configuration File

Now that you know what your options are, here's an example of a Secure Shell daemon configuration file sshd_config. You can set yours however you like; this is just for illustration purposes.

```
# This is ssh client systemwide configuration file.
# This file provides defaults for users, and the values
# can be changed in per-user configuration
# files or on the command line.
# Site-wide defaults for various options
# This allows users to connect to all hosts
Host *
# This allows the authentication agent to forward to
# remote hosts
ForwardAgent yes
# Turn off X11 forwarding
ForwardX11 no
# Authentication options. Turn off any form of rhosts and
# TIS authentication
RhostsAuthentication yes
RhostsRSAAuthentication no
RSAAuthentication yes
TISAuthentication no
# Make sure password authentication is turned on
PasswordAuthentication yes
# Turn off any form of rsh connectivity
FallBackToRsh no
UseRsh no
# Turn on batch mode for those who want to run ssh in
# scripts
```

```
BatchMode yes
# Use IDEA for our first choice in ciphers
Cipher idea
# Leave these defaults
StrictHostKeyChecking no
IdentityFile ~/.ssh/identity
Port 22
EscapeChar ~
```

Other Secure Shell Client Configuration Files

In addition to the Secure Shell client system and user configuration files, you need to be aware of other files that affect the way the Secure Shell client behaves. The configuration files are stored either in the /etc directory for system-wide configurations or in $HOME/ .ssh for individual settings.

The /etc Directory

The files listed below are found in the /etc directory and are not configuration files for the ssh client itself, but they are important to how ssh behaves. This includes the /etc/shosts.equiv file, the /etc/sshrc file, and the /etc/ssh_known_hosts file.

/etc/shosts.equiv These are trusted hosts for Secure Shell only. If you use the .rhosts and /etc/hosts.equiv, both Berkeley services and Secure Shell will trust the hosts. The user equivalent of this file is in the user's home directory called .shosts. If you are implementing a Secure Shell environment, you may want to use only the shosts.equiv and .shosts files.

/etc/sshrc This file has similar functionality to a /etc/login file. This file sets global login-time initializations before a user's shell starts after they have logged in. Variables can be set on a per host basis. This file should only be writable by root; you don't want users to change the login initializations for everyone.

/etc/ssh_known_hosts This file contains a list of known host keys for the local host. This file should be managed by the system administrator only and should contain only the host keys of the LAN or the hosts that the administrator feels are trustworthy. This file only contains public keys with the critical information in this format:

```
public key hostname bits-per-modulus public exponent comments
```

Keep in mind that the comments are optional. If you have a different hostname but the same physical host, separate listings must be made for each hostname.

The ~/.ssh Directory

The files listed below are found in the ~/.ssh directory and are not configuration files for the client itself (the ~/.ssh/config file for the user). This includes the following files in the ~/.ssh directory: environment, known_hosts, random_seed, identity, identity.pub, authorized_keys, and rc files.

$HOME/.ssh/authorized_keys This file contains all the RSA public keys that are used for RSA authentication from this account from remote sites. This file should only be accessible by the user, not by anyone else. The format for this file is similar to the ~/.ssh/identity.pub file.

$HOME/.ssh/config This is the user configuration file, as discussed previously in this chapter.

$HOME/.ssh/identity This is the user's RSA private key. Like the ~/.ssh/random_seed, the user should not modify the permissions or change the file in any way. Because this is how the Secure Shell client recognizes the user, it is strongly recommended that you specify a passphrase when generating the key. This passphrase is used to encrypt the data with the IDEA cipher. This file is unreadable by people.

$HOME/.ssh/identity.pub This is the user's RSA public key. Unlike the ~/.ssh/identity file, this file is readable by humans and looks a lot like a PGP public key. This file should be added to any remote host you want to log in to in the ~/.ssh/authorized_keys file. It isn't necessary for Secure Shell; however, the user may feel more secure using it.

$HOME/.ssh/known_hosts This file keeps record of the public host keys for all the hosts that the user has logged in to, including hosts that are not in the /etc/ssh_known_hosts file.

$HOME/.ssh/random_seed This file is used for seeding the random number generator; it is specific to the user and the user should not modify the permissions or change the file in any way. This is used in the public key exchange for the user files and is unreadable by people.

$HOME/.ssh/rc This file sets the user's login-time initializations before a user's shell starts after they have logged in. Variables can be set on a per host basis. This file should only be writable by the user.

Environmental Variables

Even after learning about all the other files that affect the Secure Shell client's behavior, you can set some environmental variables as well. These variables are set by Secure Shell, and the user should not be configuring them on their own because they directly affect Secure Shell's behavior. You may be able to set other environmental variables, but this varies from operating system to operating system. For example, the following information might be read from either /etc/environment or $HOME/.ssh/environment:

DISPLAY This variable sets the location of the X server. It is usually defined by the user when not using Secure Shell. However, because Secure Shell sets this variable dependent on authorization cookies, you do not want to manually set this variable. The format of DISPLAY usually looks like this:

```
DISPLAY=hostname:number
```

where number is greater than or equal to one. Zero is usually used on a local host.

LOGNAME or USER This variable sets the username.

MAIL Sets the directory to the user's mailbox. It may be something like $HOME/inbox.

PATH Sets the default path for the user, as defined in /etc/environment. This may be overridden by the user's shell initialization files, such as ~/.cshrc or ~/.profile.

SSH_AUTH_SOCK If SOCKS is configured, this specifies the UNIX domain socket's path used to talk to the authentication agent.

SSH_CLIENT Locates the client. This variable includes the client's IP address, the client's port number, and the server's port number. It may look something like this:

```
111.22.3.44 1025 22
```

SSH_ORIGINAL_COMMAND If you are using the Secure Shell client to remotely execute a command, this variable is set to show the original command line that the user sent.

SSH_TTY This sets the path to the tty device that is associated with the prevalent shell. If there is no tty (for example, Secure Shell is not set in an interactive mode), this variable will not be set.

Summary

The Secure Shell server client, ssh and scp, is the main interface to Secure Shell. Secure Shell can be used either in an interactive mode like `rlogin` or in a command mode like `rsh`. The server is authenticated with RSA keys, and the user authenticates with a RSA public key cryptography. The user can also authenticate with a password or other authentication devices such as SecurID cards. Before the user authentication takes place, the session is encrypted with a symmetric key: IDEA, 3DES, DES, Blowfish, or Arcfour.

The Secure Shell server client connects to the server on port 22, which is a well-known port for Secure Shell. Before it connects, it reads the configurations passed through command lines, the user's configuration files, or system-wide configuration files. When the connection is established and the symmetric key algorithm is determined, the Secure Shell client encrypts the packets before even sending the password over the network. If a command needs to be executed, it is stored in a buffer before the connection is established. If the session is interactive, then the Secure Shell client allocates a tty.

The Secure Shell clients have many options; some can be taken at the command line, whereas others can be passed through a configuration file. The default system-wide configuration file is `/etc/ssh_config`, and individual users have `~/.ssh/config`. For the options you can define, they include the types of authentication, compression, X, port forwarding, and some specific options for `scp`, such as recursive copying and keeping the current file attributes.

Secure Shell 2 (SSH2)

Secure Shell 2 Server Daemon—`sshd2` and `sftp-server2`

In this chapter:

- SSH 2.0 Protocol

- The nuts and bolts

- Usage

- Files

- Secure File Transfer Server—`sftp-server`

Now that you've installed and configured Secure Shell on your UNIX system, you'll want to know how to use the Secure Shell 2 server daemon, sshd2, and its FTP server as well. You don't need to use sshd2 unless you are using the Secure Shell 2 clients (ssh2, scp2, or sftp) to connect.

SSH 2.0 Protocol

The second release of Secure Shell is built on the SSH2 protocol. This protocol defines how it works, how the packet is assembled, and what the protocol provides. Secure Shell has two different protocols: SSH 1.5 is used in Secure Shell releases 1.2.26 and earlier, and SSH 2.0 is used in version 2.0.0 and higher. SSH 2.0 is covered in this chapter, and SSH 1.5 is covered in *"Secure Shell 1 Server Daemon*—sshd*"* on page 55.

How It Works

Secure Shell 2 works very similarly to Secure Shell 1, but with some fundamental changes. The code has been 98% rewritten according to the README file, which means that the functions work differently from SSH1. It also means that the SSH1 and SSH2 protocols are incompatible. There is built-in support for DSA[1] public key exchange, which does the same thing that the RSA authentication provides, except with none of the legal issues[2]. The only way you can get the RSA authentication method with SSH2 is by purchasing the commercial version.

Secure Shell 2 also uses a different set of protocols that comply with the proposed secsh charter to the IETF. (This is currently in draft form.) This makes Secure Shell 2 more flexible and more secure than Secure Shell 1 and allows Secure Shell 2 to integrate with digital certificate infrastructures including X.509 certificates used for Public Key Infrastructure (PKI), DNSSEC, and Simple Public Key Infrastructure (SPKI). Additionally, Secure Shell 2 can work without a central key management structure just like Secure Shell 1.

Secure Shell 2 also has support for platform-independent modules that implement specific functions. This enables a system admin-

---

1. Digital Signature Algorithm (DSA)
2. RSA is under U.S. patent until the year 2000. After that, free implementations will be legal in the United States.

istrator to incorporate specific functions from the operating system into the Secure Shell transport. Secure Shell 2, like Secure Shell 1, operates on layer 7 of the OSI model on the TCP/IP protocol.

Some other cool things that Secure Shell 2 has done is to implement a secure file transfer client and server, sftp. Also, Secure Shell 2 has built-in SOCKS support for SOCKS 4.x, so you can connect using the SOCKS proxy much easier than with Secure Shell 1.

Most of the encryption and authentication functionality works like Secure Shell 1. The Secure Shell server is also responsible for executing shell commands or logins on the remote host and sending the information securely to the remote site from the client and vice versa. Other things that the Secure Shell server secures are X11 and port forwarding, and the Secure Shell Agent, ssh-agent2, connections.

The encryption cipher is decided on by the Secure Shell Server daemon, which is on the remote side. This controls the host key checks and makes sure they work properly. If you have problems with your host key, you'll probably want to run the remote SSH server in debug mode as well as the client. Other critical encryption functions that the server handles is error-checking with encryption to not allow sensitive information outside.

Unlike other TCP/IP applications, Secure Shell is designed to work on its own instead of with wrappers or through the Internet daemon inetd. Nonetheless, many people do want to run the Secure Shell daemon through TCP wrappers. You can run it through inetd for the TCP wrappers (tcpd), which is run from inetd; however, this is not necessary. Using TCP wrappers is covered in *"Other Cool Things You Can Do With Secure Shell"* on page 239.

The Connection

The SSH 2.0 protocol handles connection establishment, key exchange, user and server authentication, and TCP connections such as forwarding, pty allocation for interactive sessions, X11, and the Secure Shell agent. It handles everything in separate layers: the connection layer, the user authentication layer, and the transport layer. This does not include the reliable unsecure transport that might be forwarded to SSH. See Figure 5.1 to see the difference between the SSH 1.5 and SSH 2.0 protocols.

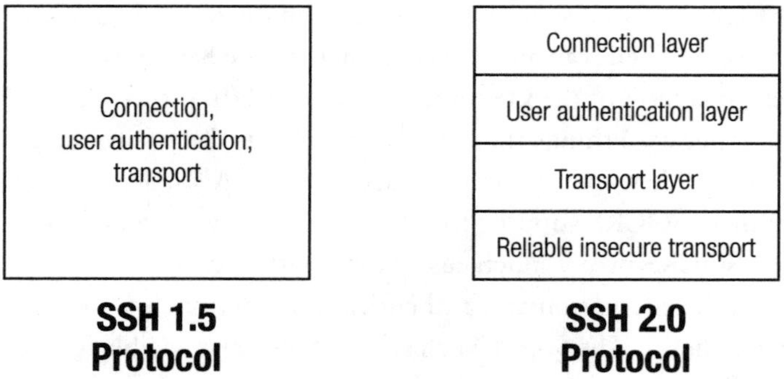

**SSH 1.5
Protocol**

**SSH 2.0
Protocol**

Figure 5.1 *The difference between the SSH 1.5 and SSH 2.0 protocols.*

The connection layer can handle multiple channels through a single connection. These channels are independent of the sessions and are flow-controlled. This handling function of the SSH 2.0 protocol provides interactive sessions, remote command execution, and forwarded connections including X11 and other TCP traffic. All of these are considered channels, and they can be opened from either the local or remote side.

The user authentication layer handles any type of authentication such as passwords, public key, and any other third party that may be incorporated in a later date. The only form of authentication that is required for SSH 2.0 is the public key authentication—all others are optional. Even though public key authentication is required, SSH 2.0 can include other custom means of authentication.

Note   Kerberos and TIS authentication are not currently supported in the SSH 2.0 protocol.

The transport layer has a flexible key exchange method, which authenticates the server, not the user, and is handled by the user authentication layer. It provides the basic symmetric encryption for SSH2, including IDEA, Blowfish, and Twofish. Also, it has hooks for future support with PKI. It provides additional integrity with an optional MAC address.

The packet itself is a TCP packet and contains the following: the packet length, the padding length, the payload itself, padding, and an optional MAC address. Out of all of this, everything is encrypted except for the packet length. If this packet is compressed, it becomes about half the size. Figure 5.2 shows how the Secure Shell 2 packet looks.

Figure 5.2 *SSH 2.0 packet.*

The Nuts and Bolts

When you start the Secure Shell server, the sshd is executed and starts listening on port 22 by default. You'll find this out through a port scan on a host to see where the Secure Shell daemon is listening. You can also see if the process is running on your ps command.

> Since you don't want to type sshd every time you boot your system **Note**
> (which shouldn't occur often anyway), you'll want to start this daemon at boot, and this is covered later in the chapter.

To start the Secure Shell daemon, simply type:

```
# sshd
```

> Looks the same as running the Secure Shell 1 daemon, right? If **Note**
> you've already installed SSH1 and install SSH2, the symbolic links to
> /usr/local/sbin/sshd will be changed to link to sshd2 from sshd1.

This does not display anything and brings you back to your prompt. If you want to make sure that sshd is running, you can check your processes:[3]

```
bash# ps -aux | grep sshd
root 49 0.0 3.3 704 962 ? S Jan 8 0:00 /usr/local/sbin/sshd
```

---

3. Depending on your UNIX system, you may have to use different options for the ps command. The option -eaf usually works if -aux doesn't. Anyway, check your man pages to be on the safe side.

After the Secure Shell daemon is started, it starts listening on a port for a socket. Like Secure Shell 1, the default port that the Secure Shell daemon runs on is port 22. This is now a well-known port with the release of SSH2. This can be changed; however, make sure that other TCP/IP daemons are not using or listening on those ports.

Usually the Secure Shell daemon does listen for a socket, unless it is started from the Internet daemon inetd. Then inetd will listen for the socket instead. For now, let's assume you're not going to run Secure Shell through inetd. When the Secure Shell daemon starts listening for a socket, it waits until it connects. Once it connects, the Secure Shell daemon spawns a child process, which in turn generates an DSA server key. When the key is generated, the Secure Shell daemon is ready for the remote client to connect to the Secure Shell daemon or waits for a connection from a remote system. See Figure 5.3 for an illustration of how this works.

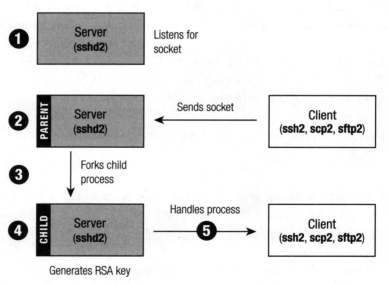

Figure 5.3 *How the sshd2 daemon connection works.*

At this point the Secure Shell daemon is sitting around and listening for a socket. When it hears a connection, the socket is bound to a particular port. Usually the socket comes in on a non-privileged port (1023 or higher) and is bound to port 22. Before the port is bound, Secure Shell needs to get the IP address of the client. This is used for the log, but if the connection is not a socket, the IP address 0.0.0.0 is assigned.

Now that the connection is made, the client and server exchange host public keys. When the keys are validated, the client and server exchange the supported cipher information. The local client may support Triple DES, Blowfish, IDEA, and Twofish, and the remote server may only support DES and IDEA.

> DES support is not the default setting, and most SSH2 implementa- **Note**
> tions are compiled without it. With the release of SSH2, Twofish is
> now a supported symmetric key cipher.

Both the client and server list what ciphers they support, and each selects the first cipher on the client's list that is also supported by the server. See Figure 5.4 for an illustration of how this default behavior works.

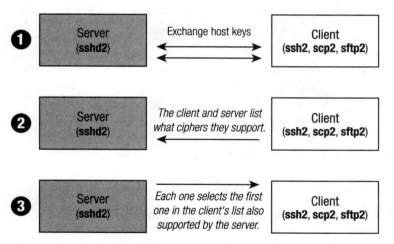

Figure 5.4 *How SSH2 chooses its cipher.*

Now that the host keys are validated and a cipher is chosen, the local server recognizes the connection and forks a dchild process to manage the connection between the local and remote server. This key exchange works the same as SSH1. Now the client will start transmitting encrypted data. This happens before the user is prompted for a passphrase.

SSH2 does not use server keys. Instead, SSH2 only relies on the encryption to prevent spoofing.

The connection between the Secure Shell daemon and the client continues until the client has ended its connection. Then the server keeps listening for connections until the daemon is killed, either intentionally or through a system crash. Then, if a socket is heard, the connection process repeats itself. If Secure Shell exits with an error, it does not dump the core to prevent from leaking the private information. See Figure 5.5 to see what happens at the end of a connection.

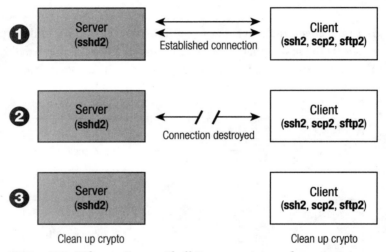

Figure 5.5 *When a Secure Shell 2 connection ends.*

So, the overall connectivity looks like this:

- connection request on port 22 from client

- server forks a child process

- systems exchange host keys

- session key and local host key exchanged from client

- supported cipher decided on by servers

- encrypted data transferred

- connection broken down

Secure Shell Daemon Processes

Now that you understand how the daemon functions, you'll want to know how to handle the processes. Usually after a connection is negotiated, a child process is spawned from the parent to handle the interaction between the client and the remote server. Keep in mind that the client can be started on either end—the local host or the remote host.

After the Secure Shell daemon is started, the process identification number (PID) is stored in /etc/sshd_pid. This makes it easier to kill the appropriate daemon. If a child process is running, you don't want to accidentally kill it, especially while it's binding to a socket.

One of the ways that the Secure Shell daemon handles processes is that it works like inetd. You can send it a SIGHUP signal (which is a kill -HUP signal), and the sshd will execute itself. As a result, it will reread its configuration file and regenerate its server key. Remember that inetd handles the SIGHUP signal the same way.

The Parent Process

As in all implementations that are UNIX, you have files and you have processes. Because sshd is the Secure Shell daemon file that runs the Secure Shell daemon processes, we have two processes from sshd to be concerned with: the parent and the child processes. So, a daemon is a process that runs in the background on its own and controls the application it is running. The initial process that is started from the daemon is the parent process.

One of the features that was not changed when converting to SSH2 is the way the server spawns processes; it's the same process as the SSH1 daemon. The parent's job is to listen (unlike human parents) and to fork child processes. And that's all it does. The connections themselves are run through the child processes. So the parent says, "Aha! We have a connection here!" and then spawns the child process to complete the session. The parent tells the child process to make the connection with the socket. In the meantime, the parent keeps listening for more sockets. If there are more connections, the parent forks additional child processes. See Figure 5.6 on page 132 for an illustration of this process.

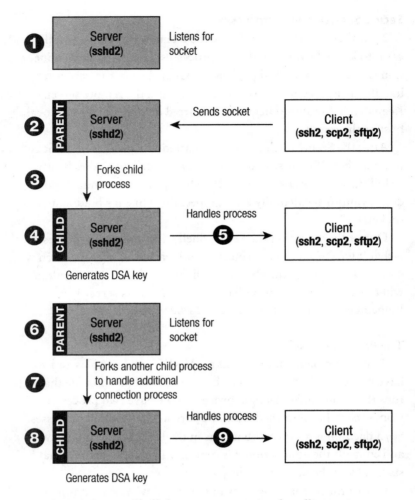

Figure 5.6 *Secure Shell daemon connection handling.*

Before the child process makes the connection, the session key is given to the child process to encrypt the session and the parent process marks that key as "used." At this point, the host key is cleared.

Naturally, we don't want to listen endlessly, waiting for an authentication from the remote server. The daemon has a built-in "alert" which causes the server to exit when the authentication is made or the alert times out. The alert is turned off during debugging mode to help detect problems with authentication.

The Child Process

With the parent process actively listening for sockets and forking child processes, the child process makes the connection with the other server. When the child process starts, it starts running with the user (the person who started the client) UID, not root. This keeps someone from running processes as root on your system.

To start the session, the child process closes the listening socket and starts using the accepted socket to make the session. Next, the logging is restarted because the process identification number has changed. The child process then authenticates the user. If the session is not interactive, the session is connected and then torn down. Otherwise, the child process allocates for an interactive session— things like pseudo terminals, X11 connections, TCP/IP protocols, and the authentication agent (`ssh-agent2`).

Now that the connection is made, the client needs to know that we are the local server, and that it can request a connection to any port it wants to. The client starts from port 22, and the server side connects to any port (this is usually port 1023 or higher). When the connection is done, the connection is torn down and the encryption is cleared up.

The Encryption of Secure Shell

The Secure Shell daemon is useful in that it does a few checks on key lengths, public keys, check bytes, and authentication, but it's the encryption that comes with Secure Shell that offers a major part of the functionality of the server. Some of the encryption is split between the child and the parent processes. The parent process generates the host key and gives it to the child process to negotiate with the remote server. The child process also handles the session itself, which consists of the user authentication and the symmetric key encryption for the data transfer. Keep in mind that SSH2 has added the Twofish cipher to its collection of encryption mechanisms. Table 5.1 on page 134 breaks down the encryption task to either the parent or child process.

Table 5.1 *Encryption task by parent or child process*

Encryption-related task	Process
Generates host key	Parent
Keeps list of keys	Parent
Key exchange	Child
Handles session encryption	Child
Handles session authentication	Child
Handles destruction of keys	Child

Key Exchange

When the connection is identified by the parent, the child process makes the incoming connection. At this point, version identifiers for Secure Shell have been exchanged by the two servers. After the appropriate version identification is made by the server, it is ready to send the server key and do the key exchange with the remote server.

You have two keys on the local system: a DSA 1024-bit host key, which is used to authenticate the host and make sure that it's not being spoofed, and a DSA 768-bit server key, which is regenerated every hour if it has been used. The reason the server key is regenerated every hour is that this is enough time to keep the key alive without being cracked. Also, the server key is not stored on the disk but in memory. Checks are done to make sure that both keys have significantly different lengths. The host key is stored locally on the disk, which defaults to /etc/ssh2/hostkey for the private key and /etc/ssh2/hostkey.pub for the public key. Key management is covered in *"Secure Shell Key Management"* on page 191.

For key exchange, Secure Shell 2 uses Diffie-Helman. This is different than the authentication process, which uses the DSA algorithm. In Secure Shell 1 and the commercial version of Secure Shell 2, RSA is used for both key exchange and authentication. The DSA and RSA keys use different algorithms, and each type of key is kept in different files to keep Secure Shell from getting confused.

After the keys are exchanged and validated, the keys are not needed for any other encryption functions. The next thing the Secure Shell daemon does is really cool—it generates a series of check bytes that the client sends to the remote server through a user packet.

These check bytes, a packet that includes 64 bits of random data, must be matched by the remote host. If these check bytes match, the Secure Shell connection is established. This is how Secure Shell protects against IP spoofing. However, this only protects against a remote host *outside* of your local network from IP spoofing attacks, but not against someone sniffing your network and obtaining the check bytes that way. For password-protected accounts, this is not an issue. For authentication using Berkeley services (using the `.rhosts` or `/etc/hosts.equiv` for authentication), the check bytes can be picked up and someone can log in to your host. It is not recommended to use Berkeley services for authentication!

When we send out our public key, we include our check bytes. The check bytes must be included in the encrypted reply to establish a secure connection. The next packet we receive should be encrypted using our host public keys, and we decrypt it. At the end of this packet, there should be a set of check bytes that match those we sent earlier with our public key. This is used to verify that the remote host has properly received our connection.

Encrypting the Session

We receive a couple of things in this packet: our check bytes and the session key. Our check bytes verify that this is the remote server that we sent this to, and the session key is in the decrypted integer from the check bytes. After the session key is extracted, the connection between the remote and local host is now encrypted with a supported symmetric key cipher. This is the way that the secret key is sent to the server without divulging it publicly.

So the encryption steps work like this:

1. Generate check bytes.

2. Attach check bytes to local public key and send to remote server.

3. Receive encrypted packet including remote public key and check bytes.

4. Verify the check bytes are what was originally sent.

5. Extract session key from the decrypted integer from the encrypted packet.

6. Start the session key and encrypt the session from now on.

7. Send an encrypted acknowledgement packet.

8. Established connection sends only the encrypted packets.

9. Connection is torn down; session keys are destroyed.

Next, we send our acknowledgement packet, which is now encrypted with the session key along with any other packets we send to the remote server from this point on. After the connection is broken down and the socket connections are destroyed, the session key is destroyed.

Authenticating the Users

Now that we are sending everything over an encrypted channel, it shouldn't bother you to be typing your password over the network (unless you are using a weak form of encryption), because it is now being sent encrypted through the tunnel. The session to you will look like any other client session, such as telnet or rsh; however, we'll go over this in the next chapter. In the meantime, let's see how the actual authentication works.

The Secure Shell client (be it ssh2, scp2, sftp) checks for the /etc/nologin message in case the remote system is shutting down or rebooting. If this is not the case, the login process kicks in and the client sends the appropriate username to the remote server. After the username is accepted, the authentication type is checked.

The purpose of using Secure Shell is to have strong security—it is highly recommended that you use some form of public key authentication with Secure Shell. You can also use it conjunction with rhosts authentication and password authentication. When you are authenticating with public key, the passphrase protects the private key. This passphrase is different than what you type in to log in to your account—this passphrase is what you entered when your keypair is generated.

If the Secure Shell client is coming from a privileged port, then it is checked for rhosts authentication (which includes `$HOME/.rhosts` and `/etc/hosts.equiv`). If no rhosts authentication occurs (and there shouldn't be if you want this to be really secure), you are then prompted for your login password.

Next, the password is read. You can authenticate with rhosts (which can include public key authentication), public key host authentication, public key challenge-response authentication, or password-based authentication. You can use password-based authentication with the public key host authentication (and this is recommended).

> You can authenticate to Secure Shell without a password; however, this can create a security hole if done incorrectly.   **Note**

A Word on Not Using Passwords to Protect Your Secure Shell Keys

On the Secure Shell mailing list, this is a popular question: how do I use Secure Shell without a password? (This is not only popular for SSH1, but also for SSH2—so I'm including the same information that is provided in *"Secure Shell 1 Server Daemon—*`sshd`*"* on page 55.)

Think of the reason you're using Secure Shell, and you'll realize why this is a bad thing to do. Secure Shell is designed to prevent someone from hijacking a session and obtaining access to your host remotely through poor methods of authentication (bad passwords, Berkeley services, NFS, NIS, and the like).

So, why would you not password-protect your key? Many people want to do this for convenience, especially for script writing. You do have one easy way around this: run the Secure Shell authentication agent. After starting the agent, all you need to do is add the keys into memory. This makes it so that you don't have to worry about passwords while the daemon is running. If the system gets rebooted or the daemon crashes, then you'll have to re-enter the passwords.

If this is too much of a bother for you, you probably should be aware of the risks that can very likely happen if you are not password-protecting your keys:

- If someone accesses your computer, they have instant access to your keys even if the Secure Shell authentication agent is not running.

- Someone can hijack your private and public host keys and spoof your host.

- If you are doing this with rsh authentication enabled, you are vulnerable to several rsh attacks. If you must use a host authentication file along with the DSA or RSA keys, you have to use the shosts files ($HOME/.shosts or /etc/shosts.equiv) for Secure Shell only. This only protects against rsh attacks, not the private keys being hijacked.

The following are some recommendations for increasing your security with passwords:

- Use strong passwords for all keys and account access. This includes not using dictionary or well-known words and using a combination of upper- and lowercase letters, numbers, and special characters (!@#$%^&*).

- Do not embed passwords in a script. Especially with the growing popularity of Expect, putting passwords in remote access scripts is becoming a common practice. This is really bad because you are storing your password in a cleartext file.

- Realize that on a multi-user machine, you are risking the root account by not password-protecting your keys. If you are not password-protecting your user keys, always password-protect the keys in the root account!

Basically, this falls under the rationale for using strong passwords in the first place. Make sure you password-protect every key with strong passwords. If you do not, be aware of the risks you are taking, and know that you are seriously putting the security of your system—and the systems you connect to—at risk.

Usage of the Secure Shell Daemon

Now that you have some understanding of how the Secure Shell daemon works, you have several options to work with when running the daemon. Like most UNIX networking daemons, you can set the debugging mode, change the location of key files, and set the level of verbosity. You can also change the key sizes and change the port which the daemon is listening on. Those options are:

-b bits You can specify the number of bits in the server key. This defaults to 768 bits; however, you can make this larger or smaller, depending on whether or not you are running from `inetd` or want stronger security.

-d Debug mode. This is the same as `sshd1`. The Secure Shell daemon is started but does not run in the background nor does it fork any child processes. The higher the debugging level, the more information you receive. The debugging output goes to the system log, and the "alert" mechanism is turned off. This option should only be used for debugging the server, not for increasing logging messages.

-f config_file This is the same as `sshd1`. You can specify a specific configuration file. The default is `/etc/ssh2/sshd_config`, but if you're running Secure Shell without root privileges, you will need to define this file elsewhere.

-g login_grace_time This is what sets the "alert" mechanism in the Secure Shell daemon and is the same as `sshd1`. It gives the client a certain grace time to authenticate with the server, which defaults to 600 seconds (10 minutes). If the client does not authenticate, the server process disconnects from that socket. You can set this to zero, which means there is no limit on authentication time. If you put the Secure Shell daemon in debug mode, this is set to zero automatically.

-h host_key_file This is the same as `sshd1`. This specifies which file you are using for the private host key. You have to use this option if you are not running the Secure Shell daemon as root. Normally, the private host key file is not readable by anyone but the root account; however, this is not the case if you are running it from a user account. Also, if you are using an alternative file, make sure you set the permissions to something like 400.

-i You can specify whether or not to run Secure Shell from inetd. This is the same as sshd1. You can choose whether or not to run the Secure Shell daemon with TCP wrappers or if you want to run Secure Shell from inetd. Running Secure Shell from inetd causes its own problems, because the Secure Shell daemon needs to generate the server client before it responds to the client, and this can become a latency issue. Clients would have to wait too long for a normal length or stronger server key for when the keys are regenerated. However, you could use a smaller server key to increase performance; but be aware that the weaker the key, the easier it is to crack.

-o option You can specify options that are used in the configuration file but for which there is no command-line option.

-p port This is the same as sshd1. You can specify which port the server listens for sockets on. The default is port 22, which is reserved for Secure Shell. Keep in mind that this is also the port defined in the /etc/services file, unless you change it. You may want to define an alternate port if port 22 is already being used for another application or if you are running the Secure Shell daemon from another user besides root.

-q This is the quiet mode, which means that nothing is sent to the system log. This is the same as sshd1. Usually what is sent is the start of a connection, the authentication of the user, and the termination of the connection. You may not want to enable this option unless your logs fill up quite quickly. Audit trails are always good for checking to see if someone has illegally gained access to your system.

-v This puts the Secure Shell daemon in verbose mode. This is the same as giving sshd the -d 2 option. This also means that you cannot really run sshd2 with the verbose mode, because no child processes will be spawned.

Note   There are no server keys in SSH2.

Using SSH1 and SSH2 Daemons on the Same Host

For compatibility reasons, you probably want to make sure you have compatibility with SSH1. In order to do this, you need to have the latest version of SSH1 (currently 1.2.27) and a copy of SSH2. You need to run at least both server daemons (`sshd1` and `sshd2`) in order to accept and send Secure Shell client connections from both versions. If you do not run both versions, you will not be able to send and receive connections from the Secure Shell clients.

As far as actual compatibility, there is none between SSH1 and SSH2. However, you can use the most recent version of SSH1 with SSH2. If a connection is requested from a SSH1 client, the SSH2 server daemon forwards the connection to the SSH1 server daemon. However, you cannot connect a SSH1 client to a SSH2 server daemon and vice versa.

Also, if you see a message that says that the packet length is bad, check to see if you're running an earlier version of SSH1. You may need to upgrade.

Some Examples

These options are not set by default. The default setting for the Secure Shell daemon is to use a 768-bit server key that regenerates every hour, an authentication timeout of 10 minutes, listens on port 22 for connections, and finds its configuration files in the `/etc/ssh2` directory. So the default Secure Shell daemon runs like this:

```
# sshd
```

These next examples are similar to those in Chapter 3 on the SSH1 server daemon. This way you can see that there are minimal differences in the usage.

Or you can pass it these options and it does the same thing as the default:

```
# sshd -b 768 -f /etc/ssh2/sshd_config -g 600 -h /etc/ssh2/ssh_host_key -p 22
```

You can define the Secure Shell port as something greater than 1024 for a non-privileged Secure Shell daemon:

```
# sshd -p 2022
```

Using a different configuration file for a different port? No problem!

```
# sshd -p 2022 -f /etc/sshd_config_weird_port
```

And if you want to run Secure Shell through inetd, you can do that too, but don't forget to shrink the server keys. Keep in mind, though, that you don't want your keys very weak. With a timeout of 10 minutes and a weak key or a weak algorithm, you're in trouble. Also, you really wouldn't run this on the command line—you would run it from a script to run it from inetd.

```
# sshd -i -b 512
```

Note   You should edit /etc/inetd.conf before running sshd from it.

Initiating Secure Shell from the Startup Scripts

Most administrators who are running Secure Shell want it running all the time, and probably want to have it run without having to start it all the time. To solve this, simply put it in a startup script. This is the same way you start up SSH1 server daemon as described in *"Secure Shell 1 Server Daemon*—sshd*"* on page 55. Table 5.2 shows by operating system some locations to start the Secure Shell daemon from.

Table 5.2 *Location of startup scripts per operating system*

Operating system	Startup script
Slackware Linux	/etc/rc.d
Redhat Linux	/etc/rc*.d
Solaris	/sbin/rc*.d
HP-UX	/sbin/rc*.d
Irix	/etc/rc*.d
AIX	/etc
DEC UNIX	/sbin/rc*.d

I found that in Linux installations the script installs it automatically. However, if you find you need to edit your scripts to add it, you can include the following script snippet to your startup script.

My UNIX system is a Slackware Linux system, and the networking initialization script is /etc/rc.d/inet2. In this script, you will find the Secure Shell daemon is started here. If you need to, you can edit your startup script to put Secure Shell daemon in the correct path and specify the options you want.

```
#!/bin/sh
#
# rc.inet2  This shell script boots up the entire INET
#           system. Note, that when this script is used to
#           also fire up any important remote NFS disks
#           (like the /usr distribution), care must be
#           taken to actually have all the needed binaries
#           online _now_ ...
#
# Author:   Fred N. van Kempen,
<waltje@uwalt.nl.mugnet.org>
#
# Constants.
NET="/usr/sbin"
IN_SERV="lpd"
LPSPOOL="/var/spool/lpd"
# At this point, we are ready to talk to The World...
# echo "Mounting remote file systems..."
# /sbin/mount -a -t nfs # This may be our /usr runtime!!!
echo -n "Starting daemons:"
# Start the SYSLOGD/Klogd daemons. These must come first.
if [ -f ${NET}/syslogd ]; then
   echo -n " syslogd"
   ${NET}/syslogd
   sleep 1 # prevent syslogd/klogd race condition on SMP
           # kernels
   echo -n " klogd"
   ${NET}/klogd
fi
# Start the SUN RPC Portmapper.
if [ -f ${NET}/rpc.portmap ]; then
    echo -n " portmap"
    ${NET}/rpc.portmap
fi
# Start the INET SuperServer
if [ -f ${NET}/inetd ]; then
  echo -n " inetd"
```

```
    ${NET}/inetd
else
  echo "no INETD found. INET cancelled!"
  exit 1
fi
# Look for sshd in the two most common locations
# (compiled with --prefix=/usr or with --prefix=/usr/local)
# and if we find it, start it up
if [ -x /usr/local/sbin/sshd ]; then
  echo -n " sshd"
  /usr/local/sbin/sshd
elif [ -x /usr/sbin/sshd ]; then
  echo -n " sshd"
  /usr/sbin/sshd
fi
# Start the various INET servers.
for server in ${IN_SERV} ; do
  if [ -f ${NET}/${server} ]; then
    echo -n " ${server}"
    ${NET}/${server}
  fi
done
# # Start the various SUN RPC servers.
if [ -f ${NET}/rpc.portmap ]; then
  # Start the NFS server daemons.
  if [ -f ${NET}/rpc.mountd ]; then
    echo -n " mountd"
    ${NET}/rpc.mountd
  fi
  if [ -f ${NET}/rpc.nfsd ]; then
    echo -n " nfsd"
    ${NET}/rpc.nfsd
  fi
fi # Done starting various SUN RPC servers.
# The 'echo' below will put a carriage return at the end
# of the list of started servers.
echo
# Done!
```

Note

If you look at the startup script for the SSH1 server daemon in Chapter 3, you will see that the script is the same one. This is because even if you have installed both sshd1 and sshd2, the symbolic link is always the more recent release.

Logging Your Connections

The Secure Shell daemon, by default, logs the initial request for a connection, the authentication, and the closing of the connection. Since this code is free, you are more than welcome to edit it to make more information logged. This is from the /var/adm/messages log file on Slackware Linux. When a connection is made, your log files may look something like this:

```
Jul 9 08:19:25 tigerlair sshd2[1880]: log: Connection from 206.184.139.144 port 926
Jul 9 08:19:34 tigerlair sshd2[1880]: log: Password authentication for stripes accepted.
Jul 9 08:19:42 tigerlair sshd2[1880]: log: Closing connection to 206.184.139.144
```

You can also turn on verbose logging or turn logging off completely with the quiet option.

Also, you can use TCP wrappers with the -D PARANOID option to log each socket. This may duplicate some of the efforts of the Secure Shell daemon, or you can configure it to provide you with more information.

Keep in mind that where your logs go is system-dependent. Linux distributions may put the information in the system log, located in /var/adm/syslog, and HP-UX or AIX may put the logging information in a completely different location. Check your operating system manuals for log file locations.

Configuring Secure Shell

Secure Shell has a configuration file where you can define options. Some of these options are not definable by the command-line options, but you can configure lots of extras to work with Secure Shell. Like most configuration files and shell scripts, empty lines and lines starting with the "#" are not read. The default configuration file for Secure Shell is /etc/sshd2/sshd_config.

The following are the options that you can set in the sshd_config file for Secure Shell. The format for defining these options in the /etc/sshd2/sshd_config file is:

```
OptionType Argument
```

If you have multiple arguments, they are separated by a space. This format applies to all the options listed below.

Allowing by Username or Hostname

You can filter usernames or hostnames via Secure Shell 2. This does not allow you as many filter options as you have in SSH1, but you do have some that can help you, such as the ability to ignore rhosts files and permitting or denying root logins.

IgnoreRhosts This is the same configuration option as in `sshd1`. This defines whether or not `.rhosts` and `.shosts` will be used for authentication. This does not have any effect on the system-wide files `/etc/hosts.equiv` and `/etc/shosts.equiv`. The default for this option is "no." If you do want to use this, please use `.shosts` instead of `.rhosts` for improved security.

Usage:

```
IgnoreRhosts yes
```

PermitRootLogin You can define whether or not root can login via `ssh2`. The default is "yes," but you may want to turn this off. Keep in mind that it does not affect root logins via FTP, Telnet, or any other means.

Usage:

```
PermitRootLogin nopwd
```

Authentication

Secure Shell provides different authentication methods: passwords, rhosts, and public keys. You can either use one or a combination of any of the above for accessing accounts via Secure Shell. However, be aware that rhosts authentication is the weakest, and that any combination with the public key is going to be your strongest form of authentication. Note that in SSH2 you have no options for TIS or dKerberos authentication as of the time of publication of this book.

PasswordGuesses This option specifies how many attempts a user has to type their password correctly for password authentication. This number must be an integer. The higher you set it, the higher the chance someone has to brute force a password if you have password-only authentication enabled.

Usage:

```
PasswordGuesses 4
```

PasswordAuthentication You can define whether or not you want to use passwords to access accounts via Secure Shell. This is the same as the sshd1 configuration option. The default is "yes," and what the passwords do is protect the public key, not the account itself, by more conventional means. You may opt to turn off password authentication, but you're better off using it in addition to PubKeyAuthentication.

Usage:

```
PasswordAuthentication yes
```

PermitEmptyPasswords This defines whether or not you want to use passwords to help authenticate. This is the same as the sshd1 configuration option. You can allow null passwords; however, this is strongly advised against. If someone accesses your host (desktop, laptop, server, and so on), it's one less thing that they need a password to have access to. The default is "yes," but ignore that. Always use strong passwords and set this to "no."

Usage:

```
PermitEmptyPasswords no
```

RHostsAuthentication This option sets your authentication to be based on the .rhosts or /etc/hosts.equiv alone. This is the same as the RhostsAuthentication configuration option for sshd1. This doesn't require a password or a public key, but it opens your system up to Berkeley services attacks that are well known and the reason you are using Secure Shell in the first place. The default is "no," and you're best leaving it that way. If you do want to use Rhosts authentication, use it in conjunction with the public key authentication in RHostsPubKeyAuthentication.

Usage:

```
RHostsAuthentication no
```

RHostsPubKeyAuthentication This option is not currently implemented in the most recent release of Secure Shell 2. It sets your authentication to be based on the .rhosts or /etc/hosts.equiv with the public key and is the same as the RhostsRSAAuthentication configuration option for sshd1. This doesn't require a password, but it does require that the remote side has a DSA or RSA key to

authenticate against. This opens your system up to Berkeley services attacks, but the threat is minimized because of the required
public key authentication. If you do leave this option at "yes" (the
default), you may want to set some stricter login requirements for
hosts. Again, if you want to lean on the more secure side of things,
turn off any type of rhosts authentication.

Usage:

```
RHostsPubKeyAuthentication no
```

PubKeyAuthentication You can use a myriad of authentication
types; or as you can see, you can use a sole type as well. If you want
to define only public key authentication to be accepted, you can.
This is the same as the RSAAuthentication option for sshd1. This
does not require rhosts or passwords to help authenticate. The
default is "yes" and this is fine to leave as is.

Usage:

```
PubKeyAuthentication yes
```

Server Options

These options are specific to how the Secure Shell daemon functions. This includes TCP forwarding, listening on specific addresses
and ports, sending keepalive messages, and server key settings.

Ciphers You can specify which ciphers you want to use for
encrypting. The currently supported ciphers are DES, 3DES, Blowfish, Twofish, IDEA, and Arcfour. You do have other options you
can specify: any, any standard (anystd), and anycipher. This option
includes any cipher according to the restraints, except for none.
Use "none" only if you are debugging or testing.

Usage:

```
Ciphers anycipher
```

Ssh1Compatibility This option specifies whether or not to be
compatible with SSH1 daemon. This option will execute the SSH1
daemon if the client only supports SSH1. This is good if you have
SSH1 clients still connecting to your server. Keep in mind that you
need to install both SSH1 and SSH2 to get this to work. Your argument is either "yes" or "no," depending on if you want backward
compatibility.

Usage:

```
Ssh1Compatibility yes
```

Sshd1Path If you are going to have SSH1 compatibility, you may want to specify the SSH1 path, especially if you have installed `sshd1` in a non-common directory.

Usage:

```
Sshd1Path /usr/local/security/sbin/sshd1
```

ForwardAgent This option specifies whether or not you can forward the Secure Shell authentication agent (`ssh-agent2`) to the remote host. You can either turn this on (yes) or turn it off (no).

Usage:

```
ForwardAgent yes
```

KeepAlive The Secure Shell daemon can be set to send keep-alive messages or not to send them. Keepalive messages let the remote server know whether or not the connection has died; and as a result, kills the active process. This is the same as in the configuration options for `sshd1`. However, if the route temporarily goes away, it can get frustrating to see a message like this:

```
Connection down; disconnecting.
```

OK, so that's annoying. But if you don't send keepalives, you may have hanging sessions that leave ghost processes and eat your server's resources. The default setting is "yes," which means that the server sends keepalives. If you want to disable keepalive messages, you'll have to disable both the server and client configuration files. Be aware that this may leave you with hanging processes if you decide to turn them off.

Usage:

```
KeepAlive yes
```

ListenAddress If you are running a multi-homed host, you can specify which address you want the server to listen on. This is the same configuration option that `sshd1` has. This defaults to your main IP interface if you don't have more than one (and if you have only one, you don't have to set this).

Usage:

```
ListenAddress 1.2.3.4
```

Port You can specify a port for the Secure Shell daemon to listen on. The default port is 22; however, you may want to define another port for application purposes or because port 22 is in use. This is the same configuration option for sshd1, and it is the same as the -p option.

Usage:

```
Port 21
```

StrictModes You can have the server check the file modes (permissions) and ownership of the user's home directory (and rhosts if applicable) before making the login connection. This is the same configuration option that sshd1 has, and it's a good idea because a user may have accidentally left their directory and files world-writable. If they did, make sure you shoot them. The default setting for StrictModes is "yes."

Usage:

```
StrictModes yes
```

ForwardX11 This option defines whether or not X forwarding is allowed through the Secure Shell daemon. This is the same configuration option as X11Forwarding for sshd1. Like other TCP traffic, this can be overridden by user-defined forwarders. It is up to you to allow X traffic through. However, if you are going to let X traffic through remotely, you'll want to forward it through Secure Shell. The default setting is "yes."

Usage:

```
ForwardX11 yes
```

File Locations

These options define where the Secure Shell daemons key files are located. This includes the key files, the random seed, and the process identification file.

AuthorizationFile This option specifies the name of the user's authorization file. The default is ~/.ssh2/authorization, and it provides a list of private keys on how the Secure Shell server will identify the user.

Usage:

```
HostKey $HOME/.ssh2/ssh2_identity
```

HostKeyFile This specifies which file you are using for the private host key. This is the same configuration option as `HostKey` in `sshd1`. You have to use this option if you are not running the Secure Shell daemon as root. Normally, the private host key file is not readable by anyone but the root account; however, this is not the case if you are running it from a user account. The default file is `/etc/ssh2/hostkey`. Also, if you are using an alternative file, make sure you set the permissions to something like 400. This is the same as the `-h` option.

Usage:

```
HostKey /usr/local/etc/ssh2_host_key
```

PublicHostKeyFile Like the `HostKeyFile` option, this specifies the public host key. You'll want to pick the `HostKeyFile` option first before specifying this one. This will prevent you from getting your configuration files messed up.

Usage:

```
HostKey /usr/local/etc/ssh2_host_key.pub
```

RandomSeedFile This defines the location of the random seed file used to generate server keys. This is the same as the `sshd1` configuration option `RandomSeed`. The default location is `/etc/ssh2/random_seed`.

Usage:

```
RandomSeed /usr/local/etc/ssh2_random_seed
```

Account Activity Options

This options define what affects a remote account's environmental settings when you log in via Secure Shell. Most of these settings are set during login using environmental settings such as `.profile` or `.cshrc`. However, you can make sure they take effect by setting them in the Secure Shell daemon configuration file.

LoginGraceTime This is what sets the "alert" mechanism in the Secure Shell daemon. This is the same configuration option as in sshd1. It gives the client a certain grace time to authenticate with the server, which defaults to 600 seconds (10 minutes). If the client does not authenticate, then the server process disconnects from that socket. You can set this to zero, which means there is no limit on authentication time. If you put the Secure Shell daemon in debug mode, this is set to zero automatically. This is the same as the -g option.

Usage:

```
LoginGraceTime 660
```

PrintMotd This defines whether or not the user account prints the system message of the day located in /etc/motd. This is the same configuration option as in sshd1. It is only for interactive logins (not scp or ssh with a command after it). The default setting is "yes." This can also be set in the user's environmental initialization file.

Usage:

```
PrintMotd no
```

Logging Options

These options affect the output that is sent to the log files. You can either increase the logging, which violates users' privacy, or turn it off completely—minus a few error messages.

QuietMode This is the quiet mode, which means that nothing is sent to the system log. This is the same configuration option that sshd1 has. What is usually sent is the start of a connection, the authentication of the user, and the termination of the connection. You may not want to enable this option unless your logs fill up quite quickly. Audit trails are always good for checking to see if someone has illegally gained access to your system. This is the same as the -q option. The default for this is "no."

Usage:

```
QuietMode no
```

VerboseMode This causes the sshd2 to print level 2 debugging messages. Remember that the Secure Shell 2 server daemon will

not fork child processes with this turned on. This is the same as the
-v option.

Usage:

```
VerboseMode no
```

A Sample Server Configuration File

Now that you know what your options are, here is an example
of a Secure Shell daemon configuration file sshd_config. You can
set yours how you like; this is just for illustration purposes:

```
# This is ssh2 server systemwide configuration file.
# These are some settings that we set through the TCP
# wrappers
# (commented for notes, we don't need to define them here)
# Date created - 30 Dec 98
# AllowHosts *.myhost.com goodguys.atotherhosts.com
# DenyHosts lowsecurity.knownhosts.com evilhosts.com
Port 22
ListenAddress 0.0.0.0
HostKeyFile /etc/ssh2/hostkey
RandomSeedFile /etc/ssh2/random_seed
LoginGraceTime 600
PermitRootLogin no
IgnoreRhosts no
StrictModes yes
QuietMode no
ForwardX11 yes
PrintMotd yes
KeepAlive yes
RhostsAuthentication no
PubKeyAuthentication yes
PasswordAuthentication yes
PermitEmptyPasswords no
```

Secure File Transfer Server—sftp-server

Even though this is a new feature with Secure Shell 2, the Secure
FTP server is not well documented. The Secure FTP server,
sftp-server2, is run by the Secure Shell 2 daemon, which listens
for a connection on port 22. Because this is more of a client application than a server application (the server handles all requests to
sftp-server, so nothing has to be done by the administrator), the
secure FTP will be covered more in *"Secure Shell 2 Clients—*ssh2,
scp2, *and* sftp2*"* on page 155.

Summary

The Secure Shell 2 server daemon, sshd, is the controlling feature of Secure Shell 2. Secure Shell 2 has some improvements over Secure Shell 1, including digital certificate support like Public Key Infrastructure and a Secure File Transfer server. Currently, there is no actual support for PKI, just "hooks" in the application.

Secure Shell 2 server daemon, like its predecessor, listens on port 22, which is a well-known port for Secure Shell. When the daemon hears a socket, it forks a child process that handles the host and server key authentication and client connections. After the connection is torn down, the child process goes away and the parent process remains listening for other Secure Shell connections.

The Secure Shell 2 daemon has many options; some can be taken at the command line, whereas others can be passed through a configuration file. Keep in mind that some of the configuration and command-line options from SSH1 have been changed or removed, and some new options have been added. The default configuration file is /etc/ssh2/sshd_config. The options you can define include the types of authentication, X and other TCP network traffic, logging features, and filtering by hostname or username.

Secure Shell 2 Clients—
ssh2, scp2, and sftp2

In this chapter:

- How it works

- The nuts and bolts

- Usage

- Files

Now that you know how the server works, you'll need to understand how the client works as well. As you've seen, most of the communication is handled by the server, including authentication and encryption.

How It Works

If you read *"Secure Shell 1 Server Daemon*—sshd*"* on page 55 on how the Secure Shell 2 server daemon works, you'll probably remember the drive-through bank teller analogy used for Secure Shell 1. Going back to that analogy, the Secure Shell daemon on both sides would be the driver and the teller, and the Secure Shell client would be the tube and the data it passes between the two in the canister.

The Secure Shell client negotiates the encryption type, the type of connection (interactive or command line), compression if desired, the information passed between the remote and local servers, and forwarding. The forwarding includes the TCP/IP forwarding and X11 traffic. The client is basically what the user deals with, so it also defines what the user uses for authentication files, passwords, hostname, and username.

The client portion of Secure Shell 2 provides the user with an interface, and it's what most people are familiar with when they talk about Secure Shell. To most users, this will look like a remote login like telnet, rsh, or rlogin, or even a remote copy such as rcp.

Most of the actual connection is handled on the Secure Shell daemon side, which is covered in *"Secure Shell 2 Server Daemon*— sshd2 *and* sftp-server2*"* on page 123. The client does provide the user with an interface and a set of options that allow a user to log in, send commands to a remote server, or copy files securely. The client also requests the connection from the local host to a remote host.

In addition, the client initiates the connection between the server and usually cuts the connection with a user command. The client also provides the user authentication via password or via rhosts. The user public keys, which are stored in the user's home directory, are what the client uses so that the user can log in remotely.

Secure Shell 2 uses three clients: `ssh`, `scp`, and `sftp`. The `ssh` client allows secure remote logins and commands to be issued from a remote server, and the `scp` client allows secure file copying over networks. The `sftp` client allows secure file transferring to any remote host running the Secure Shell 2 daemon. There is no `slogin` alias for Secure Shell 2.

The Nuts and Bolts

Before any connection from the client takes place, both Secure Shell daemons need to be running on both the remote and local host. A connection is always initiated by the client side. This includes both clients, `ssh` and `scp`. The server listens on a specific port—usually port 22—waiting for connections. The clients usually connect on port 1021 or higher.

The basic syntax for the Secure Shell 2 client is the same as the Secure Shell 1 client:

```
$ ssh hostname [command]
```

The command is optional. Without the command parameter, the Secure Shell client goes into interactive mode. Otherwise, Secure Shell executes the command on the remote server, then exits. You can also forward TCP/IP traffic like POP, NTP, and X with Secure Shell as an agent. This is covered in *"Other Cool Things You Can Do With Secure Shell"* on page 239.

Connecting

The client does not have to connect to a remote server; it can also connect to the same server machine that the client is located on. This happens through the local host, so it is through a TCP/IP socket connection. This specific socket is for bi-directional communication, which is defined by the secsh IETF draft. However, Secure Shell 2 handles the transport and connection running on top of the TCP protocol.

After the server daemon makes the connection to the socket, the client handles the interaction between the user and the remote host. The client reads files as the specified user (either by the default user or by specifying in a command-line option). If we're running the Secure Shell client as root, we'll need to initialize the root account.

Even with Secure Shell 2, the Secure Shell client will fall back on rsh or rcp, depending on whether the Secure Shell daemon is found on the remote server or not (if it isn't, the remote server is not accepting Secure Shell connections). Because Secure Shell always connects 8-bits clean, it will not connect this way unless defined by rlogin (rlogin uses the -8 to define the connection as 8-bit instead of 7-bit). However, you probably don't want to fall back on rlogin or rsh if you want to keep secure connections.

The basic steps for the client connection are the following:

1. Reads user and system configuration files

2. Negotiates connection

3. Authenticates user account (against the public key, password, rhosts or any combination thereof)

4. Forks process (if being run in the background)

5. Run on a tty or standard input, depending on the type of connection

6. Close connection

Before Establishing the Connection

The Secure Shell client needs to do several things before running the connection on a remote host. One is to set a default umask of 022, which makes the files writable by the owner only, but world-readable. Because the modes are not set explicitly, this provides for a basic default set of permissions for the files.

In addition, the Secure Shell client needs to set an effective UID because it runs as root (SUID bit is on) when executed. Secure Shell does use an effective UID bit for executing commands on the remote host, as opposed to the real UID, which is defined on the local host.

Next, the Secure Shell client reads the configuration files. The first configuration files it reads are the user configuration files, which are located in the $HOME/.ssh directory. If the user does not specify any files such as known hosts, the Secure Shell client looks

toward the system-wide configuration settings, which are stored in
/etc/ssh2/ssh_config.

If that file does not exist, some defaults are set up by the client
itself, such as the username, which defaults to the username running the Secure Shell client locally. Hostnames and usernames are
limited to 255 characters maximum.

When a connection is opened to the remote host, the only time
the Secure Shell client needs root privileges is for rhosts authentication. However, it does run as root. Even though this is necessary
for rhosts authentication, the SUID bit is not set for scp or sftp.

```
tigerlair:/home/stripes- ls -l /usr/local/bin/ssh /usr/local/bin/scp
-rws--x--x 1 root other 1383412 Sep 11 11:29 /usr/local/bin/ssh*
-rwxr-xr-x 1 root other 1383412 Sep 11 11:29 /usr/local/bin/scp*
-rwxr-xr-x 1 root other 1383412 Sep 11 11:29 /usr/local/bin/sftp*
```

If the connection fails, the Secure Shell client will try to run rsh.
If it succeeds, the host private key is loaded for public key authentication. This is usually done before the Secure Shell client is no
longer running as root, because the host private key is only readable by root.

```
tigerlair:/home/stripes- ls -l /etc/ssh2/hostkey
-r-------- 1 root other 1383412 Sep 11 11:29 /etc/ssh2/hostkey
```

> The current public key authentication for the public domain version   **Note**
> of SSH2 is Digital Signature Standard (DSS), which uses the Digital
> Signature Algorithm (DSA). These will be referred to interchangeably.
> The RSA algorithm is implemented only in the commercial release.

During the Connection

As the connection is being established, the $HOME/.ssh2 direc-
tory is created—if it doesn't already exist on the local host. This
creates several files for the user, including the user private and public identity files (which is a DSA keypair), known hosts, and the
random seed for that user. After the keypair is exchanged success-
fully between the host and the user accounts, a connection is established. Figure 6.1 shows how the client functions during an
interactive and non-interactive connection to the remote server.

If it is interactive, the session is established on a tty. Also, if compression is enabled, it will be enabled after the successful key exchange. When the connection is established, the host private key is cleared from memory in case of a core dump.

Non-interactive connection

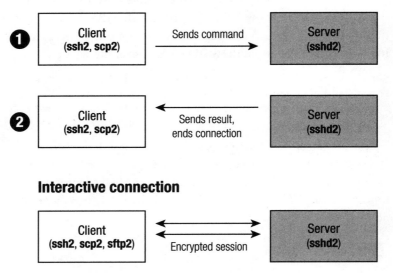

Interactive connection

Figure 6.1 *The difference between an interactive and non-interactive connection.*

If a tty is located, the Secure Shell client will create the packet and store the TERM information inside. Like the commands, there is no limit on the string length, just on the packet size. This packet includes the window size of the terminal and the tty modes. The client then sends it to the remote server and awaits a response.

To execute a command on the remote host, it has to be specified. For example, if you are going to be using scp2 or ssh2 with a command, you specify it at the end of the command line. If you are going to be using a terminal, a tty will be allocated so you can execute the remote commands interactively. This does not store any commands in the buffer, because they are executed real-time.

Otherwise, if you do provide a command, the Secure Shell client will recognize that it is a command and store it in the buffer. It can be any length because there is no limit on the length of the command itself—only the packet that sends it. This prevents buffer overflows.

As the client is sending output, it does not actually get logged. Instead, all the output goes directly to the terminal on the local host, including the status line for scp2, as well as any active terminal for the Secure Shell client—interactive or not.

Closing the Connection

When the user decides to end the session, either because the command has been completed or logged out of an interactive session, the connection must be closed. The client must receive a signal and trap it, and the signal must be something that signals an exit. When the session is closed, the connection to the remote server is severed. Before the client exits, it returns a status.

Secure Copying—scp2

Another nice functionality of the Secure Shell client is that it allows you to copy remotely through Secure Shell. It uses the same ports as the ssh2 client for copying. In fact, the scp2 client is a modified version of the Berkeley services rcp that uses ssh2 as a transport, but because the Berkeley services rcp uses rcmd to execute the command remotely, it's not very secure. Using ssh2 allows scp2 to copy files using the same security that ssh2 does: public key authentication, symmetric key encryption, and anti-spoofing mechanisms. See Figure 6.2 on page 162 to see how scp2 uses ssh2 for making connections.

The syntax is a little more complicated than ssh. It looks like this:

```
$ scp2 user@source:/directory/file user@destination:/directory/file
```

Later in this chapter the syntax for scp2 is reviewed.

Unlike the ssh client, scp2 does not run as SUID root. This is because it uses ssh to manage the connection, and that already runs as SUID root. Before connecting, scp2 establishes its functionality: verbose, statistics, compression, batch, cipher type, and non-privileged ports. The verbosity is how much information scp2 presents, statistics show you the status line on how much has downloaded,

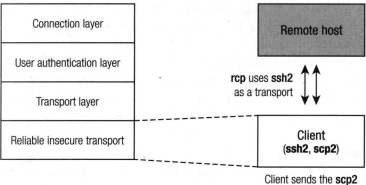

Figure 6.2 *How scp2 uses ssh2 for connections.*

compression is used for increasing performance, batch mode is whether or not scp2 prompts for a password, and non-privileged ports is for using scp2 for any ports above 1023. The cipher type is the type of symmetric encryption used during the connection.

Before the connection is made, scp2 creates a socket pair for communicating with ssh2. When the connection is made, the key-pairs are exchanged and the remote copy command is executed on the remote system. After the remote copy command is executed as the user on the host, the function returns a value before it closes: zero or higher if it succeeds and less than zero if it fails.

Secure File Transfer—sftp2

A new feature added to the Secure Shell protocol with release 2 is the *secure file transfer* client—sftp3. This is an FTP-flavored client that works in a similar fashion to scp2. The separate FTP client runs as a non-SUID user and uses the Secure Shell 2 for its data connections. As a result, the connection is secure. This security feature is especially crucial with FTP because there are known security flaws with the FTP protocol itself, including the bounce attack.

Usage of the Secure Shell Clients

Now that you have some understanding of how the Secure Shell clients work, you need to know about the options you can pass to them. The ssh2 and scp2 clients function in very similar ways to the SSH1 counterparts. This includes the agents, the ciphers, the escape characters, how to send the client into the background, the verbosity, ports and port forwarding, and compression. This section covers usage on both ssh and scp clients.

Usage for ssh2

Both Secure Shell clients, ssh2 and scp2, use different syntax for the command options. The ssh2 client has many more options because it is has more functionality than just copying files. And because scp2 uses ssh2 as a transport, the ssh2 client needs to provide some functionality for scp as well.

For all intents and purposes, ssh2 has a very simple syntax:

```
$ ssh2 [options] hostname [command]
```

> **Note** You do not have to type ssh2 or scp2 to run any of the Secure Shell 2 clients. After you install the SSH2 applications, the symbolic links for ssh and scp should link to ssh2 and scp2, respectively. If you have both SSH1 and SSH2 clients installed, you will need to run ssh1 and scp1 to run the SSH1 clients.

Command-Line Options

Command-line options for SSH2 are much more robust than the command-line options for SSH1. You'll find many more functions are available in SSH2, including enabling the authentication agent, disabling compression, setting the debugging level, and enabling X traffic.

Notice that -k for Kerberos ticketing do not exist for ssh2.

-a With this option, you can disable forwarding for the authentication agent. This is the same as the ssh1 client. It prevents the passphrase that was loaded into memory from being used for this issuance of the Secure Shell client. If you want, you can specify this in the configuration file per host instead of globally.

+a This option enables the authentication agent to forward. This is the default.

-c cipher This is the same option that is defined in ssh, since it is passed directly to ssh. Also, this is the same option that scp1 uses. You can choose which symmetric key cipher you want to encrypt the network traffic with. This does not affect the authentication, which uses DSA or RSA public key. Your choices for ciphers are IDEA, DES, 3DES, Blowfish, and Twofish. You can also choose "none," but this disables any encryption and renders the Secure Shell client unsecure. The "none" choice should be used for debugging and testing purposes only, not for actual use. Your best bet is to use 3DES, IDEA, or Blowfish. Blowfish and Twofish are the fastest supported algorithms for SSH2. For the best security, use IDEA. If IDEA is not supported for both Secure Shell servers, use 3DES.

+C Compresses all the data being sent through the Secure Shell client, including input, output, error messages, and forwarded data. This is the same as the -C option for ssh1. Don't get them mixed up. This uses the gzip algorithm, and the compression level can be defined through the configuration file option CompressionLevel. This works great for slow lines like modems, but it doesn't help much on an already fast network. Also, using the configuration file allows you to configure this option on a per-host basis.

-C This option disables compression. Remember that this is the opposite of what this option does with ssh1. Also, this is the default for ssh2.

-d debug_level This prints debugging information at whatever level you want. The higher the number, the more information you get. The numbers range from 0 to 99. Remember that the -v option prints out debugging information for level 2.

-e escape_character This defines the escape character. The default is "~", but can be set to any character or control character. This is also the same for ssh1. You can also define "none," which makes the session transparent, but you may want to leave it as a default in case the connection gets hung. To use the escape character, type the escape character followed by a period, and this closes the connection. If you type the escape character followed by a **control+Z**, the connection gets suspended.

-f Sends the ssh connection to the background. This is the same option as ssh1. This happens after authentication has been completed and forwarding for TCP/IP has been established. It is really great for starting X programs at the remote host. The user is prompted for a password (provided the authentication agent isn't running), and the connection is then sent to the background.

-F configuration_file This option specifies which user configuration file to use. The default is ~/.ssh2/ssh2_config. However, you can have both your default file and another configuration file. The alternative file is read first, then the default file options are added.

-h Prints a summary of help commands, then exits. This does not run the ssh2 client.

-i identity_file This defines the DSA private key, or identity file from which authentication is read. This has similar functionality to the same option in ssh1. The default file is $HOME/.ssh2/id_dsa1024_a. You can define multiple files for different hosts. If you do define different files, you may want to name them per host (for example, id_dsa1024_a.thishost, id_dsa1024a.thathost).

-l login_name This specifies the username that you log in with on the remote host. This is the same option as for ssh1. The default is the same username as the one on the local host. This may also be defined on a per-host basis in the configuration file. This is a very useful option because in today's world many people have access to different hosts with different accounts.

-L port:host:hostport This forwards any connection to the local host on the specified port to the hostport on the remote host. This is the same option in ssh1. The socket listens to the port on the local host, and whenever a connection is made to this port (port 110 for POP, for example), the connection is forwarded to the secure channel and the connection is made to the remote host on the hostport. Port forwarding can also be defined on a per-host basis via the configuration file. For privileged ports, only root can forward them.

basis via the configuration file. For privileged ports, only root can forward them.

-n This option works similar to the -f option; however, it will not work if you need to type a password. This is the same option that ssh1 has. Standard input is redirected from /dev/null, and it must be used when the Secure Shell client is being sent to the background. This is commonly used for scripts and to send X traffic that's being run on the remote host. It's good to use this option with the authentication agent.

-o option This is used for passing options in the configuration file when no defined command-line option is defined. This is the same option as for ssh1. This includes StrictHostKeyChecking and UseRsh, which do not have their own command-line option. These options and others are covered later in this chapter. This has the same format as if it were in the configuration file.

-p port You can specify which port the client connects to the server on. This is the same option that ssh1 has. The default is port 22, which is reserved for Secure Shell. Keep in mind that the port defined in the /etc/services file is for the server, unless otherwise specified. This may be specified on a per-host basis in the configuration file.

-P Use a port above 1023, a non-privileged port. This is the same option as ssh1. You cannot use this for rhosts authentication (either combined with public key authentication or by itself). However, this is very helpful for connecting through some firewalls that do not have configurations for it.

-q This is the quiet mode, which means that nothing is displayed. This is the same option that is used for ssh1 and usually pertains to warning and diagnostic messages. If you use this option, you'll want to turn it off if you're running into authentication or connection problems.

-R port:host:hostport This forwards any connection from the remote host on the specified port to the hostport on the local host. This is the same option in ssh1. This works in the reverse way from the -L option. A socket listens to a port on the remote host, and whenever a connection is made to this port, it is forwarded to the local host and the hostport. The port forwarding can be specified on a per-host basis in the configuration. If you use a privileged port, it can only be forwarded when logging in as root on the remote host.

-S This specifies for the Secure Shell client to not request a session channel. This is used for port forwarding requests and when a tty doesn't need to be allocated for use (non-interactive mode).

-t This option forces the Secure Shell client to work in interactive mode. This is the same option that is used in ssh1. It forces a pseudo tty, even if a command is given. This can be used for executing screen-based programs on a remote host.

-V This prints the client's version number and exits. It does the same thing in ssh1.

-v Verbose mode. Causes ssh to print debugging messages about its progress. This is helpful in debugging connection, authentication, and configuration problems. This is the equivalent of running in debug mode at level 2. It does the same thing in ssh1.

-x Disables forwarding for X traffic. This is the same option used in ssh1. Because X is known to be unsecure, paranoid sites may want to use this option. This option can be defined on a per-host basis via the configuration file.

+x If you want to enable X traffic to be forwarded, use this option. This also happens to be the default for ssh2.

Some Examples

Like SSH1, these options are not set by default. The default setting for the Secure Shell client is to run in the foreground (if no command is passed) and start at terminal. Also, the traffic is not compressed by default. When compressing data, the process may slow down traffic and only waste CPU cycles so that you may not get any increased bandwidth out of it. X traffic is automatically forwarded, but you can turn it off if it causes errors to send it.

If you were to use options to get the same results as the default, your command line would look like this:

```
$ ssh2 +a -C -e ~ -l $USER -p 22 +x host.com
```

So, to log in to a remote account using Secure Shell, you can use:

```
$ ssh2 host.com
```

This allows you to log in with a different username. For example, the local host I'm on has the username "anne." The account I have on the remote host is "ahc." Note that this is the same thing you do with ssh1. To log in with "ahc," I use the following:

```
$ ssh2 -l ahc host.com
```

Because I'm using a modem line, I need to turn on compression. I also want to use the IDEA cipher:

```
$ ssh2 +C -c idea host.com
```

If you want to connect to the remote host and run the process in the background, you can do that very easily. This is most often used in conjunction with X programs or in shell scripts. Keep in mind that this will prompt for authentication. You'll also want to turn off the escape character.

```
$ ssh2 -f -e host.com xload
```

If you want to send the output to /dev/null and run the remote program in the background, use the -f option's related option: -n. This does not prompt for passwords, so make sure you use this with .shosts or the authentication agent. Again, you'll probably want to turn off the escape character.

```
$ ssh2 -n -e host.com xclock &
```

If you want to connect to the remote server on a different port from port 22, use the -p option.

```
$ ssh2 -p 2023 host.com
```

Usage for scp2

Like the SSH1 scp client, the syntax for scp2 is a little more complicated than ssh2. It looks like this:

```
$ scp2 user@source:/directory/file user@destination:/directory/file
```

The nice thing about scp2 is you can copy to the remote host or copy to the local host. So, depending on the location of file you are sending (either the remote or local host), you need to specify the username, the hostname, the directory, and the file. This may sound complicated and like a lot to remember, but if you are doing this right, you should be OK. I use scp2 to copy files to and from my Linux host at home and to and from my ISP account.

Command-Line Options

If you need to toggle between setting the cipher, defining the identity files, preserving file attributes, setting up the ports, enabling compression, setting batch mode, and defining options for ssh2 (since scp2 uses ssh2 as a transport). This has some new options that were not in scp1.

Notice that options -a, -A, -B, -C, -i, -L, -o, -q, and -Q no longer exist in this implementation of scp.

-1 Makes scp2 run scp1. This is a 1 (one) not an l (L). This is good for compatibility with SSH1 servers, so if you're going to run this option, you must use this one first, followed by any other scp1 options. Note that scp2 options will not work after this option is used. You can use the -t and the -f options with this. See *"Secure Shell Clients—*ssh *and* scp*"* on page 89 for more information on scp1.

-c cipher This is the same option that is defined in ssh2, since it is passed directly to ssh2. Also, this is the same option that scp1 uses. You can choose which symmetric key cipher you want to encrypt the network traffic with. This does not affect the authentication, which uses DSA or RSA public key. Your choices for ciphers are IDEA, DES, 3DES, Blowfish, Arcfour, and Twofish. You can also choose "none," but this disables any encryption and renders the Secure Shell client unsecure. The "none" choice should be used for debugging and testing purposes only, not for actual use. Your best bet is to use 3DES, IDEA, or Blowfish. Blowfish and Twofish are the fastest supported algorithms for SSH2. For the best security, use IDEA. If IDEA is not supported for both Secure Shell servers, use 3DES.

-d This is a sanity check to make sure the copy destination is a directory. If it is not a directory (say that it's a file, for instance), scp2 will complain with an error message, then exit.

-D debug_level_spec This defines the amount of debugging information you receive. It's the same option that ssh2 uses.

-h Prints a command usage summary, then exits. It doesn't run the scp2 program.

-n Previews what scp2 would do, but it doesn't copy any files. This a nice way to make sure you're copying the right files to the right place before you do it.

-p Preserves the file attributes from the source host. This includes modification times, access times, and modes from the original file. This option is taken directly from rcp and is the same option used in scp1. You'll find this very useful if you are backing up files and want to ensure file integrity.

-P port You can specify which port the client connects to the server on. This is the same as the scp1 command-line option. The default is port 22, which is reserved for Secure Shell. Keep in mind that this port is defined in the /etc/services file for the server, unless otherwise specified. This may be specified on a per-host basis in the configuration file. This is different than ssh2 because rcp uses -p to preserve file attributes.

-r Recursively copies entire directories and the files inside. This should copy all the files and subdirectories in that directory. This is the same option used for scp1. This option won't be supported until release 2.0.13.

-S path_to_ssh2 This option specifies the path to ssh2. This is similar to the option used in scp1. This is used if you've installed ssh in a non-standard directory.

-u This option uses scp2 more like a secure mv function. Instead of leaving the source files (and directories), it removes them after copying them to the destination. Use this option carefully.

-v Verbose mode. Causes scp2 to print debugging messages about its progress. This prints out information on debug level 2. This is helpful in debugging connection, authentication, and configuration problems. This is similar to the same option used in scp1.

Some Examples

The following options are not set by default. The default setting for the scp is to run in the foreground and display the statistics. Also, the traffic is not compressed by default as well, because this may slow down traffic and only waste CPU cycles. Also, batch mode is not set and port 22 is used by default. We'll assume that the local host account name is "anne" and the remote host account name is "ahc."

So, to copy a file from my local host to my remote host:

```
$ scp2 filename ahc@host:/home/ahc/
```

To copy a file from the remote host to the current directory on the local host, I use the same command. However, it looks a little different:

```
$ scp2 ahc@host:/home/ahc/filename
```

If you want to see statistics, they look something like this:

```
$ scp2 ahc@host:/home/ahc/filename
```

If you want to see what scp2 is going to do without actually copying the files:

```
$ scp2 -n ahc@host:/home/ahc/filename
```

If you want to copy files to the tools directory and make sure tools is a directory with the IDEA cipher:

```
$ scp2 -d -c idea ahc@host:/home/ahc/filename tools
```

You can copy an entire directory structure (for backing up a Web site, for instance) over port 2000:

```
$ scp2 -r -P 2000 ahc@host:/home/ahc/tools
```

If you want to copy a file to the tools directory and remove the file from the remote host:

```
$ scp2 -u ahc@host:/home/ahc/filename tools
```

Usage for sftp2

Like the scp2 client, the sftp2 has some funky syntax:

```
$ sftp2 hostname [port number] [username]
```

The nice thing is that you can use this with any host running the Secure Shell 2 server daemon. There is no "separate" daemon for the FTP connections; all the work is done from the client, which is an FTP-flavored client. This does not use FTP itself, but a similar client. Notice that the syntax is very similar to FTP itself, but you have some command-line options you can specify with sftp2 that are different from FTP.

Command-Line Options

If you need to toggle between setting the cipher, defining the port, and setting the path for ssh2, these options will help. There are also two debugging options, but you should only use those if you're running into problems. Because sftp2 is a new application to Secure Shell, not very many options are available.

-c cipher This is the same option that is defined in ssh, because it is passed directly to ssh. Also, this is the same option that scp1 uses. You can choose which symmetric key cipher you want to encrypt the network traffic with. This does not affect the authentication, which uses DSA or RSA public key. Your choices for ciphers are IDEA, DES, 3DES, Blowfish, Arcfour, and Twofish. You can also choose "none," but this disables any encryption and renders the Secure Shell client unsecure. The "none" choice should be used for debugging and testing purposes only, not for actual use. DES and Arcfour are both known to be unsecure ciphers, so don't use them. Your best bet is to use 3DES, IDEA, or Blowfish. Blowfish and Twofish are the fastest supported algorithms for SSH2. For the best security, use IDEA. If IDEA is not supported for both Secure Shell servers, use 3DES.

-d debug_level_spec This defines the amount of debugging information you receive. It's the same option that ssh2 uses. Note that scp2 uses -D, where sftp2 uses -d.

-p port You can specify which port the client connects to the server on. The default is port 22, which is reserved for Secure Shell. Keep in mind that this port is defined in the /etc/services file for the server, unless otherwise specified. This may be specified on a per-host basis in the configuration file. Note that this is the same as the ssh2 option for port selection.

-S path_to_ssh2 This option specifies the path to ssh2. This is the same option used in scp2. This is used if you've installed ssh in a non-standard directory.

-v Verbose mode. This is like all the other clients for Secure Shell 2 and causes sftp2 to print debugging messages about its progress. This prints out information on debug level 2, which is helpful in debugging connection, authentication, and configuration problems. This is similar to the same option used in `scp1`.

Some Examples

The following options are not set by default. The default setting for the `sftp2` is to run on port 22. If you want to set options like compression and the ciphers that relate mostly to `ssh2`, not the `sftp2` client, then you should set them in the configuration file as shown later in the chapter.

So, the default command with options looks something like this:

```
$ sftp2 -p 22 hostname.com
```

To send a file using port 2000 for Secure Shell and using the Blowfish cipher with the username ahc:

```
$ sftp2 -p 2000 -c blowfish hostname.com ahc
```

Configuring the Secure Shell Client

Secure Shell has a configuration file in which you can define options by default. This sets options for `ssh`, `scp`, and `sftp` clients. Some of these options are not definable by the command-line option, but you can configure extra functions to work with Secure Shell. Like most configuration files and shell scripts, empty lines and lines starting with the "#" are not read. The default configuration file for Secure Shell is `/etc/ssh2/ssh2_config`. This sets the options for both the `ssh2` and `scp2` clients.

With the client, the user can have their own specified settings in the `$HOME/.ssh2/ssh2_config` file. This has the same format as the `/etc/ssh2/ssh2_config` file. The order in which options are applied to the client is:

1. Command-line options

2. The user's configuration file

3. The system-wide configuration file

The following are options that you can set in the `ssh2_config` file for Secure Shell. The format for defining these options in the `/etc/ssh2/ssh2_config` file is:

```
OptionType Argument
```

If you have multiple arguments, they are separated by a space. This format applies to all the options listed below.

Hostname Options

You can define some options affecting the remote host you connect to through some configuration options. All of these options also apply to IP addresses as well as network host names. There is no HostName configuration option for ssh2 as in ssh1. With wildcards, you can filter a range of addresses or by entire domains.

Host This defines which host is affected by the options configured in the configuration file. This is the same option used in ssh1. You can use wildcards ('*' for multiple characters and '?' for single characters). This is the same as the hostname that is given on the command line.

Usage:

```
Host tigerlair.com
```

StrictHostKeyChecking This is the same option that is implemented in ssh1, but is not currently implemented as of the 2.0.11 release of SSH2. This can be used to configure the client on whether or not to add host keys to the $HOME/.ssh2/known_hosts file automatically or to ask for them. If you frequently connect to different hosts (let's say you are using a shell account from an ISP and your connection gets a dynamically allocated IP address, for example), this may not be a good idea and could become quite irritating. If you are setting up Secure Shell to run on a production environment where the hosts should not be changing, you'll probably want to set this to "no." Your options are "no," "yes," and "ask." The "ask" option prompts you if you want to add a host to your known_hosts file.

Usage:

```
StrictHostKeyChecking ask
```

Authentication

Secure Shell provides different authentication methods: passwords, rhosts, public keys, and TIS authentication mechanisms. You can either use only one or a combination of any of these for accessing accounts via Secure Shell. However, be aware that rhosts authentication is the weakest, and any combination with the public keypair is going to be your strongest form of authentication.

Note that `NumberOfPasswordPrompts`, `TISAuthentication`, and the `Kerberos` options are not implemented for Secure Shell 2.

BatchMode This is the same configuration option used in `ssh1`, but it is not currently implemented for `ssh2`. This turns off prompting for passwords if it is turned on. This is great if you're using Secure Shell in scripts or running cron or batch jobs. Remember, it helps to have the authentication agent going instead of using rhosts for this. The default is "no," and your choices are "yes" and "no."

Usage:

```
BatchMode no
```

PasswordAuthentication You can define whether or not you want to use passwords to access accounts via Secure Shell. This is the same option used in `ssh1`. The default is "yes," and what the passwords do is protect the private key, not the account itself, by more conventional means. You may opt to turn off password authentication, but it's better to leave it on because it protects your private and public keys. This is similar to the `PasswordAuthentication` for the Secure Shell daemon.

Usage:

```
PasswordAuthentication yes
```

PasswordPrompt This specifies whether or not to include the remote hostname and username in the password prompt. This option combines both `PasswordPromptHostname` and `PasswordPromptLogin` from `ssh1` into one option. The variables `%U` and `%H` represent the username and hostname, respectively. This only has an effect on what the user sees, not on what the program actually does.

Usage:

```
PasswordPrompt "%U password"
```

RHostsAuthentication This option sets your authentication to be based on the `.rhosts` or `/etc/hosts.equiv` alone. This doesn't require a password or a public keypair. This is the same as the `RhostsAuthentication` option used in `ssh1`, and it opens your system up to Berkeley services attacks that are well known and the reason you are using Secure Shell in the first place. The default is "no," and you're best leaving it that way. If you do want to use rhosts authentication, use it in conjunction with the public key authentication in RHostsPubKeyAuthentication. This is similar to the Secure Shell server daemon setting RHostsAuthentication. However, it does not have the same significant effect on security the way that the server-side configuration does.

Usage:

```
RHostsAuthentication no
```

RHostsPubKeyAuthentication This option sets your authentication to be based on the .rhosts or /etc/hosts.equiv with the public keypair. This is similar to the RhostsRSAAuthentication option for ssh1 and can be used for SSH1 compatibility. This doesn't require a password, but it does require that the remote side has a public keypair to authenticate against. This opens your system up to Berkeley services attacks, but the threat is minimized because of the required public keypair. If you do leave this option at "yes" (the default), you may want to set some stricter login requirements for hosts. Again, if you want to be on the more secure side of things, turn off any type of rhosts authentication. This is similar to the Secure Shell server daemon configuration option RHostsPubKeyAuthentication.

Usage:

```
RhostsPubKeyAuthentication no
```

PubKeyAuthentication You can use a myriad of authentication types; or as you can see, you can use a single type. This is similar to the RSAAuthentication option for ssh1 and can be used for SSH1 compatibility. If you want to define only public key authentication to be accepted, you can. This does not require rhosts or passwords to help authenticate. The default is "yes" and this is fine to leave as is. This is similar to the Secure Shell server daemon configuration option RhostsAuthentication.

Usage:

```
PubKeyAuthentication yes
```

Client Options

These options are specific to how the Secure Shell client functions overall. These general settings include options such as the username on the remote host, connection attempts, proxy commands (if used), the cipher, forwardings, the escape character, and using `rsh`.

Note that `CompressionLevel`, `ClearAllForwardings`, `ConnectionAttempts`, and `ProxyCommand` are no longer supported options for Secure Shell 2.

DontReadStdin With this option, the user does not require a passphrase, in which case Secure Shell Authentication Agent should be running. This option redirects input into `/dev/null`.

Usage:

```
DontReadStdin no
```

Cipher This option is where you can choose the cipher you connect with. You can use IDEA, 3DES, Blowfish, DES, and Arcfour. This is the same option used in `ssh1`. You can also pick "none," but don't do this unless you are debugging. Your best bets are to pick either IDEA, 3DES, or Blowfish. Because IDEA is not supported by all servers, if you pick IDEA and it's not supported, it will fall back to 3DES.

Usage:

```
Cipher idea
```

Compression This defines whether or not you use compression. This is the same option used in `ssh1`. This is the same algorithm that the gzip application uses. You have two obvious choices: "yes" or "no." Keep in mind if you're on a fast network, you don't want to bother turning on compression because it actually slows things down as opposed to speeding them up.

Usage:

```
Compression yes
```

EscapeChar This defines the escape character and is the same as the `ssh1` option. The default is the tilde (~). This is the same as the `-e` option you can pass on the command line. The argument should be a single character only, a single character followed by a carat (^)

to indicate a control character, or "none" to disable the escape character (which makes the connection transparent).

Usage:

```
EscapeChar z^
```

FallBackToRsh You can define the Secure Shell client so that if it fails to connect (usually because no daemon is running on the remote or local side), it will try to connect to the remote client via rsh. Before running rsh, you will get a warning that the session is not encrypted. This is the same option used in ssh1. It looks something like this:

```
tigerlair:/home/ahc: ssh www.trusting.host.com
Secure connection to www.trusting.host.com refused;
reverting to insecure method.
Using rsh. WARNING: Connection will not be encrypted.
```

Usage:

```
FallBackToRsh no
```

ForcePTTYAllocation This option forces a tty even if a command is given. This is used for such things as menu command interfaces. As of the 2.0.11 release, this is not currently implemented.

Usage:

```
ForcePTTYAllocation No
```

GoBackground This forces ssh2 to run as a background process after authentication. This is useful if the process needs to be run in the background, but the user needs to enter the passphrase.

Usage:

```
GoBackground Yes
```

KeepAlive The Secure Shell daemon can be set to send keepalive messages or to not send them. This is the same format that ssh1 uses. Keepalive messages let the remote server know whether or not the connection has died; and as a result, kills the active process. However, if the route temporarily goes away, it can get frustrating to see a message like this:

```
Connection down; disconnecting.
```

OK, it's annoying. But if you don't send keepalives, you may have hanging sessions that leave ghost processes and eat your server's resources. The default setting is "yes," which means that the server sends keepalives. If you want to disable keepalive messages, you'll have to disable both the server and client configuration files. Be aware that this may leave you with hanging processes if you decide to turn them off. This is similar to the Secure Shell server daemon configuration setting `KeepAlive`.

Usage:

```
KeepAlive yes
```

User This is where you specify a username to log in on the remote host. This is the same option as `ssh1`. You may want to define this if you are constantly logging on to a remote host with a different username than you have on your local host. This way you don't have to constantly type it on the command line with the `-1` option.

Usage:

```
User ahc
```

UseRsh This option specifies whether or not `rsh` should be used for this host. If the host does not support the SSH protocol, then `rsh` or `rlogin` is automatically executed. This is the same option used in `ssh1`. If this option is specified, all other options are ignored. So, aside from the inherent security issues with `rsh`, you may not want to use this particular option.

Usage:

```
UseRsh no
```

File Locations

These options define where the Secure Shell client files are located. This includes the user's identity file and the known host files for the system and the user.

Note that there are no longer options for `GlobalKnownHostsFile` and `UserKnownHostsFile`.

AuthorizationFile This option specifies the name of the user's authorization file. The default is `$HOME/.ssh2/authorization`.

Usage:

```
AuthorizationFile ~/.ssh2/newauth.file
```

RandomSeedFile This option specifies where the user's random seed file is and is used for generating a random number to create the public keypair. The default is $HOME/.ssh2/random_seed.
Usage:

```
RandomSeedFile ~/.ssh2/newrandom.file
```

IdentityFile This specifies where the user's DSA or RSA private key is located. The default is $HOME/.ssh2/id_dsa1024_a. This is similar to the IdentityFile option for ssh1. You can define various identity files that can be used by the authentication agent. You can define an identity file for each host that you are going to connect to as well. You can use the tilde (~) instead of $HOME to represent the user's home directory.
Usage:

```
IdentityFile ~/.ssh2/id_dsa1024_a.thishost
```

Ports
With Secure Shell, you can do a lot of things with the ports. This includes defining ports for fowarding both locally and remotely, the actual port that the Secure Shell client connects on, and whether or not privileged ports are used. GatewayPorts is no longer implemented for ssh2.

LocalForward This forwards any connection to the local host on the specified port to the hostport on the remote host. This is the same option used in ssh1. The socket listens to the port on the local host, and whenever a connection is made to this port (say, port 110 for POP, for example), the connection is forwarded to the secure channel and the connection is made to the remote host on the hostport. For privileged ports, only root can forward them. This is the same as the -L option for the ssh1 client.
Usage:

```
LocalForward 1025:remotehost:110
```

Port You can specify a port for the Secure Shell daemon to listen on. The default port is 22; however, you may want to define another port for application purposes or when port 22 is in use. This is the same option as the -p option used in ssh1 and is similar to the Port option for the Secure Shell server daemon configuration file.

Usage:

```
Port 21
```

RemoteForward This forwards any connection from the remote host (on the specified port) to be forwarded to the hostport on the local host. This is the same option used in ssh1. This works in the reverse way the -L option does. A socket listens to a port on the remote host, and whenever a connection is made to this port, it is forwarded to the local host and the hostport. If you use a privileged port, it can only be forwarded when logging in as root on the remote host. This is the same as the -R option for the ssh1 client.

Usage:

```
RemoteForward 110:remotehost:1025
```

UseNonPrivilegedPort Use a port above 1023, a non-privileged port. You cannot use this for rhosts authentication (either combined with public key authentication or by itself). However, this is very helpful for connecting through some firewalls that do not have configurations for it. This is the same option as UsePrivilegedPort for ssh1, although this is not yet implemented as of release 2.011. This is the same as the -P option.

Usage:

```
UsePrivilegedPort yes
```

Forwarding

These options are used to define forwarding for ssh2. They include forwarding the authentication agent to remote hosts and forwarding X11 traffic.

ForwardAgent This option can be configured to forward the connection to the authentication agent on the remote host. This is the same option used in ssh1. This helps when you are not using passwords and want to use Secure Shell for things like shell scripts.

Usage:

```
ForwardAgent yes
```

ForwardX11 This option defines whether or not X forwarding is automatically sent through the Secure Shell channel and the DIS-PLAY environmental variable gets set. This is the same option used in ssh1. Like other TCP traffic, this can be overridden by user-defined forwarders. It is up to you to allow X traffic through. However, if you are going to let X traffic through remotely, you'll want to forward it through Secure Shell. This is similar to the X11Forwarding option on the Secure Shell daemon.

Usage:

```
ForwardX11 yes
```

SSH1 Compatibility

These options specify SSH1 compatibility with SSH2. This includes using the SSH1 compatibility code, making the SSH1 authentication agent compatible, and the path for ssh1.

Ssh1AgentCompatibility This option defines whether or not the Secure Shell 2 authentication agent should be compatible with Secure Shell 1. The options you can use are "none," "traditional," and "ssh2." If you are using the Secure Shell 2 Authentication Agent in SSH1 compatibility mode as defined in the option Ssh1Compatibility, you can only use the "ssh2" value. Otherwise, "none" will not forward any SSH1 agent at all, and "traditional" will forward like it was running SSH1.

Usage:

```
Ssh1AgentCompatibility ssh2
```

Ssh1Compatibility If you want to support both SSH1 and SSH2, you'll want to set this to "yes." This executes the ssh1 client if you connect with a server that only supports ssh1.

Usage:

```
Ssh1Compatibility yes
```

Ssh1Path This option specifies the location of the ssh1 client. This defaults to /usr/local/bin/ssh1. This is the application that is run whenever a connection to a server daemon only supports Secure Shell 1.

Usage:

```
Ssh1Path /usr/local/security/bin/ssh1
```

Verbosity

These modes determine how much you want the Secure Shell client to tell you. You have two modes: VerboseMode, which gives you a lot of information, and QuietMode, which gives you very little information.

VerboseMode This mode causes the ssh2 client to print debugging messages. This means that you should not run in this mode unless you are troubleshooting or testing. This information is helpful for connection, authentication, and configuration problems.

Usage:

```
VerboseMode no
```

QuietMode This is opposite from VerboseMode. The only information printed is the fatal errors which cause ssh2 to not function the way it should. You can do this if you know exactly what's going on. Most people leave this as "no."

Usage:

```
QuietMode no
```

A Sample Client Configuration File

Now that you know what your options are, here is an example of a Secure Shell 2 client configuration file ssh2_config. You can set yours however you like; this is just for illustration purposes.

```
# This is ssh2 client systemwide configuration file.
# This file provides defaults for users, and the values can
# be changed in per-user configuration files or on the
# command line.
# Site-wide defaults for various options
# This allows users to connect to all hosts
Host *
# This allows the authentication agent to forward to
# remote hosts
ForwardAgent yes
# Turn off X11 forwarding
ForwardX11 no
# Authentication options. Turn off any form of rhosts and
# TIS authentication
RHostsAuthentication yes
PubKeyAuthentication yes
```

```
# Make sure password authentication is turned on
PasswordAuthentication yes
# Turn off any form of rsh connectivity
FallBackToRsh no
UseRsh no
# Turn on batch mode for those who want to run ssh in
# scripts
BatchMode yes
# Use IDEA and Blowfish for our first choice in ciphers
Cipher idea blowfish
# Leave these defaults
# StrictHostKeyChecking no
# IdentityFile ~/.ssh2/id_dsa1024_a
# Port 22
# EscapeChar ~
```

Other Secure Shell Client Configuration Files

In addition to the Secure Shell client system and user configuration files, you need to be aware of other files that affect the way the Secure Shell client behaves. The configuration files are stored either in the /etc directory for system-wide configurations or in $HOME/.ssh2 for individual settings.

The /etc/ssh2 Directory

The files listed below are found in the /etc/ssh2 directory and are used for public keys and key generation. They are /etc/ssh2/hostkey, /etc/ssh2/hostkey.pub, and /etc/ssh2/random_seed. Most of the other files that Secure Shell 2 uses are in the user's home directory, which is covered in the next section.

/etc/ssh2/hostkey The private key for the host. This is usually created during the "make install" process. This file should not be readable by anyone but root, nor should it be password-protected. You can re-create it using ssh-keygen2, which is covered in *"Secure Shell Key Management"* on page 191.

/etc/ssh2/hostkey.pub The public key for the host. This is usually created during the "make install" process. This file can be readable by anyone, and it should be passphrase-protected. You can re-create it using ssh-keygen2, which is covered in *"Secure Shell Key Management"* on page 191.

/etc/ssh2/random_seed Like Secure Shell 1, this file contains the random number seed generated for the key generation. This file should not be read by anyone and only root should have the ability to access it. This is also covered more in *"Secure Shell Key Management"* on page 191.

The ~/.ssh2 Directory

The files listed below are found in the ~/.ssh directory that are not configuration files for the client itself but for the user. This includes the following files in the ~/.ssh directory: environment, known_hosts, random_seed, identity, identity.pub, authorized_keys, and rc files.

$HOME/.ssh2/authorization This file contains all the DSA public keys that are used for logging in to this account from remote sites. This file should only be accessible by the user and not by anyone else. This file should list all the applicable identity files.

$HOME/.ssh2/environment This is the user environmental variable configuration file. These environmental variables are discussed in the next section of this chapter.

$HOME/.ssh2/id_dsa1024_a This is the user's DSA private key. Like the ~/.ssh2/random_seed, the user should not modify the permissions or change the file in any way. This is how the Secure Shell client recognizes the user. It is strongly recommended that you specify a passphrase when generating the key. This passphrase is used to encrypt the data with the IDEA cipher. This file is unreadable by people.

$HOME/.ssh2/id_dsa1024_a.pub This is the user's DSA public key. Unlike the ~/.ssh2/id_dsa1024_a.pub file, this file is readable by humans and looks a lot like a PGP public key. Add this file to any remote host you want to log in to in the ~/.ssh/authorized_keys file. This file isn't necessary for Secure Shell; however, the user may feel more secure using it.

$HOME/.ssh2/identification This file sets the user's identification file per host. If a user wants to use another identification file in addition to the one he has as his default, use this file to recognize that key.

$HOME/.ssh2/random_seed This file is used for seeding the random number generator. It is specific to the user, and the user should not modify the permissions or change the file in any way.

This is used in the public key exchange for the user files. This file is unreadable by people.

$HOME/.ssh2/ssh2_config This is the user configuration file as discussed previously in this chapter.

Environmental Variables

Even after learning about all these other files that affect the Secure Shell client's behavior, you can set some environmental variables as well. These variables are set by Secure Shell, and the user should not be configuring these on their own, because they directly affect Secure Shell's behavior. There may be other environmental variables you can set—this varies from operating system to operating system. For example, this information may be read from /etc/environment or $HOME/.ssh2/environment.

DISPLAY This variable sets the location of the X server. It is usually defined by the user when not using Secure Shell. However, because Secure Shell sets this variable dependent on authorization cookies, you do not want to manually set this variable. The format of DISPLAY usually looks like this:

```
DISPLAY=hostname:number
```

where number is greater than or equal to one. Zero is usually used on a local host.

LOGNAME or USER This variable sets the username.

MAIL Sets the directory to the user's mailbox. It may be something like $HOME/inbox.

PATH Sets the default path for the user, as defined in /etc/environment. This may be overridden by the user's shell initialization files, such as ~/.cshrc or ~/.profile.

SSH2_AUTH_SOCK If authentication agent is forwarded, this specifies the UNIX domain socket's path used to talk to the authentication agent.

SSH2_CLIENT Locates the client. This variable includes the client's IP address, the client's port number, and the server's port number. It may look something like this:

```
111.22.3.44 1025 22
```

SSH2_ORIGINAL_COMMAND If you are using the Secure Shell client to remotely execute a command, this variable is set to show the original command line that the user sent.

SSH_SOCKS_SERVER This defines the location of the SOCKS server that the Secure Shell client and server access to go through the SOCKS proxy.

SSH2_TTY This sets the path to the tty device that is associated with the prevalent shell. If there is no tty (for example, Secure Shell is not set in an interactive mode), this variable will not be set.

Summary

The Secure Shell 2 clients—`ssh2`, `sftp2`, and `scp2`—are the main interface to Secure Shell 2. Secure Shell can be used either in an interactive mode like `rlogin` or in a command mode like `rsh`. The user authenticates with public key cryptography, and the session is encrypted with a symmetric key: IDEA, 3DES, DES, Blowfish, Twofish, or Arcfour.

The Secure Shell 2 client connects to the server on port 22, which is a well-known port for Secure Shell. Before it connects, it reads the configurations passed through command line, the user's configuration files, or system-wide configuration files. When the connection is established and the symmetric key algorithm is determined, the Secure Shell client encrypts the packets before sending even the password over the network. If a command needs to be executed, it is stored in a buffer before the connection is established. If the session is interactive, the Secure Shell client allocates a tty.

The Secure Shell clients have many options; some can be taken at the command line whereas others can be passed through a configuration file. The default system-wide configuration file is `/etc/ssh2/ssh2_config`, and individual users have `~/.ssh2/ssh2_config`. For those options you can define, they include the types of authentication, compression, X, port forwarding, and some specific options for `scp`, such as recursive copying and keeping the current file attributes.

Advanced Usage of Secure Shell

Secure Shell Key Management

In this chapter:

- Host keys

- User keys

- Key generation

- Making your keys publicly available

- The authentication agent

This chapter is a bit of a misnomer—it is not key management in the sense of Public Key Infrastructure, rather it's more like how to manage your private and public keys properly for Secure Shell. As of press time, there is no available implementation of Secure Shell and digital certificates which use the X.509 standard. However, look for that just before the millennium.

Part of working with Secure Shell is protecting your keys. You want to make sure that your keys are secure (so it helps to harden your host as best as possible). You have some key management functionality that's built in to Secure Shell, such as making certain hosts known and storing some keys into memory. You can also add keys to memory when you feel it's necessary.

Because each client and server (SSH1 and SSH2) behave differently, they use different key files. In additional, SSH1 only provides for RSA keypairs where SSH2 provides for DSA (and RSA in the commercial release) keypairs. In this chapter, you will see how each protocol handles keys and how you can manage your keys.

Host Keys

For each Secure Shell protocol, you'll find a set of system-wide key files that are used for the identity of the host and the identity of the Secure Shell server. We'll talk about some other files that relate to the host key later in this chapter. Table 7.1 shows you how your host and server keys relate to each other and the authentication process.

Table 7.1 *Your host and server key regeneration time*

Key	Regeneration time	Size
Host key	Every 3-6 months or never	1024-bit
Server key	Every hour	768-bit

SSH1

In SSH1, you'll find three main files for the host key. As you can see, the key files all begin with ssh_. Keep in mind that all files that begin with ssh_ are not necessarily related to the host keypair. They are:

- /etc/ssh_host_key
- /etc/ssh_host_key.pub

The /etc/ssh_host_key is your private host key. This file should not be accessed by anyone other than root. This file should also not be readable by anyone other than root. This is the system-wide private key, and it should remain protected as much as possible.

If you were to list the /etc/ssh_host_key file, you would see the permission as follows:

```
# ls -l /etc/ssh_host_key
-r-------- 1 root bin 533 Feb 25 1997 /etc/ssh_host_key
```

If there is any other read or write permissions set on this file, you should run the following command:

```
# chmod 400 /etc/ssh_host_key
# ls -l /etc/ssh_host_key
-r-------- 1 root bin 533 Feb 25 1997 /etc/ssh_host_key
```

The /etc/ssh_host_key.pub is your public host key. This file does not provide a service for the Secure Shell application, and it is used to match the host private key. This is so that the administration can either copy the contents into the /etc/ssh_known_hosts file for the system or copy the contents for the user's known host file—~/.ssh/known_hosts. This will be covered later in the chapter.

The /etc/ssh_random_seed character is not a key, but is used for generating the RSA keypair for the system. This is covered under the section on key generation later in this chapter.

Checking Your Host Keys

You should make sure your host keys are fine. This defines your host to other Secure Shell daemons and clients without having to worry about spoofing. These are the most important ones to make secure, especially the private host key. By default, your private host key is /etc/ssh_host_key. The permissions should be that root is the only account that has read access to the file, and root should own it (unless you are running Secure Shell from a non-privileged user account).

```
# ls -l /etc/ssh_host_key
-r-------- 1 root bin 533 Feb 25 1997 /etc/ssh_host_key
```

This is the key you must have protected. Therefore, it doesn't hurt to install security patches and stop network traffic that you don't need for your host. The contents of the key itself look like this:

```
# more /etc/ssh_host_key
(Garbage printed here)
```

You can see that this key prints garbage to the human eye. This file is unreadable because there is no reason that someone should be looking at the host's private key. Again, store a copy of the key off-line on a disk or CD somewhere. You may also want to sign your keys with a PGP key. This file is used to determine the identity of the host. Note that it should not be password-protected, because the computer does not need a password in the same way a human account should.

You'll notice that the public key has very different permissions and doesn't seem to be as protected. By default, this file is /etc/ssh_host_key.pub.

```
# ls -l /etc/ssh_host_key.pub
-rw-r--r-- 1 root bin 337 Feb 25 1997 /etc/ssh_host_key.pub
```

The reason the public key has more visibility is because you want to share this key with the public. You don't want anyone to write to it—this can cause a denial of service for Secure Shell, and someone may substitute your key with theirs. If you want to look at this key, you'll see that it looks similar to the private key, but with a different set of characters. This uses either RSA or DSA with Diffie-Helman for the key exchange.

```
# more /etc/ssh_host_key.pub
1024 35 160579799557319038214843810180424236917774412381246
835521324554378682240708290924252583569827349017782132057740
034738959603238883023412410907819508331027461099184975192116
524445749057422620398441716901869660083374436965732523503599
746728577515538018405803950424495221434299166856546314038856
25429573282666473 root@tigerlair.com
```

A Word about the Server Keys

As discussed in Chapters 3 and 5, the server keys are what the Secure Shell daemon uses to recognize that the Secure Shell server daemon is running. This key is not stored anywhere and is regenerated every hour. The regeneration time is an hour by default; however, this can be changed by the Secure Shell server daemon configuration file. However, SSH2 does not use server keys.

If this key is intercepted, it cannot be cryptanalyzed in enough time before it is regenerated. This increases the security of Secure Shell. The host key and the user identity key does not change unless a new key is generated for each. The server key is also an RSA key-pair, just like the host key and the identity key.

You can set your server key to zero so it does not regenerate; however, this does not provide you any security if your machine is cracked or physically compromised.

Building Your `ssh_known_hosts` with `ssh-keyscan`

If you are looking to farm SSH1 public host keys, you can use a utility called `ssh-keyscan` by David Mazieres. This utility is designed to obtain and verify public host keys as well as build the `ssh_known_hosts` files. An optimized version of the `ssh-make-known-hosts` Perl script—`make-host-list`—is also available.

This doesn't require you to be able to log in to the systems you are scanning and has the ability to scan thousands of hosts in a matter of minutes. To use `ssh-keyscan`:

```
# ssh-keyscan host
```

Another way to use `ssh-keyscan` is to build an `ssh_known_hosts` file. To do this, simply run the following command:

```
# make-host-list domaintoscan.com | ssh-keyscan -f-
```

The bad news is `ssh-keyscan` does not use regular expressions, and you have to modify this program to make it do so. But the good news is that it is GNU source, so you can.

Just so you know, `ssh-keyscan` causes the Secure Shell daemon to print out the log message "Connection closed by remote host" on the machines it scans. `ssh-keyscan` looks for open port 22 on the remote Secure Shell servers and grabs the host public key. If someone has Secure Shell running on another port, `ssh-keyscan` will not grab the host public key.

CD-ROM   Look for a copy of `ssh-keyscan` on the CD-ROM that comes with this book.

SSH2

From Chapter 5, you can see that the system files for SSH2 are stored in the `/etc/ssh2` directory, including your key files `/etc/ssh2/hostkey` and `/etc/ssh2/hostkey`. These files are created from the "make install" process, where they need to be manually configured in SSH1. These are DSA host keys, not RSA host keys as in SSH1, unless you are running the commercial version of SSH2.

- `/etc/ssh2/hostkey`
- `/etc/ssh2/hostkey.pub`
- `/etc/ssh2/random_seed`

The `/etc/ssh2/hostkey` is your private host key. Like its SSH1 counterpart, this file should not be accessed by anyone other than root and it should also not be readable by anyone other than root. This is the system-wide private key, and it should remain protected as much as possible. Again, remember that if permissions other than "read-only by root" are set, change the permissions using the `chmod` command as shown for the `ssh` example.

The `/etc/ssh2/hostkey.pub` is your public host key. This file does not provide a service for the Secure Shell application, and it is used to match the host's private key. This is so that the administration can either copy the contents into the `/etc/ssh_known_hosts` file for the system or copy the contents for the user's known host file—`~/.ssh2/known_hosts`. This will be covered later in the chapter.

The `/etc/ssh2/random_seed` character is not a key but is used for generating the DSA or RSA keypair for the system. This is covered under the section on key generation later in this chapter.

Your host keys and server keys should have the same permissions and attributes as the SSH1 counterparts.

User Keys

As well as a set of system keys, Secure Shell has a set of user-specific key files, which are used for the user's identity and the identity of the host that they log in to. Some other files that relate to the user's key are covered later in this chapter. Figure 7.1 shows you how your user's keypair functions with the client and server.

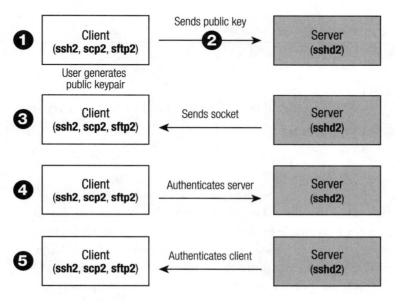

Figure 7.1 *User keypair functions with the Secure Shell client and server.*

Table 7.2 shows you how the host key files correlate with the user key files for SSH1. As you can see, a lot of similarity exists between the host key management and the user key management.

Table 7.2 *Location of keys for user and hosts*

Key file	Host	User
Private Key	/etc/ssh_host_key	~/.ssh/identity
Public Key	/etc/ssh_host_key.pub	~/.ssh/identity.pub
Random Seed	/etc/ssh_random_seed	~/.ssh/random_seed

Table 7.3 shows you how the host key files correlate with the user key files for SSH2. Again, you can see the similarity to the host key management and the user key management.

Table 7.3 *Host key and user key management for SSH2*

Key file	Host	User
Private Key	/etc/ssh2/hostkey	~/.ssh2/ id_dsa1024_a
Public Key	/etc/ssh2/hostkey.pub	~/.ssh2/ id_dsa1024_a.pub
Random Seed	/etc/ssh2/random_seed	~/.ssh2/random_seed

SSH1

In SSH1, you'll find three main files for the host key. They are:

- ~/.ssh/identity
- ~/.ssh/identity.pub
- ~/.ssh/random_seed

The ~/.ssh/identity is your private user key and this file should not be accessed by anyone other than the user. It should also not be readable by anyone other than the user. This is the user's private key because it identifies the user for the ssh login, and it should remain protected as much as possible.

If you list the ~/.ssh/identity file, you'll see the permission as follows:

```
# ls -l ~/.ssh/identity
-r-------- 1 stripes users 533 Feb 2 1999 ~/.ssh/identity
```

If any other read or write permissions are set on this file, you should run the following command:

```
# chmod 400 ~/.ssh/identity
# ls -l ~/.ssh/identity
-r-------- 1 stripes users 533 Feb 2 1999 ~/.ssh/identity
```

The ~/.ssh/identity.pub is your user's public key. This file does not provide a service for the Secure Shell application, and it's used to match the user's private key. This is so that the user can copy the authorized keys into the remote host's ~/.ssh/known_hosts file. This will be covered later in the chapter.

If you list the ~/ssh/identity.pub file, you'll see the permission as follows:

```
# ls -l ~/.ssh/identity.pub
-r--r--r-- 1 stripes users 533 Feb 2 1999 ~/.ssh/identity.pub
```

If any other read or write permissions are set on this file, you should run the following command:

```
# chmod 444 ~/.ssh/identity.pub
# ls -l ~/.ssh/identity.pub
-r--r--r-- 1 stripes users 533 Feb 2 1999 ~/.ssh/identity.pub
```

The ~/.ssh/random_seed character is not a key but is used for generating the RSA keypair for the user. This is covered under the section on key generation later in this chapter.

Checking Your User Keys

This file should be treated in a similar fashion as the /etc/ssh_host_key file for the host. You need to make sure your user's identity keys have the correct permissions. This defines your account to other Secure Shell accounts that you log in to without having to worry about who you really are. For the user, these files are the most important ones to make secure, especially the private identity key. These are protected by a password that the user provides. If someone does get root access, all the user keys will be password-protected (provided you reminded your users to do so). By default, your private identity key is ~/.ssh/identity. The permissions should be that only the user is able to view and write to the file, and the user should own it.

```
$ ls -l ~/.ssh/identity
-rw------- 1 stripes users 413 Feb 4 1998 identity
```

This is the key you must have protected. Therefore, it doesn't hurt to install Tripwire to check file integrity or download the user account Trojan horse detector available at http://www.cs.purdue.edu/COAST, which is critical for keypairs, especially the private keys. You'll also want to store a copy of the signature off-line on a disk or a burned CD somewhere. For additional protection, you can sign the key with a PGP key. The contents of the key itself look very similar to the contents of the /etc/ssh_host_key file:

```
$ more ~/.ssh/identity
(Garbage printed here)
```

You can see that this key prints garbage to the human eye. This file is unreadable because there is no reason that someone should be looking at the host's private key. This file is used to determine the identity of the host.

You'll notice that the user's public key has the same permissions as the private identity key file. By default, this file is ~/.ssh/identity.pub.

```
$ ls -l ~/.ssh/identity.pub
-rw------- 1 stripes users 413 Feb 4 1998 identity.pub
```

The reason the public key has more visibility is because you want to share this key with the public. You don't want anyone to write to it—this can cause a denial of service for Secure Shell, and someone may substitute your key with theirs.

If you list the /etc/ssh_host_key.pub file, you'll see the permission as follows:

```
# ls -l /etc/ssh_host_key.pub
-r--r--r-- 1 root bin 337 Feb 25 1997 /etc/ssh_host_key.pub
```

If any other read or write permissions are set on this file, you should run the following command:

```
# chmod 444 /etc/ssh_host_key.pub

# ls -l /etc/ssh_host_key.pub
-r--r--r-- 1 root bin 337 Feb 25 1997 /etc/ssh_host_key.pub
```

If you want to look at this key, you'll see that it looks similar to the private key but with a different set of characters.

```
$ more ~/.ssh/identity.pub
1024 37 1605797995573190382148438101804242369177744412381247
6835521324555687694330708290967987883569827349017782132057
4003473895960323888302341241090781950897882746109918497519
1165244457490574226203984417169018696600833744369657325235
9797746728577515538018405803950424495221434299166856546314
3885625429573282666473 stripes@tigerlair.com
```

SSH2

In SSH2, you'll find three main files for the host key. They are:

- `~/.ssh2/ id_dsa1024_a`
- `~/.ssh2/id_dsa1024_a.pub`

The `~/.ssh2/ id_dsa1024_a` is your DSA private user key. This file should not be accessed by anyone other than the user, and it should also not be readable by anyone other than the user. This is the user's private key because it identifies the user for the `ssh` login, and it should remain protected as much as possible.

The `~/.ssh2/ id_dsa1024_a.pub` is your DSA user's public key. This file does not provide a service for the Secure Shell application, and it is used to match the user's private key. This is so that the user can copy the authorized keys into the remote host's `~/.ssh/known_hosts` file. This will be covered later in the chapter.

The `~/.ssh/random_seed` file is not a key but is used for generating the DSA keypair for the user. This is covered in the following section on key generation.

Your user keys should have the same permissions and attributes as the SSH1 counterparts.

Key Generation

One of the most important things Secure Shell does is to generate keypairs. You can do this either from an administrator for the host key or as a user for your identity key files. This file determines the identity of the host (not the server, remember, which is regenerated regularly at every hour by default) and of the user who is logging in to a remote host. Because SSH1 and SSH2 use two different public key encryption algorithms, you'll find different files for both, as well as a different procedure for both. Figure 7.2 on page 202 shows you how the key is generated for the host and the users.

SSH1: ssh-keygen

SSH1 uses a program called `ssh-keygen` to generate the RSA authentication keypair. The system administrator may use this to generate host keys, but that should only be on a regularly scheduled time to update the host key `/etc/ssh_host_key` and

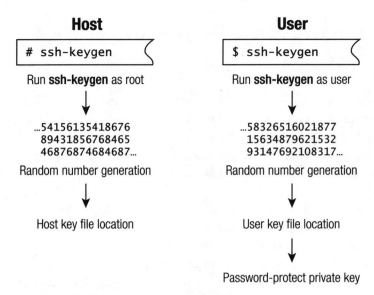

Figure 7.2 *The key generation process.*

/etc/ssh_host_key.pub. As a system administrator, you'll want to update the host key every few months (every 3 to 6 months) or so to keep the key from being compromised. You'll want to regenerate in case someone has stolen your host key and is trying to compromise your system. If your host key does change, a warning is generated. This can either be a system administrator changing the key or an unauthorized change.

To generate a host keypair:

```
# ssh-keygen
```

The next thing you'll see is:

```
Initializing random number generator...
Generating p:  ................++ (distance 222)
Generating q:  ....................++ (distance 366)
Computing the keys...
Key generation complete.
```

After you see the key generation, you are prompted for the host key file location:

```
Enter file in which to save the key (/etc/ssh_host_key):
```

Next, you're prompted for your password, twice. This is not shown onscreen.

```
Enter passphrase:
Enter the same passphrase again:
```

Next, you see where your private host key was saved. Then you see what your public key looks like and where it is stored. It should have the same name as your host key with .pub on the end of the filename.

```
Your identification has been saved in /etc/ssh_host_key.
Your public key is:
1024 37 1175275181282873279808475024838238821152558383447 25
796225405791695880888191784113149677706787726977209067224 63
976255073111504953634361979758777836485389337280874747214 44
376154637043034543426640229512653318818727242987903791380 89
628349120338426345267048083862401613959808620532824589949 55
9852899081907422484567 root@tigerlair.com
Your public key has been saved in /etc/ssh_host_key.pub
```

As a user, you'll want to run the ssh-keygen file to generate your identity keypair. This creates your ~/.ssh/identity and ~/.ssh/identity.pub files. A user can create as many identity files as is needed.

To generate a user keypair:

```
shell13:/home/stripes- ssh-keygen
```

The next thing you'll see should look very similar to the host key generation:

```
Initializing random number generator...
Generating p:  .................++ (distance 222)
Generating q:  .....................++ (distance 366)
Computing the keys...
Key generation complete.
```

After you see the key generation, you are prompted for the user identity key file location. Again, this step is the same as the host key generation.

```
Enter file in which to save the key
(/home/stripes/.ssh/identity):
```

You know the drill:

```
Enter passphrase:
Enter the same passphrase again:
```

And the location of your private and public keys should also look very familiar:

```
Your identification has been saved in
/home/stripes/.ssh/identity.
Your public key is:
1024 37 11752751812828732798084750248382388211525583834725
79622540579169588088819178411314967770678772697720906722463
97625507311150495363436197975877783648538933728087474721444
37615463704303454342664022951265331881872724298790379138089
62834912033842634526704808386240161395980862053282458994955
9852899081907422484567 stripes@shell13.ba.best.com
Your public key has been saved in /home/stripes/.ssh/identity.pub
```

Passphrases

OK, I'm going to be blunt here: use it for your user account. The only time you want an empty passphrase is for the host key, because the computer does not need to unsecure the key the same way a user has to. Because we can't really make a computer "remember" a passphrase the same way a person does, you do not want to pass-phrase-protect your host key. However, a password *does* protect the user's private key. Make sure you come up with something that is not easily guessable—password crackers are getting more and more sophisticated as hacking becomes more popular.

Note   This password is different from the password you use to log in to your account.

The following are some rules that may help you pick a strong passphrase:

1. Use upper- and lowercase letters, numbers, and symbols (!@#$%^&*(){}[]~`).

2. Keep your passphrase long (the man page recommends 10 to 30 characters).

3. Don't use simple sentences that can be found in a book, for instance.

4. Start with a phrase that means something to you, like "airlines really suck when you have to travel," and using numbers and symbols in it thus: air4lines@reall5. It gives you a frame of reference and still makes for a difficult passphrase to crack.

5. Don't write it down somewhere that is not password-protected or secured itself.

It's important to keep in mind that if you forget your passphrase, there is no way to recover it. If you do lose it, you will have to generate a new keypair. If you do this, you will have to change the public key in the /etc/ssh_known_host file on remote hosts as well as the ~/.ssh/known_host file as well.

This passphrase does have a use—it encrypts the private key with a symmetric key cipher (usually IDEA) and it uses the passphrase as its key.

Usage

The ssh-keygen command can be used on its own or you can pass command-line options to it. To generate an RSA keypair, simply run:

```
# ssh-keygen
```

Remember that running ssh-keygen from root will create the host key.

-b bits This option specifies the number of bits to use in the key. The default is 1024 bits, which is the strongest key you can generate without decreasing the performance. Making a larger key may slow things down, depending on your processor. The minimum key you can set is 512 bits, and the maximum key you can set is 2048 bits.

-c This option changes the comment field in the private and public keys. This does not generate a new key, and you will be prompted for the passphrase.

-C This option lets you change the comment on the command line.

-f This option specifies the key file name. It automatically adds on the .pub for the public key.

-N This option creates a new passphrase on the command line.

-p This option changes the passphrase of the current private key instead of creating a new one. You will be asked for the old passphrase and must then enter the new passphrase twice to change it.

-P This option lets you define the old passphrase on the command line.

-u This option changes the cipher that the key is encrypted with. The cipher is changed to the default cipher chosen at the configure and compile time, which is usually 3DES.

You can use `ssh-keygen` in four "general" ways: to create a new key, to change the passphrase, to change the comment, and to change the encryption.

The syntax for creating a new keypair is:

```
$ ssh-keygen [-b bitsinkeypair] [-f filename] [-N newpass-
phrase] [-C comment]
```

This enables you to define the number of bits in the keypair, the file location of the private key (the public key will be the same with `.pub` added onto the end), the new passphrase, and the comment. Keep in mind unless you're running an encrypted session or you're not immediately connected to a network, your passphrase will be visible to those running a "w" on the system or those running a packet sniffer.

The syntax for changing the passphrase on a keypair is:

```
$ ssh-keygen -p [-P oldpassphrase] [-N newpassphrase]
```

Keep in mind you have the same problem with the `-P` option any time you use it; it will change the passphrase. Providing the old passphrase on the command line shouldn't be an issue as long as you manage to change it before someone picks it up with a password sniffer on your local system.

The syntax for changing the comment on a keypair is:

```
$ ssh-keygen -c [-P yourpassphrase] [-C newcomment]
```

This only changes the comment in both your public and private key. The comment is your email address (or root's email address) by default.

The syntax for changing the encryption on a keypair is:

```
$ ssh-keygen -u [-f file] [-P passphrase]
```

This changes the encryption type back to the default, which is usually 3DES. You cannot define any other encryption type here—you can only change your default at compile time.

Examples

Now that you know what the options are, the following are some different ways you can use `ssh-keygen` to help you manage your Secure Shell keys.

To generate a key with 768 bits and put it in a file called `/etc/ssh_insecure_host_key`:

```
# ssh-keygen -b 768 -f /etc/ssh_insecure_host_key
```

To change the passphrase of the keypair:

```
# ssh-keygen -p
```

To change the comment on the keypair (you will be prompted for the passphrase):

```
# ssh-keygen -c -C "The Crypto Tiger, stripes@tigerlair.com"
```

To change the encryption for the user ahc's identity file:

```
# ssh-keygen -u -f ~ahc/.ssh/identity
```

SSH2: `ssh-keygen2`

SSH2 uses a program called `ssh-keygen2` to generate the DSA authentication keypair. You don't have to do this manually because the installation procedure automatically creates the host keypair for you. The system administrator may use this to generate host keys, but that should only be on a regularly scheduled time to update the host key `/etc/ssh2/hostkey` and `/etc/ssh2/host-key.pub`. You'll want to regenerate in case someone has stolen your host key and is trying to compromise your system.

> You will not need to run `ssh-keygen2` to create the host keypair. You only need to run `ssh-keygen2` for generating the user's keypair. **Note**

Usage

The usage for `ssh-keygen2` is very similar to its SSH1 counterpart. The following are the options that `ssh-keygen2` needs. Some of these options differ from the `ssh-keygen` options.

-b bits This option is the same for `ssh-keygen`. It specifies the number of bits to use in the key. The default is 1024 bits, which is the strongest key you can generate without decreasing the performance. Making a larger key is useless because it does not improve security by as much as it slows things down. The minimum key you can set is 512 bits, and the maximum is 2048 bits.

-c This option is the same for `ssh-keygen`. It changes the comment field in the private and public keys. This does not generate a new key, and you will be prompted for the passphrase.

-e file This option lets you edit the specified key file interactively, and change the comment or passphrase. This works very similarly to using `ssh-keygen -c -p`.

-h or -\? This option prints a summary of `ssh-keygen2` commands and usage. It does not generate any new keypairs.

-l file This option converts a `ssh1` key to `ssh2` format. You do not want to do this if you plan on using both SSH1 and SSH2.

-o output_file This option is the same as the `-f` option with `ssh-keygen`. It specifies the key file name and automatically adds on the `.pub` for the public key.

-p passphrase This option lets you specify the passphrase on the command line.

-P This option lets you generate a key with an empty passphrase. This should only be used for the host key. Keep in mind this is different from the `-P` option used in `ssh-keygen`.

-q Quiet mode. This does not print the indicator information to standard output.

-r Include random data from standard input to create the random seed to generate the keypair.

-t key_algorithm This option specifies the cipher used in the key generation (which is DSS/DSA in the current release), but can include RSA in some of the distributions (in the commercial version). This is not the same as the `-u` option for `ssh-keygen`.

-v This option prints the version, then exits. It does not generate any new keypairs.

Examples

The following are some examples for using `ssh-keygen2` that will create the same situations as those for `ssh-keygen`.

To generate a key with 768 bits and put it in a file called `/etc/ssh_insecure_host_key`:

```
# ssh-keygen -b 768 -o /etc/ssh_insecure_host_key
```

To change the passphrase of the keypair:

```
# ssh-keygen -p
```

To change the comment on the keypair (you will be prompted for the passphrase):

```
# ssh-keygen -c
```

To change the key algorithm (not the encryption) for the user ahc's identity file:

```
# ssh-keygen -t RSA -o ~ahc/.ssh/identity
```

The Random Seed

The random seed file is used for creating the host and user identity keys and is necessary for Secure Shell in case you want to regenerate the keys—and for the user accounts, these keys are regenerated on a regular basis. Neither file is readable by people and prints garbage to the screen (like the private key files do). Figure 7.3 shows how the random seed is used to generate the keypairs. Other than for generating keypairs, these files have no other use to Secure Shell.

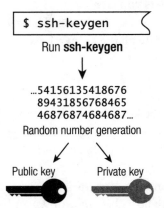

Figure 7.3 *How the random seed is used to create the keypairs.*

SSH1

The system-wide random seed file that is used to generate the host key is usually located at /etc/ssh_random_seed. This file is used to create the /etc/ssh_host_key and /etc/ssh_host_key.pub files. For the user accounts, the ~/.ssh/random_seed is used to generate the ~/.ssh/identity and ~/.ssh/identity.pub files. The random_seed files are generated with SSH key generation programs ssh_keygen and ssh_keygen2.

SSH2

The system-wide random seed file that is used to generate the host key is usually located at /etc/ssh2/random_seed. This file is used to create the /etc/ssh2/host_key and /etc/ssh2/host_key.pub files. For the user accounts, the ~/.ssh2/random_seed is used to generate the ~/.ssh2/id_dsa1024_a and ~/.ssh2/id_dsa1024_a.pub files.

Making Your Keys Publicly Available

After you have created your keys, you'll want to make them publicly available. If someone has strict host-checking turned on, you'll definitely want to give copies of your public keys to your trusted servers. This is good key management, and if the keys change and are regenerated, make sure you send the updates to other servers you trust.

SSH1

For SSH1, there is a Perl script that lets you create a ssh_known_hosts file. This script is make-ssh-known-hosts. The system administrator should run this to create all the known hosts and should manage this file accordingly.

System-wide keys

To create your system-wide RSA public keys, you need to run make-ssh-known-hosts, which is a Perl script that helps create the /etc/ssh_known_hosts file from DNS. This is a global file used for all users, not just specific users like the ~/.ssh/known_hosts file. This file is maintained by the system administrator (the root account), which updates this file as more hosts become known and others become obsolete.

The main name server (which can be defined with the `--initialdns` option) is queried for its Start of Authority (SOA) record, and then proceeds to find its host public key (`/etc/ssh_known_hosts.pub`). It does this by connecting via Secure Shell and tries to copy its host public key to the `/etc/ssh_known_hosts` file. In order for this to work, you need to have RSA authentication turned on. Note that you must have DNS and BIND running for this to work.

Usually this is done for the entire domain name (for example, `tigerlair.com`) and all the public host keys are added to the `/etc/ssh_known_hosts` file. You can run this for multiple files and combine the results into one file. This makes administration of Secure Shell very easy and simply needing to be updated as the hosts are updated.

To create an `/etc/ssh_known_hosts` file:

```
# make-ssh-known-hosts > /etc/ssh_known_hosts
```

To create an `/etc/ssh_ hosts_different_domain` file for a different domain:

```
# make-ssh-known-hosts different.domain.com >
/etc/ssh_hosts_for_different_domain
```

To create an `/etc/ssh_known_hosts` with a different DNS server:

```
# make-ssh-known-hosts --server different.dns.server.com >
/etc/ssh_known_hosts
```

To create a set of trusted subdomains:

```
# make-ssh-known-hosts --subdomains subdomain.tiger-
lair.com > /etc/ssh_known_subdomain
```

User Keys

In the same way that a user manages their keys on a local basis, the concept of copying the public keys to a file is very similar. You can do this by getting all the public keys from all the user accounts you plan to access from remote hosts and copy them into your `~/.ssh/known_hosts` file on the local system. All of the keys in the `~/.ssh/known_hosts` are allowed access.

You will also want to copy your local public key (`~/.ssh/identity.pub`) into your `~/.ssh/known_hosts` file. This is especially true if you are doing some local host connections (which most people do from time to time). You can also mail your user account known_hosts file to the other accounts you plan on using. Then your user key management is complete until you have any changes.

To create your ~/.ssh/known_hosts file:

```
$ cp ~/.ssh/identity.pub ~/.ssh/known_hosts
$ cat ~/otherkeyfiles >> ~/.ssh/known_hosts
```

SSH2

For SSH2, there is no ssh_known_hosts file. Therefore, there is no make-ssh-known-hosts Perl script either. There are also no global known hosts files like the /etc/ssh_known_hosts in SSH1. Instead, each user has their own authorization file usually located in ~/.ssh2/authorization. This file contains the key file name for each public key allowed to authenticate to this server.

An example of the ~/.ssh2/authorization file is:

```
# authorization file for stripes@tigerlair.com
# Local public key
Key id_dsa_1024_a.pub
# ISP public key
Key id_dsa_1024_ISP.pub
```

Authentication Agent

Secure Shell has a nice feature that enables the user to store keys in memory—this is the Secure Shell authentication agent. This provides the user the ability to use RSA keys without having to type the password all the time. This is very beneficial for the convenience of not having to type in passwords all the time for logins, X sessions, or running scripts.

SSH1

The Secure Shell authentication agent is ssh-agent. It gets the authentication agent running—it does not add keys. Keys are added with the ssh-add command, which is discussed later in the chapter. However, the authentication agent is used only for that X terminal session or for that login session.

For any child processes started from the Secure Shell authentication agent, the agent connection is inherited by any of those processes, including child and grandchild processes. This provides the

Secure Shell authentication agent the ability to manage keys from the parent process locally.

The authentication agent creates a UNIX socket, which is stored in `/tmp/ssh-username/agent-socket-processID`. The socket name is located in the environmental variable SSH_AUTH_SOCK. One of the things Secure Shell does to maintain the security of the authentication agent is to make it accessible only to the user. However, root can access it, and if the same user starts another `ssh-agent` process, this may create problems.

Starting `ssh-agent`

Starting the `ssh-agent` is easy. All you have to do is type the command. To start the Secure Shell authentication agent:

```
$ ssh-agent
```

This automatically sends the authentication agent to the background. However, you can run the Secure Shell authentication agent with a shell:

```
$ ssh-agent $SHELL
```

> **Tip** You can tell the `ssh-agent` what type of shell you want to pass. If you want to use some `csh` type of shell, all you have to do is use the `-c` option. For a Bourne-ish shell, use the `-s` option.

This will spawn another process. If you do not want the overhead of having another process running in memory, you can use exec:

```
$ exec ssh-agent $SHELL
```

Then it will look like all you did was start another shell. If you want to do this all the time from a login session, you can put this in your `~/.login` file for an account or your startup scripts if you're booting a host. To include the `ssh-agent` in your `.login` file, all you need to add to the end of the file is:

```
echo "Running the Secure Shell authentication agent…"
exec ssh-agent $SHELL
```

If you want to run the authentication agent with X, do the following:

```
$ ssh-agent startx &
```

This starts the authentication agent for running in X.[1] You can put this in your ~/.xinitrc file as well so that you don't have to type this all the time. An example of an .xinitrc file that has the ssh-agent running is:

```
#!/bin/sh
# .xinitrc sample file running ssh-agent
SSHAGENT="exec ssh-agent"
$SSHAGENT $HOME/.xinitrc
# Start up some local X applications, notice that these do
# not need the ssh-agent.
xclock &
xload &
# Start up some X terms with the ssh-agent
$SSHAGENT xterm -geometry 80x24 &
$SSHAGENT xterm -geometry 80x24 &
$SSHAGENT xterm -geometry 80x24
```

Note

Remember that running ssh-agent will not load your keys into memory. You have to do that on your own with the ssh-add command.

The ssh-agent is designed to help the user by giving them the convenience of not having to deal with passwords. So this can be kept on a local computer. The passphrases used for authentication are not sent over the network, and the connection is forwarded over remote Secure Shell logins. This provides a user with the ability to go from network to network in a secure manner with the identities stored in memory.

Managing Keys in Memory with ssh-add

When you've got the agent running, you need to add RSA keys to it. To add keys to the ssh-agent, you need to run ssh-add. This adds private RSA keys to the ssh-agent and allows it to forward the keys through a Secure Shell connection. This means that after

---

1. Depending on your system, you may use another command to start X. The startx command is specific to Xfree86, which runs on Linux and FreeBSD.

the keys are added and the `ssh-agent` is running, you will only need to type the password once to get it to run.

To add your identity key, all you need to do is run `ssh-add`:

```
shell3:/home/stripes- ssh-add
```

Then you are prompted for entering your passphrase:

```
Need passphrase for /home/stripes/.ssh/identity
(stripes@tigerlair.com).
Enter passphrase:
```

After you have entered your passphrase properly, you will see that your identity file has been added to the Secure Shell authentication agent:

```
Identity added: /home/stripes/.ssh/identity (stripes@tiger-
lair.com)
```

When you run the `ssh-add` command without any arguments, it loads your `~/.ssh/identity` file by default. When you are running `ssh-add`, it must be a child process of the `ssh-agent`. Otherwise, this will not work.

> **Note** Keep in mind that you must be running `ssh-agent` before running `ssh-add`.

You can use the `-p` option to read the passphrase from standard input or from a pipe. If you want to list all your current identities stored in your authentication agent, use the `-l` option:

```
$ ssh-add -l
1024 37 117527518128287327980847502483823882115255838344725
796225405791695880888191784113149677706787726977209906722463
976255073111504953634361979758777836485389337280874747721444
376154637043034543426640229512653318818727242987903791380089
628349120338426345267048083862401613959808620532824589994955
985289908190742248456 7 stripes@tigerlair.com
1024 37 117527518128287327980847502483823882115255838344725
796225405791695880888191784113149677706787726977209906722463
976255073111504953634361979758777836485389337280874747721444
376154637043034543426640229512653318818727242987903791380089
628349120338426345267048083862401613959808620532824589994955
985289908190742248456 7 ahc@sherekhan.tigerlair.com
```

Notice that you can store multiple identities in the `ssh-agent`.

You can also remove identities from the Secure Shell agent using `ssh-add`. To remove an identity, use the `-d` option followed by the identity filename:

```
$ ssh-add -d ~/.ssh/identity
```

To remove all the identities, use the `-D` option:

```
$ ssh-add -D
```

This means you don't have to log in to every remote host to remove the identity—you can do this locally.

Killing the `ssh-agent`

You can remove the `ssh-agent` very easily. You can either kill the process when you log out from the X session or terminal by killing the `SSH_AGENT_PID`.

```
$ kill -9 $SSH_AGENT_PID
```

Or you can do this the easy way:

```
$ ssh-agent -k
```

This is really nice because it kills your process and unsets the environment variables `SSH_AUTH_SOCKET` for the UNIX socket and `SSH_AGENT_PID` for the process ID. You should probably do this after ending your session just to remove the RSA keys from memory.

SSH2

The SSH2 protocol has a very similar implementation of the Secure Shell authentication agent called `ssh-agent2` (and `ssh-add2` works very similarly to `ssh-add`, its SSH1 counterpart). The command-line options are the same as in `ssh-agent` and `ssh-add`; however, there are compatibility issues. First of all, the freeware version of SSH2 will not have a compatible authentication agent because it does not support RSA. Also, the environment variables that `ssh-agent2` sets are `SSH2_AUTH_SOCKET` and `SSH2_ AGENT_PID` instead of `SSH_AUTH_SOCKET` and `SSH_AGENT_PID`. SSH2 may also set variables from SSH1 for comatibility.

Summary

The Secure Shell protocols SSH1 and SSH2 provide very similar key management structures. Note that all the public keys in both SSH1 and SSH2 have a `.pub` extension, whereas the private keys do not have any extension. Keep in mind that SSH1 uses RSA for the keypairs, but the public domain version of SSH2 uses only DSA/DSS. The commercial version of SSH2, however, does implement RSA as well as DSA.

System keys for SSH1 are defined as `/etc/ssh_host_key` and `/etc/ssh_host_key.pub`; and for SSH2, they are defined as `/etc/ssh2/hostkey` and `/etc/ssh2/hostkey.pub`. The user keys for SSH1 are defined as `~/.ssh/identity` for the user's private key and `~/.ssh/identity.pub` for the user's public key. You need to make sure you that you use a strong passphrase for your user keypairs and no passphrase for your host keypair.

Both SSH1 and SSH2 also contain random seed files for both the host keypair and the user keypair that help generate the keys. For SSH1, you have to manually generate both the host and user RSA keypair by running `ssh-keygen` as root. To create the user RSA keypair, you need to run `ssh-keygen` as the user. For SSH2, the host keypair is automatically generated when first installing the program. For the user keypair or to regenerate the host keypair, use the `ssh-keygen2` command.

To make your keys publicly available in both SSH1 and SSH2, you need to copy your user and host public keys to the appropriate accounts, both locally and remotely. This provides you with the authentication you need if you are running public key authentication. SSH2 checks this more strictly than SSH1 unless you are running SSH1 under strict host-checking.

The Secure Shell authentication agent allows you to store your keys in memory as a user. This enables you to keep the keys in memory for multiple identity files, and you only have to enter the password one time, as long as the key stays in memory. You can start the Secure Shell authentication agent from either an X session or a terminal.

Secure Shell and Firewalls

In this chapter:

- Defining firewalls

- Firewalls and Secure Shell

- Beyond basic configuration

As with any TCP/IP application, you probably want to know how it's going to work through a firewall. With the growing necessity of firewalls and the growing use of Secure Shell, this chapter will cover some of the quirks and kinks you may run into when combining these two technologies. Additionally, you'll read an introduction on the definition of a firewall, the different types of firewalls that exist, and the different firewall architectures that are possible.

Defining Firewalls

Whenever people talk about network security, it is usually synonymous with the word "firewall." Fortunately for security professionals, it is just a small part of network security, so we're still employable. So, what is a firewall anyway? A firewall is a choke point between a trusted and non-trusted network. This choke point defines what type of network traffic is trusted and non-trusted. The problem with this is that firewall vendors allow people to trust any type of network traffic without offering warnings of possible vulnerabilities.

Note   The non-trusted network is usually the Internet in most firewall diagrams. As firewall architecture becomes more and more complex, administrators are designing their networks and separating internal networks with firewalls.

As a result, many firewalls will let you send through whatever traffic you want: this includes NFS, Berkeley services, X, whatever. Enter Secure Shell. If you want, you can forward the above unsecure traffic through Secure Shell (see *"Other Cool Things You Can Do With Secure Shell"* on page 239) and not have to worry about the possibility that your traffic is being sniffed or being hijacked.

Many freeware sniffers and session hijackers are available on the Internet. Even though you are using a firewall to separate your network from a non-trusted network, be aware that even with the use of Telnet you run the risk of someone reading your text or hijacking your session. Since that traffic is not encrypted, you are opening yourself up to attacks that firewalls can't prevent. This includes denial of service (DoS), one of the most popular attacks. Table 8.1 shows you what firewalls typically will not protect against.

Table 8.1 *What firewalls do not protect against*

Attack	Why firewalls can't protect against this
Password sniffing	Cleartext traffic can be read
Malicious internal user	Considered trusted, not expected to abuse network services
Virus	Allowed in through a trusted port
Flooded open ports (DoS)	Considered trusted, not expected to be abused

Types of Firewalls

With all of the new firewall products available, there are basically three general types of firewalls: a *packet filter*, which is essentially a router; an *application gateway*, which is usually a proxy server coupled with an access list; and *stateful inspection*, which is a hybrid firewall between an application gateway and a packet filter.

Packet Filter

A packet filter is a router designed to filter traffic to and from the network. This router may or may not run routing protocols such as RIP, IGRP OSPF, or EIGRP, but for all intents and purposes, its job is to decide which packets are allowed in and out of the network. Basically, it does a few things: checks the IP address and port and whether the packet is going the right way (either inbound or outbound). And then it makes the decision to send or drop the packet.

Using the OSI model, the router acts like a layer 3 firewall—it checks by IP address and port. Other checks that can be configured are: source routing, protocol type, and established connection. Even if it's not the right application going through, as long as the packet matches the allowed IP address and port, there aren't any problems. See Figure 8.1 on page 222 for how a packet filter works with a trusted and non-trusted network.

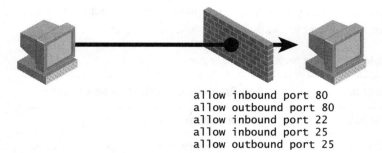

```
allow inbound port 80
allow outbound port 80
allow inbound port 22
allow inbound port 25
allow outbound port 25
```

Figure 8.1 *Packet filter firewall.*

Routers usually make a good "poor man's" firewall, but as
described, they only work on the IP layer. As a result, they are not
very scalable nor do they provide maximum security. Because a
packet filter does not check the application type, you do have
speed; however, you're not guaranteed that the packet will be legitimate and without malicious intent.

Application Gateway

An application gateway, or proxy, is designed so that a network
packet will be checked per application type before it is sent out to
the non-trusted network or before it is allowed inside to the trusted
network. This provides a network with quite a bit of security,
because the packets have to go through a check that decides
whether or not this packet belongs to the application or not.
Therefore, trusted applications are secured but are also limited in
the applications that proxies are written for. This provides quite a
bit of security on trusted applications. Fortunately, some application gateways do allow Secure Shell traffic to pass through as they
recognize it as a common network application.

Using the OSI model, the application gateway is designed to
work on layer 7, even though it does perform checks through layer
3 or layer 4, depending on the product. Because of all this checking, application gateways tend to be a lot slower than a packet filter. See Figure 8.2 for how an application gateway typically works
with a trusted and non-trusted network.

Application gateways do have their benefits—such as being able
to screen an application from the datalink layer through the appli-

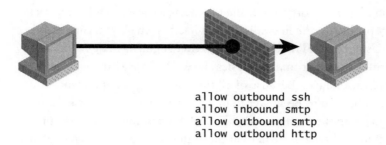

```
allow outbound ssh
allow inbound smtp
allow outbound smtp
allow outbound http
```

Figure 8.2 *Application gateway firewall.*

cation layer—but if you are on a substantial network, you may take a very big performance hit. Also, keep in mind that application gateways may be limited in their application support (including Secure Shell), especially if you are using esoteric applications that may not be mainstream. Application gateways can easily be brought down to their knees using a Quality of Service (QoS), Time of Service (ToS), or Denial of Service (DoS) attack.

These application gateways are also relatively more expensive than a packet filter if you do not opt for any freeware packages; so the cost should be carefully considered. The user may have additional configurations that they need to make with an application gateway that they would not have to for a packet filter firewall.

Stateful Inspection

Since both packet filters and application proxies have their share of problems, Checkpoint has produced a stateful inspection firewall—this is a hybrid of the application gateway and the packet filtering. Checkpoint modified the application gateway so that it works transparently like a packet filter, but provides the same amount of security that the application gateway provides. This achieves increased performance similar to a packet filter along with the security of the application gateway.

In addition to Checkpoint FW-1, the most recent versions of Cisco's PIX boxes are stateful inspection. Also, hardware firewalls have their benefits. Thus, the Cisco PIX and the Nokia IP 400 series are both stateful inspection engines that offer more protection than any UNIX- or NT-based firewalls which require OS hardening prior to having an effective firewall. The reasoning is you don't have to worry about the operating system itself having security problems; the firewall product itself is where you can focus.

Using the OSI model, the inspection engine is designed to work on all 7 layers, from the physical layer all the way through to the application layer. Because of all this checking, stateful inspection firewalls tend to be slower than a packet filter, but are still faster than an application gateway. The analysis of the packets occurs within the kernel instead of at the application level, which explains the speed increase.

The stateful inspection engine seems to be the best compromise between the two; however, it does have its issues as well. Like a packet filter, you can define for any type of traffic to go through your firewall because the vendor allows you to, including inherently unsecure programs like NFS and Berkeley services.

Note   No matter what the vendor allows you to pass through the firewall, you should seriously analyze the risk you are taking before you allow the traffic through your network.

Standard Firewall Configurations

Firewalls can be designed in many different architectures. Since the focus on this book is Secure Shell and not firewalls, this will only provide you with a basic overview of some very basic firewall architectures. If you are interested in more specific information related to firewalls, please take a look at McGraw-Hill's "Firewalls Complete" book.

Screening Firewall

With just a single firewall or router, you have achieved a screening firewall architecture. This provides you with a single point of failure connection to the non-trusted network. Depending on the importance of your connection, you may want to have redundant firewalls. This architecture provides you with one "checkpoint" for the packet to go through where the firewall decides whether or not the packet has the right to go through to the trusted network. See Figure 8.3 for how the screening firewall provides the trusted network with security.

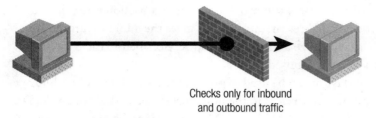

Checks only for inbound
and outbound traffic

Figure 8.3 *Screening firewall.*

Screened subnet

If you do need to provide services to an non-trusted network, you will need to put up a DMZ network segment. This provides you with a single point of failure connection to the non-trusted network, and you are able to provide services to the non-trusted network without sacrificing your trusted network. The first point of contact is usually the screening router, followed by the DMZ, and then, finally, the firewall before hitting your trusted network. This gives you at least two "checkpoints" for the packet to go through before the firewall decides whether or not the packet has the right to go through to the trusted network. See Figure 8.4 for how the screened subnet firewall provides the trusted network with an extra layer of security.

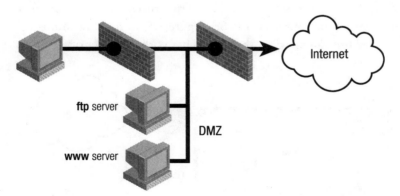

Figure 8.4 *Screened subnet firewall.*

As you can see, the screening router is used to protect the DMZ and the trusted network; and you can place as many bastion hosts as needed on the DMZ. The DMZ gives an extra safety layer for the trusted network to provide services on bastion hosts that can be trashed and restored. Also, this gives the administrator more time to recognize a threat and stop services before the trusted network is compromised.

This layout can be used to protect the trusted network while not providing any services to the non-trusted network through the *De-Militarized Zone* (DMZ). A DMZ has a safety layer for the trusted network to provide services on bastion hosts that can be trashed and restored. A *bastion host* is a computer that provides services for a particular function external to your network (such as DNS, WWW, FTP, SMTP, and the like) and is "hardened" so that unnecessary system services can be disabled. Because the unnecessary system services can be disabled, an attacker has no way to take over the host and circumvent your firewall configuration.

Multi-homed Firewall

As with the screened subnet, you can provide services through bastion hosts on a DMZ with a multi-homed firewall. This allows you to have a DMZ without the extra cost of a second firewall or screening router. However, like the screening firewall configuration, you have one "checkpoint" for all internal and DMZ traffic to go through. If you have a lot of network traffic going between the DMZ, non-trusted network, and the trusted network, this may be a strain for your network. See Figure 8.5 for how the multi-homed firewall provides the trusted network with security.

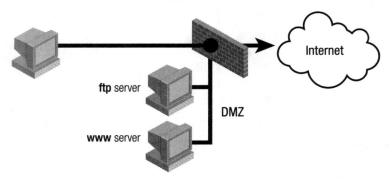

Figure 8.5 *Multi-homed firewall.*

You can see how the DMZ protects the trusted network, yet does not provide any services to the non-trusted network. It does this because most inbound traffic to the firewall usually has to go through the DMZ bastion hosts before getting to the internal network. This causes an extra hop for the network packet, and you still may find that configuration issues with the firewall allow unwelcome traffic through even though you did not intend to.

Other Firewall Architectures

You can design a multitude of other firewall architectures. You can have multiple DMZs to several networks, which can include Internet access, as well as an *extranet*.[1] You can also have your router segment off to internal network to one connection on the DMZ. This lets you segment your trusted networks off from each other as well as segment off the DMZ. See Figure 8.6 for how an extranet could be defined with additional access to the Internet and an internal screening router that divides the trusted network into two segments.

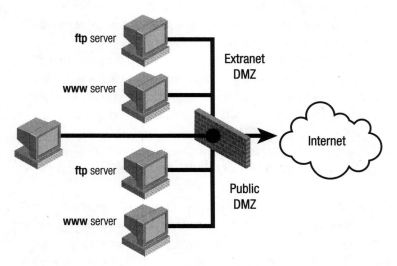

Figure 8.6 *Multi-homed extranet and public DMZ firewall architecture.*

1. An *extranet* is a network that usually connects a private network with another private network. For example, if VeriSign was to connect a network with one of their suppliers, this would be known as an extranet.

There are still quite a few combinations you can have. The more complex your firewall is, however, the more administration you need to maintain the security of it. Also, the more "checkpoints" you have a packet go through, the more carefully you need to configure your rulesets to allow Secure Shell through.

Firewalls and Secure Shell

You have several possibilities to consider about Secure Shell if your firewall does not already provide a service option for it. Secure Shell works slightly different than other TCP/IP services such as Telnet, NTP, POP, and the like. This section explains some of the basic configurations you'll need to do for Secure Shell, and some other tasks you'll need to do for the TIS firewall toolkit and SOCKS (an application proxy), as well.

Basic Configuration

As you know, the SSH daemon (both SSH1 and SSH2) listens on port 22, unless you configure it otherwise. This port should be open for inbound traffic if you plan to receive Secure Shell connections. If you are not receiving inbound connections, you should open the ports that the client side needs.

For the client side, you will need to open up the ports that the client connects on. In general, most application clients use any port above 1023, which is considered a non-privileged port. This means that the typical client connects to a listening server at port 1024 or higher. Well, Secure Shell does something funky—it connects at 1021 or higher. However, you can change Secure Shell—especially since you have the code for the UNIX client—to connect at 1024 or higher.

You can see which direction traffic flows and how much "fun" it is to configure Secure Shell manually through a packet filter or to set up a general rule on an application gateway or stateful inspection. This would be something you would configure on a packet filter firewall or even an application gateway. This means that the firewall you are using does not have any "canned" access for SSH. As you can see, this can easily become quite a mess.

Firewall Configuration

For basic firewall configuration, you need to consider how you want it to connect to the Internet. If you are already using Telnet to reach the Internet, you may want to consider using Secure Shell instead, which will reduce the risk of your packets being read, and even of your session being hijacked. Also, you can create a pseudo-Virtual Private Network (VPN) using Secure Shell to connect between two firewalls.

Hopefully, the firewall you are already using provides a ruleset for Secure Shell; you shouldn't have to manually set it. If you are using a packet filter or a firewall that requires you to manually enter a ruleset, you should definitely read in your firewall manual or documentation how Secure Shell is configured for both outbound and inbound traffic. Also, remember that Secure Shell is a TCP- and not a UDP-based application.

TCP establishes a connection, where UDP just sends out packets without establishing a connection. As a result, TCP connectivity is much more secure than a UDP[2] connection. Applications such as NFS and NIS use UDP, whereas connection-oriented applications like Telnet and FTP use TCP. For a general rule of thumb, you do not want inbound UDP packets going into your firewall.

> You should be very careful if you are configuring inbound Secure **Note**
> Shell access. This includes using TCP wrappers, defining Secure
> Shell's login, and disabling rhosts authentication.

Outbound

For the firewall configuration, you need to have two rulesets for defining outbound traffic. One will be for the client, the other for the server daemon. When a client is trying to make a connection, it is looking for something on the known server port (in Secure Shell's case, port 22). The server, on the other hand, is trying to listen for connections on ports 1021 or higher.

---

2. UDP is a User Datagram Protocol. The most common alternative to TCP is UDP, which is designed for applications where you don't need to put TCP sequences together. Where TCP works like a telephone, UDP works like a megaphone. TCP expects a response—UDP doesn't.

Even if you are going to have outbound traffic only, you still need to define rules for some inbound traffic to the server. If you do not have this, TCP cannot complete the handshake and exchange information such as host keys, server keys, and user identity, as well as trafficking the packets themselves. Note that any type of connection that you are going to have through the firewall is not necessarily "one-way," even though it appears to be.

So, by using a security policy that allows outbound Secure Shell traffic, you would use the following ruleset shown in Table 8.2.

Table 8.2 *Outbound Secure Shell firewall ruleset*

Connection	Source	Originating port	Destination	Target port
Client	Internal address	1021 or higher	External address	22 (on external server)
Server	External address	22	Internal address	1021 or higher (from client)

Inbound

The same rules apply for configuring the firewall for inbound traffic. You need two rulesets—one for the client, the other for the server daemon. Like the outbound ruleset, when a client is trying to make a connection, it is looking for something on the known server port (in Secure Shell's case, port 22). The server, on the other hand, is trying to listen for connections on ports 1021 or higher. The only difference is the source address and destination address. They are the "reverse" of the outbound ruleset.

Even if you are going to have only outbound traffic, you still need to have inbound traffic rules back to your client. If you do not have this, TCP cannot complete the handshake and exchange information such as host keys, server keys, and user identity, as well as the packets themselves. In this case, you're allowing the firewall to allow a complete connection.

So, for a security policy that allows inbound Secure Shell traffic, use the following ruleset shown in Table 8.3.

Table 8.3 *Inbound Secure Shell firewall ruleset*

Connection	Source	Originating port	Destination	Target port
Client	External address	1021 or higher	Internal address	22 (on internal server)
Server	Internal address	22	External address	1021 or higher (from client)

Proxy Configuration

A proxy server works something like a translator does for someone not familiar with the language in a foreign country. The proxy can take messages (usually delivered in the appropriate protocol) and decide how to get the message properly to the server on the outside of the trusted network that does all the work.

After the proxy takes the message and processes the packet and what application it belongs to, it sends the message to the appropriate proxy server. Then, in turn, the proxy server takes the information and sends it to the remote clients. Next, the proxy cleans up any extraneous junk that the clients or the server sends and then simply sends the requested information to the appropriate party.

As a result, the proxy has enabled a "checkpoint" for all the application packets to go through. It's deceptive because the connection *looks* transparent between the host on the non-trusted network and the client, and it appears that the host communicates directly with the proxy server. This seamless connection makes it easier for the users so they don't have to bounce between jump points. When used in conjunction with a packet filter, a proxy firewall becomes an extremely good way to provide border security. Examples of proxy firewalls include TIS firewall toolkit and Eagle Raptor.

Setting up TIS Firewall Toolkit Support

Secure Shell does support the TIS firewall toolkit; in fact, the program has built-in support that you can define at compile time. To get TIS firewall toolkit support, all you need to do is the following when building your installation of Secure Shell:

```
# ./configure --with-tis=/path/for/firewalltookit/goes/here
# make
# make install
```

You also need to set your configuration file for Secure Shell 1 to have TISAuthentication set to "yes." This makes sure that you have the proper configuration working.

Other Proxy Configurations

In addition to setting up TIS firewall toolkit, you may have to look at the manual for your particular firewall product on how to set up the application proxy. Even though a proxy may behave differently than a packet filter, configuration should be easy because many firewalls do provide a graphical user interface (GUIs) to implement rulesets. This includes popular commercial software like TIS Gauntlet, Eagle Raptor, and AltaVista Firewall.

An alternative you can use to configuring and rebuilding Secure Shell with support for TIS firewall toolkit is another proxy firewall option: tn-gw-nav. This is a freeware product written by John Saunders and Charlie Brady that uses Secure Shell to connect to a host on the outside of a TIS firewall toolkit Telnet gateway.

For this program, tn-gw-nav needs to be running on both the source and destination host, much like Secure Shell does. Also, this is not a program to forward Secure Shell over Telnet, but to let Secure Shell run through a proxy firewall without having to rebuild your implementation of Secure Shell with TIS support.

CD-ROM   Does tn-gw-nav sound like a great program? You can get it off the CD-ROM that comes with this book.

Here's something else that's really cool to use with proxies that will help you with SSH tunneling. Since a proxy firewall cannot check encrypted packets to check if the information is either SSL or

SSH, you can use the SSL port (443) to traverse a firewall with SSH through the SSL port.

The `ssh-tunnel.pl` script helps you use the SSL proxy for SSH traffic. Just make sure you have `sshd` listening on port 443. This freeware script was originally wirtten by Urban Kaveus, and this version has been updated by Theo Van Dinter.

> You can get `ssh-tunnel.pl` off the CD-ROM that comes with this book.   **CD-ROM**

Problems with Firewalls and Secure Shell

Despite the benefits of running SSH with firewalls, there are some problems which come mostly from lack of vendor support for proxies and default configurations. One of the concerns about application gateways and stateful inspection is that they check from the application layers, and they can't do that if they don't know about an application. You can use a "plug" to open a port, but this may not provide the same level of security as a proxy.

Beyond Basic Firewall Configuration

Once you have an understanding of how to set up an inbound and outbound connection for Secure Shell through one firewall, you can set up configurations for Secure Shell between two firewalls. If you do it this way, you can set up a pseudo-VPN between both networks. The technical reasons on why this is not a full VPN are discussed later in this section.

You can also use SOCKS, which is a circuit-level proxy. This allows you to make an application "proxy-friendly" so you can send it through. Secure Shell does have built-in proxy support for version 2; however, you can use SOCKS for Secure Shell 1. We'll cover other configuration options for both Secure Shell 1 and 2 later in this chapter.

Setting up a VPN Connection between Two Firewalls

In order to create a firewall-to-firewall VPN using Secure Shell, you need to create a firewall configuration with inbound and outbound rulesets for both firewalls. You can have several different types of configurations which vary depending on what you are trying to accomplish. All the hosts and internal networks are assumed to be behind firewalls. Your options to create a firewall-to-firewall VPN are:

- Internal network to internal network (traditional VPN)

- Internal network to host

- Host to internal network

- Internet host to internal network (Remote Access client access)

Instead of allowing address-to-address connection, you may want to set the ruleset so it allows some subnet of the network address from the other network.

Note   If port 22 is blocked by either firewall, this will not work.

If you are trying to enable the host-to-host option, you need to replace the network address with the host address inside each of the firewalls. Table 8.4 shows how this would look in a ruleset.

Table 8.4 *Secure Shell VPN firewall ruleset*

Connection	Source	Originating port	Destination	Target port
Client	Internal network	1021 or higher	External network	22 (on external server)
Server	External network	22	Internal network	1021 or higher (from client)
Client	External network	1021 or higher	Internal network	22 (on internal server)
Server	Internal network	22	External network	1021 or higher (from client)

You can't really configure Secure Shell to go through a firewall unless you are root on your system and can configure the daemon to run through a different port (like Telnet port 23 or HTTP port

80). Port forwarding is covered in *"Other Cool Things You Can Do With Secure Shell"* on page 239.

After you have the firewall rulesets working, you need to test your environment and make sure that the type of connection you want to work actually works. You also need to make sure that all hosts are running compatible Secure Shell daemons and clients.

For example, if you are trying to connect to a SSH2 server daemon and you are running a SSH1 client, this probably will not happen unless the destination is also running a compatible SSH1 server daemon. This is the same connectivity problem that's covered in the previous chapters on SSH1 and SSH2 compatibility.

Why Is This Technically Not a VPN?

There's a difference between a VPN product and Secure Shell. The similarities are that both a VPN and Secure Shell will authenticate using some known form of authentication including passwords, digital certificates, or key exchange. Also, both will encrypt the connection so that what is transmitted is not readable.

The difference is that Secure Shell is typically used for *session* encryption and authentication, and a VPN is used to encrypt the entire pipe. For a VPN, the session is always an encrypted tunnel of a certain bandwidth, whereas Secure Shell only encrypts the current session. Secure Shell only encrypts as long as the session is alive. Once the connection dies, not only is the encryption gone, but the session is gone as well.

If you're interested on how to get a Secure Shell connection VPN going, it is covered more in *"Other Cool Things You Can Do With Secure Shell"* on page 239.

Setting up Secure Shell with SOCKS

Even though you can send Secure Shell through a firewall, Secure Shell does support SOCKS—which is a circuit-level proxy that you can use to make applications "proxy-friendly." The most current version is SOCKS V5, which allows UNIX systems that are behind a firewall to connect to the non-trusted networks without requiring direct IP addressing. SOCKS is a popular substitute for firewalls for low bandwidth places, because it is easy to use and the connection through the SOCKS server is transparent to the user.

The difference between SOCKS V5 and SOCKS V4 is that there is now an added authentication function. It is set up so that a SOCKS server daemon is running on one system, and that system acts as a proxy. This provides a single point of access to the outside from the internal network.

After you have the SOCKS daemon up and running, you need to SOCKS-ify the application that you want to run through the SOCKS server daemon. Because of the popular use, the SOCKS distribution includes SOCKS-ified versions of `ftp`, `telnet`, Archie, `finger`, `whois`, `rping`, and `rtraceroute`.

Note

> SOCKS V5 is available for free at `http://www.socks.nec.com/`. You need to make sure that the all the requirements are met, including the appropriate compiler, and remember that SOCKS V5 is compatible with SOCKS V4.

In order to make sure that Secure Shell supports SOCKS, you need to compile SOCKS support into the kernel as in the following installation of Secure Shell:

```
# ./configure --with-socks5=/path/for/socks5/goes/here
# make
# make install
```

Or, if you have SOCKS V4 and want to compile Secure Shell for that, you would do this:

```
# ./configure --with-socks5=/path/for/socks4/goes/here
# make
# make install
```

Or, if you have an earlier version of SOCKS and want to compile Secure Shell for that, you would do this:

```
# ./configure --with-socks=/path/for/socks/goes/here
# make
# make install
# runsocks ssh
# runsocks scp
# runsocks sftp
```

After you have a SOCKS-ified version of Secure Shell, you'll want to put those clients in a directory that is separate from the "vanilla" Secure Shell. For example, the "vanilla" copy of Secure Shell is usually located in /usr/local/bin, but you may want to have a directory for SOCKS-ified applications such as /usr/local/socksify/bin.

Setting up Secure Shell with the Linux Router

The Linux router, which is available at http://www.linuxrouter.org, lets you create a simple router or switch from a stripped-down Debian Linux kernel. This kernel is network centric, so it has a lot of network support to let you create anything from a 100MB router to a remote access PPP/SLIP server.

Because it fully supports Secure Shell, you can do Secure Shell tunneling easily without relying on commercial support from a vendor. Also, you can use this in conjunction with datbkr and make a standalone Secure Shell backup appliance.

Summary

With any type of network application like Secure Shell, you may have to use it through a firewall. You will encounter three basic types of firewalls: packet filter, application gateway (which is usually a proxy), and stateful inspection. Packet filter is the cheapest but provides the least amount of security, whereas an application gateway is usually more costly, both in performance as well as monetary measure.

With Secure Shell, you can set up firewall configurations that allow inbound or outbound connections for the firewall. The client must be allowed to send from ports 1021 and higher, and the server must be allowed to have connections come to port 22 (or whatever the defined port is for your Secure Shell daemon). You can even set up firewall-to-firewall connections that will create a pseudo-VPN.

Secure Shell does have some built-in support for some firewall public domain software, particularly Firewall Toolkit from TIS and the Socks circuit level proxy. This enables you to use both firewall software for Secure Shell communications. Both the Firewall Toolkit and Socks are forms of firewall proxies, where a router is considered a packet filter.

Other Cool Things You Can Do With Secure Shell

In this chapter:

- Using Secure Shell as a transport agent

- Secure Shell and TCP wrappers

- Secure Shell for remote backups

- Secure Shell and other authentication methods

Although many people use Secure Shell for a Telnet replacement, you can use Secure Shell as a kind of Swiss Army knife for securing network connections. You can forward other network traffic including POP, X, PPP, and FTP through Secure Shell on a local or remote system. You can also forward other types of network traffic, including CVS and any other TCP traffic you want. Also, you can use Secure Shell with TCP wrappers to enhance the security of the connections. In addition, Secure Shell has some other neat functionality with applications such as Emacs and Oracle, and you can use Secure Shell for remote backups and additional authentication like SecurID cards.

Using Secure Shell as a Transport Agent

One of the more popular Swiss Army knife tricks to use Secure Shell for is to forward traffic. In fact, it's so popular that Secure Shell has built-in functionality for X forwarding. For other popular applications, some nice folks on the Net wrote software that ports traffic, including POP and FTP.

You have two types of forwarding: local and remote. Local forwarding involves taking a connection initiated from your local system to the remote system on a different port (such as POP or DNS) and forwarding it through Secure Shell's port 22 to secure the connection. See Figure 9.1 to see how the local forwards work.

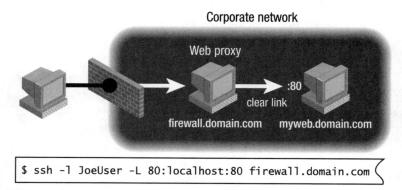

Figure 9.1 *How the local forwarding connections work.*

Remote forwarding, on the other hand, does the reverse. After receiving an initiated connection on a different port on a remote server, Secure Shell then forwards the connection back to the remote host securely. See Figure 9.2 to see how the remote forwards work.

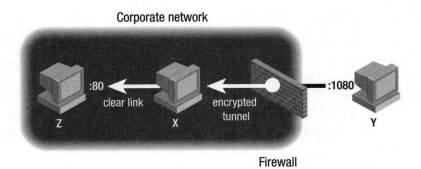

Figure 9.2 *How the remote forwarding connections work.*

Forming a VPN

Even though Secure Shell is not designed for creating a full-blown tunnel and more for session connections, you can create a VPN using Secure Shell. As is mentioned in *"Troubleshooting Secure Shell"* on page 263, you can create a VPN with Secure Shell and Point-to-Point Protocol (PPP). PPP is generally used for dial-up connections; however, you can use it in conjunction with Secure Shell to create a VPN.

The only platform that currently boasts the ability to have a Secure Shell VPN is Linux. LinuxCare wrote the Virtual Private Server (VPS), which has a strong core tunneling ability. If you're interested in the VPS, take a look at

http://www.strongcrypto.com.

You can also find VPS on the CD-ROM that comes with this book. **CD-ROM**

Forwarding X Traffic

One of the cool things about Secure Shell is that you can forward traffic over it. This includes any type of TCP/IP traffic. The most common traffic to forward is X. Because of X's popularity for running other programs, the Secure Shell client even has special functionality for it.

The way it works is X is forwarded from the remote host to the local host and then tunneled through Secure Shell. This is the equivalent of using a remote forward for ports 6000 and higher, like this:

```
$ ssh -C -l username -R 6000:xremoteserver.com:6000 localserver.com
```

The remote forwarding will be covered later in this chapter. Since there is built-in support for X, we should go over how to get a secure X connection going with Secure Shell. First, Secure Shell checks to see if the X11 forwarding is enabled and requests an X connection, then gets the information from the xauth. This provides Secure Shell with the information for the DISPLAY.

Make sure that you do not set the DISPLAY variable. If X forwarding is enabled, the DISPLAY variable gets set within Secure Shell. You don't have to define it otherwise. Next, if there isn't any authentication data from xauth, then the forwarding "code" checks the response for validity and uses this data instead. But the X server will ignore this data and use the other authentication methods for the connection instead (password, public key authentication, and so forth).

In effect, X forwarding gets the local authentication information and uses it to spoof the authentication. This provides X with the information it needs by being fooled into running the server locally. X uses its own authentication agent, xauth, for X authentication. However, it is not necessary to use xauth. If no command is specified, then a shell will be forked.

Creating Your Xauthority

The Xauthority, or xauth, allows you to control who has access to running your X server through hostname authentication. SSH works with xauth to help you run X through only trusted systems, and secures those connections by encrypting them. The first thing you probably want to do is take advantage of the Xauthority's magic cookie feature and use MD5 checksums to verify the integrity of the host.

To do this, create an .Xauthority file in the home directory of the user account:

```
$ touch $HOME/.Xauthority
```

Next you'll want to generate a checksum using a random number generator (using something like Perl or a shell script) and then pipe it through MD5:

```
$ randomnumber.sh | md5 > hostXkey
$ set KEYFILE=hostXkey
```

Then you'll want to use `hostXkey`, which is the file that will store your information on trusted hosts to run X, for the magic cookie for adding an authorized host to a file:

```
$ xauth add hostname/unix:0 . $KEYFILE
$ xauth add hostname:0 . $KEYFILE
```

> Make sure you disable `xhost` before using the Xauthority. The `xhost` **Note**
> command can destroy any security that you have set up.

Using Secure Shell with X

You can do all sorts of X usage with Secure Shell. You can do things from running your entire X session through Secure Shell to running individual applications through Secure Shell. You can also extract information from an Xauthority using Secure Shell.

The first thing you'll want to do when you compile Secure Shell is to make sure X support is enabled. You can do this by passing a switch to the configure script:

```
# configure --with-x
```

Then `make` and compile it as you usually would. For more on installation, see *"Installing Secure Shell on UNIX"* on page 19.

> Make sure you do not disable any of the other X11 options dis- **Note**
> cussed in *"Installing Secure Shell on UNIX"* on page 19.

If you want to run an entire X session through Secure Shell, you can use the Secure Shell authentication agent to start your X session:

```
$ ssh-agent startx &
```

On Linux, this will start your X session after you log in. If you are using XDM or you want to run Secure Shell X sessions auto-

matically, you can use the .xsession script that was used as an
example for starting X with Secure Shell in *"Secure Shell Key Management"* on page 191.

```
#!/bin/sh
# .xinitrc sample file running ssh-agent
SSHAGENT="exec ssh-agent"
$SSHAGENT $HOME/.xinitrc
# Start up some local X applications, notice that these do
not need
# the ssh-agent.
xclock &
xload &
# Start up some X terms with the ssh-agent
$SSHAGENT xterm -geometry 80x24 &
$SSHAGENT xterm -geometry 80x24 &
$SSHAGENT xterm -geometry 80x24
```

Assuming that you haven't used the .xsession script above, you
can define which X applications connect securely on a per application
basis. If you want to just run an X application, you only have to run it
from the command line on an xterm. To do this, start your X session[1]:

```
$ startx
```

Next, you'll either start an application or a shell. To do this
through an xterm, it helps to name the window something appropriate so that you can remember what you're doing in it. In this
case, let's call it "ssh-xterm". To start a Secure Shell connection
through a shell, do the following in an xterm:

```
$ xterm -e ssh-xterm remotehost &
```

This will spawn another xterm running Secure Shell to the
remote host. Your title bar for that xterm will become "ssh-xterm."

If you did not turn on the Secure Shell authentication agent, the
ssh-askpass program runs and prompts you for your xauth password.

You can also start X applications like xload, xclock, xterm, and
many others through Secure Shell. This way you can authenticate
the connection without having to worry about your connection
being hijacked. This will look like any other X application that you

---

1. If you already use the .xsession script listed above, running Secure Shell on
   individual X applications will be a waste of your time.

start without Secure Shell, so the security will be transparent to you. To start an X application without having to type a password:

```
$ ssh-agent xterm &
$ ssh -n remotehost xload &
```

If you're not doing any key management with Secure Shell, use the -f option so that you get prompted for a password:

```
$ ssh -f remotehost xeyes &
```

If you want to extract information for the Xauthority from your local host to another host, you'll need to start the Secure Shell authentication agent:

```
$ ssh-agent $SHELL
```

Next you'll need to run this ugly command to extract your local information to the remote host and have that information merge with the remote Xauthority file:

```
$ xauth extract - $DISPLAY | ssh -n remotehost xauth merge - &
```

This takes the display information from the target host and adds the display information to the Xauthority on the local system. However, if you want to make this secure, as in the previous example, you need to do this using the MD5 hash. Keep in mind that Secure Shell will set its own DISPLAY variable, so extracting the DISPLAY variable may not be the most secure thing to do.

Now, you should be able to run X programs on the remote host with the X forwarding turned on.

Forwarding Other Network Traffic through Local Port Forwarding

OK, so you've figured out how to do X forwarding. Now you want to run other connections securely through Secure Shell. You can forward other TCP connections without any problems, including POP3, IMAP4, SMTP, DNS, and FTP. Don't fool yourself, though, some of these connections are not very straightforward. FTP is one of the more funky TCP applications available, whereas SMTP is much more straightforward.

To forward a connection, you need to be familiar with some specific options for the Secure Shell client. For Secure Shell 1, these are the compression option, the `userid` option, and the local forwarding option, listed below:

-C Compress packets, good for mail transfers including POP3, SMTP, and IMAP4.

-l Change the username if it's different on the remote system.

-g Specify whether or not remote hosts may or may not connect to a locally forwarded port.

-c Cipher choice. Make sure you pick something compatible with the remote server.

-L Map the local port to the same port on the remote system.

In Secure Shell 2, these options should help you when you forward a connection. Note that they differ from the ones you would use for Secure Shell 1.

+C Compress packets, good for mail transfers including POP3, SMTP, and IMAP4.

-l Change the username if it's different on the remote system.

-c Cipher choice. Make sure you pick something compatible with the remote server.

-S For port forwarding that does not need a tty allocated (for non-interactive mode).

-L Map the local port to the same port on the remote system.

Table 9.1 lists some common services and their related ports that you may want to forward. This does not include all possible services. This is an abbreviated table to give you some examples of what you can do with Secure Shell.

From this you can see that you can use any type of TCP connection, whether or not you need a tty allocated for it. You can even use Secure Shell as a substitute for Secure Sockets Layer (SSL) for your HTTP connectivity. It all depends on how you want to run things.

Port forwarding can be very confusing, so here is an example of the port forwarding command. This is its most simple form; you can substitute FORWARDINGPORT for any port number you wish, provided that you have access to that port and it is not in use. The APPLICATIONPORT is what is defined in the `/etc/services` file, similar to the table above. This forwards any connection to the local host on the specified port to the port on the remote host, which is the second port defined. Note that if you are using a privi-

Table 9.1 *Some common services you may want to secure through Secure Shell*

Service	Port	What it does
Telnet	23	Virtual terminal
NTP	37	Network Time Service
FTP	21	FTP connection control
FTP data	20	FTP data connection
SMTP	25	Simple Mail Transfer Protocol
DNS	53	Domain Name Service
HTTP	80	Hypertext Transfer Protocol
POP3	110	POP email retrieval
NNTP	119	Usenet service
RPC	111	Remote Procedure Calls
IMAP4	143	IMAP email retrieval

If you want to use Secure Shell for forwarding POP connections, a script called `gwpop` is available that should do this for you. A copy is on the CD-ROM, if you want to play with it.   **CD-ROM**

leged port that both the forwarding port and the source port can be the same if you are forwarding connections from a privileged user account (most commonly `root`).

```
# ssh -L FORWARDINGPORT:service.system.com:APPLICATIONPORT
service.system.com
```

For simplicity's sake, let's say you are using the root account to access your email through an IMAP4 client on a remote machine with a specific username, say `ahc`. If you're forwarding IMAP4 using the account `ahc` with compression turned on, your command line for Secure Shell 1 may look something like this:

```
# ssh1 -C -l ahc -g -L 143:imap4.destinationhost.com:143
imap4.destinationhost.com
```

For Secure Shell 2, the same type of action may look something like this:

```
# ssh2 +C -l ahc -S -L 143:imap4.destinationhost.com:143
imap4.destinationhost.com
```

Note that in real life you may not be using a root account on a system (that is, an ISP, a work machine, and the like). In this case, the forwarding port will not be the same as the application port. You can use an entirely different port number that is not related to that application at all. Depending on if you are using a root account or not, you can use different ports instead of the privileged ports used above.

Local Forwarding for Non-Interactive TCP Connections

For example, I'm on my development system and I have the same user account on my production system; however, both are not root accounts. So, say I want to forward a POP3 connection from my production system to my development system. Given that I'm a non-privileged user, I have to use a port above 1024. Let's assume that port 1234 is the non-privileged port we are using (for illustration purposes). So, the command for Secure Shell 1 may look something like this:

```
# ssh1 -C -l ahc -g -L 1234:production.host.com:110 produc-
tion.host.com
```

Table 9.2 shows the local forwarding examples for some applications that do not need to have a session connection (that is, a tty allocation) using a non-privileged account. These examples work for both Secure Shell 1 and Secure Shell 2.

You can also define multiple secure connections for the same protocol, even on different machines. For example, say you want to have two POP3 servers connecting securely to your one host; you can do something like this:

```
# ssh1 -C -g -L 1234:pop1svr.host.com:110 -L
2222:pop2svr.host.com sshsvr.host.com
```

In this case, you don't have to use the same host that you're forwarding your ports to; instead you can use a common host that the local forwardings have access to. This creates two secure sessions

Table 9.2 *Some examples of local port forwarding and their non-interactive services for Secure Shell*

Service	Port	Example
NTP	37	# ssh -L 37:ntp.host.com:37 ntp.host.com
SMTP	25	# ssh -L 25:smtp.host.com:25 smtp.host.com
DNS	53	# ssh -L 53:dns.host.com:53 dns.host.com
HTTP	80	# ssh -L 80:http.host.com:80 http.host.com
POP3	110	$ ssh -L 1234:pop3.host.com:110 pop3.host.com
NNTP	119	$ ssh -L 1234:nntp.host.com:119 nntp.host.com
RPC	111	# ssh -L 111:rpc.host.com:111 rpc.host.com
IMAP4	143	$ ssh -L 1234:imap4.host.com:143 imap4.host.com

for POP3 connections, on systems pop1svr and pop2svr, but the Secure Shell connection can be coming from a common system that both hosts have access to.

If you are using a PPP connection, you can place a `sleep` command after the connection. This will enable you to keep the connection alive while allowing you to use the connection efficiently.

Local Forwarding for Interactive TCP Connections

Local forwarding is great for applications that do not require a session connection. So for things like DNS, SMTP, POP3, NTP, RPC, IMAP4, and the like, you can do this and you should have the connection made without any problem. But for interactive sessions, you have to add some steps to this process. This includes Telnet, FTP, and TFTP. There are other interactive network services, it just depends on what you're trying to accomplish.

Table 9.3 shows the local forwarding examples for some applications that need to have a session connection (that is, a tty allocation) using a non-privileged account. These examples work for both Secure Shell 1 and Secure Shell 2.

Table 9.3 *Some examples of local port forwarding and their interactive services for Secure Shell*

Service	Port	Example
Telnet	23	`$ ssh -L 1234:telnet.host.com:23 telnet.host.com`
TFTP	69	`$ ssh -L 1234:tftp.host.com:69 tftp.host.com`
FTP	20, 21	`$ ssh -L 1234:ftp.host.com:21 ftp.host.com`

FTP, for instance, uses both ports 20 and 21 by default. Port 20 passes the data itself, which is not the login information. Port 21, which is the FTP control connection, forwards the information, including the commands, passwords, and username. Most likely, port 21 is the one you want to protect. Unless, of course, you are passing critical documents—then you'll want to protect both.

So for an interactive local port forwarded connection, you need to add some extra steps for connecting. So, to do an interactive connection for something like Telnet, you'll need to do the following steps:

1. Create the local forwarding connection to your interactive application

2. Open a new session (xterm, shell, and so forth.)

3. Create a connection to the forwarded port using FORWARDINGPORT

So, for Telnet, you would do something like this:

```
local:/home/me- ssh -g -L 1234:telnet.host.com:23 tel-
net.host.com
password: ********
Welcome to the telnet server.
telnet:/home/me-
```

You are now connected to the remote server through the local forwarding. However, if you want to create the secure Telnet connection, you will want to open a new window and log in to the Telnet server through the forwarded local port (in this case, port 1234).

```
local:/home/me- telnet telnet.host.com 1234
password: ********
```

```
Welcome to the telnet server.
telnet:/home/me-
```

Now you are connected through a secure local port forwarding and using Telnet. You can do the same thing with FTP. When you use FTP, keep in mind that you are opening two ports (20 and 21), not just one like you do with Telnet (which is only port 23). Also, when you are transferring files with an FTP session, you are usually concerned about the username and password, not as much about the data. For illustrative purposes, we will use the FTP control port as an example:

```
local:/home/me- ssh -g -L 1234:ftp.host.com:23 ftp.host.com
password: ********
Welcome to the ftp server.
ftp:/home/me-
```

Now, as in the Telnet connection, you are now connected to the remote server through the local forwarding. However, if you want to create the secure FTP control connection, you will want to open a new window and log in to the FTP server through the forwarded local port (in this case, port 1234).

```
local:/home/me- ftp ftp.host.com 1234
Connected to ftp.
Name (ftp:me):
331 Password required for me.
Password:
230 User me logged in.
ftp>
```

Even though this is convenient for the FTP control connection, you can get a copy of ftpsshd. This program will encrypt both the FTP data and control ports (ports 20 and 21) using Secure Shell. You can find ftpsshd on the CD-ROM that comes with this book.

> **Note** Even though local forwarding a port is more secure than sending it through the clear, you still need to be careful. You could be forwarding dangerous data across the line.

You can also forward Emacs connections through Secure Shell. You can't do it through the normal local port forwarding—it's too slow that way. Instead, Noah Friedman wrote a LISP script, ssh.el, that Emacs and Xemacs version 19 can use to run Emacs remotely through Secure Shell.

To use it, just load the file into Emacs and then start it with "`Mx ssh`."

CD-ROM   You can find a copy of `ssh.el` on the CD-ROM or you can download it directly from:

`ftp://ftp.splode.com/pub/users/friedman/emacs-lisp/`

Local Forwarding for UDP Connections

Even though Secure Shell is used primarily for local forwarding TCP connections, a patch is available for using Secure Shell with NFS. This, of course, does not improve your security by completely securing NFS. If you want to do that, you'll have to remove NFS and NIS altogether.

I'm not a big fan of NFS or NIS because they use UDP, which is easily spoofed and hijacked (more so than TCP). As a result, they are inherently a bad idea. If you have to use them, you probably want to find a better way to authenticate than just the hostname (which is how NFS authenticates). Andrew Polyakov wrote a patch that uses digital certificates based on Secure Shell 1.2.26 key authentication. What happens is the keys are stored in a secure location and they are signed by a trusted third party.

This in turn creates a Certificate Authority that signs the RSA public keys, creates digital certificates, and stores them in a local file that does not get NFS exported or in a networked database like NIS/NIS+. This uses NIS/NIS+ to distribute the digital certificates. Once you have your keys in a secured location, you can also enforce digital signatures on the public keys that are signed by the trusted system, which generates digital certificates.

To patch 1.2.26 with the NFS patch:

```
# cd /usr/local/src ssh-1.2.26
# patch -p1 < ssh-1.2.26.local.patch
# ./configure
# make
# make install
```

Don't forget to add any configure switches that you may need.

It's cool to see that someone is using Secure Shell to create a Certificate Authority and use it to improve the security of NFS. However, be aware that using NIS to distribute the digital certificates is not a good idea because it can be easily spoofed (it uses UDP). If you are going to do this, use NIS+.

The Secure Shell 1.2.26 NFS patch is available on the CD-ROM that comes with this book or at:
`http://fy.chalmers.se/~appro/ssh_beyond.html`

CD-ROM

Remote Port Forwarding

Now that you have an understanding of local port forwarding, you want to know what the remote forwarding is used for. This is one of the lesser-used options for Secure Shell. Many people have a need to forward other protocols through local forwarding, but not many use the `-R` option.

Why? It doesn't have as many uses as the `-L` option, and it's also a lot more risky. Even though forwarding any type of unsecure traffic through Secure Shell is taking a risk, remote forwarding is even more so. What happens is your Secure Shell daemon accepts a forwarded port from a remote client. The remote client can remotely forward a connection through any port they want. Keep in mind that if this is a root account, then they can forward privileged ports below 1024.

In this case, the syntax for remote port forwarding looks very similar to local port forwarding:

```
# ssh -R FORWARDINGPORT:service.system.com:APPLICATIONPORT
service.system.com
```

So, if you use this command from a remote host, for example, you will connect to the remote host's Web server (port 80) through a Secure Shell connection on port 1234. This is a great way to come in through a firewall to connect to a Web server, or you can use this as a proxy:

```
$ ssh -R 1234:web.system.com:80 web.system.com
```

To connect to a Web server on the inside of a firewall, you can use the remote port forwarding connection from outside of a firewall that has an opening to receive traffic on port 1234, and securely administer the Web server this way. Note that the firewall needs to have a rule set supporting both HTTP (port 80), Secure Shell (port 22), and the remote forwarded port (1234).

To use this as a proxy, you can initiate the connection on the inside of the firewall. You can then use the `ssh -R` command from *inside* the firewall, not outside as in the example before. In this case, you do the same thing.

This may sound cool, but it does have its problems. Even though you are encrypting the session and using public key authentication, you need to remember that you are blindly accepting connections from an unknown port on a host. This can secure network packets that are being used for a designated purpose, but you are also taking the risk that you are allowing unknown, maybe troublesome, network packets through.

Note   Instead of using remote port forwarding, you can always configure a SOCKS-enabled Secure Shell daemon and client to create a proxy.

Secure Shell and TCP Wrappers

Despite Secure Shell's own security, many people want to make it even more secure. You can do so by running Secure Shell through TCP wrappers. TCP wrappers, written by Wietse Venema, is a network logger that logs the client's hostname, time of connection, and service type. It also has detection for IP or hostname spoofing, access controls, and countermeasures. If someone is trying to connect through a non-trusted TCP application (like TFTP), they can be probed with the appropriate counter (such as a `finger` probe or an `rwho` request) if they are trying to break in.

CD-ROM   You can find TCP wrappers on the CD-ROM or at: `ftp://ftp.porcupine.org/pub/security/`. Make sure you check the PGP signature to protect against Trojan horses.

So, in order to get Secure Shell to work with TCP wrappers, you need to make sure that TCP wrappers is installed and configured properly on your system. When you run a TCP application through TCP wrappers, it is considered wrapped. Next, you'll need to configure Secure Shell to run with the TCP wrappers. To do this, you need to do the following:

```
# configure --with-lib-wrap=/PATHOF/libwrap.a
```

Then you'll you need to recompile and build it as shown in *"Installing Secure Shell on UNIX"* on page 19. Make sure the Secure Shell Makefile has both these lines:

```
-I/PATHOF/tcpwrappers
WRAPLIBS = -L/PATHOF/tcpwrappers -lwrap
```

This is especially important for locating two key files for TCP wrappers: libwrap.a and tcpd.h. OK, so you're not done yet. You need to change a few more files. These include /etc/inetd.conf, /etc/hosts.deny, and /etc/hosts.allow. The two configuration files that TCP wrappers use for access control are /etc/hosts.allow and /etc/hosts.deny. You'll want to run any TCP wrapper function through inetd for added security.

To add an entry for wrapped Secure Shell through /etc/inetd.conf, add the following line:

```
ssh stream tcp nowait root /usr/sbin/tcpd  sshd -i
```

This will spawn a sshd from inetd.conf on each request to Secure Shell. Note that in /etc/services, Secure Shell is defined like this:

```
ssh 22/tcp # Secure Shell
```

You'll want to make sure you'll got your /etc/hosts.deny set properly. This prevents anyone who is not defined in /etc/hosts.allow from being allowed in. To do this, you'll want to put this entry in /etc/hosts.deny:

```
ALL : ALL
```

Next, you need to add entries for sshd to /etc/hosts.allow. You have two different entries for Secure Shell in /etc/hosts.allow—one for the Secure Shell daemon, the other for X11 forwarding (if you desire). So, a simple /etc/hosts.allow file for a wrapped Secure Shell daemon that allows X11 forwarding can look something like this:

```
sshd: ALL : allow
sshdfwd-X11: ALL : allow
```

You can also configure the /etc/hosts.allow for specific host control. This allows connections from only the defined hosts or networks in. The syntax for /etc/hosts.allow and /etc/hosts.deny looks like this:

```
deamons: clients: allow/deny
```

In this case, we will deny all default connections using the /etc/hosts.deny, but allow in only Secure Shell connections with /etc/hosts.allow. So, our /etc/hosts.allow looks like this:

```
sshd: .trusted-domain.com : allow
sshdfwd-X11: trusted-X-host.trusted-domain.com : allow
```

This will only allow hosts on the trusted domain in for Secure Shell connections. For Secure Shell X11 forwarding, we are only allowing one host to do this, the trusted-X-host on the trusted domain. With TCP wrappers, you can also be notified every time someone connects. For example, the following entry in /etc/hosts.allow will finger the remote host (with the approved safe_finger command) and mail the information to network operations (network-ops) at another host in case this host is compromised.

```
sshd: .trusted-domain.com : \
  spawn (/usr/sbin/safe_finger -l @%h | /usr/ucb/mail -s
ssh-%h \
  network-ops@centralhost.trusted-domain.com) &
```

Secure Shell for Remote Backups

Because Secure Shell has a built-in remote copy program, you can use it for remote backups. However, if you want to do something a little more sophisticated, like doing tape backups over the network, you can use a series of applications in conjunction with Secure Shell.

Using tar

For data dumping tapes from a remote connection and tarring them, you can do something like this:

```
# tar cvf - . | ssh -c twofish remotehost "dd of=/dev/rst0"
```

If you want to make this seamless, use the ssh-agent to add keys to memory. You can use this for a script and tar multiple tape data dumps at a time. To restore the data, all you need to do is reverse the process and make tar expand the archive.

```
# ssh -c twofish rmt_host "dd if=/dev/rst0" | tar xvf -
```

Or you can pipe tar through gzip to compress the archive:

```
# tar cvf - . | gzip | ssh -c twofish host buffer -o <tape-drive>
```

> **Use the Twofish or Blowfish cipher on Secure Shell. These are the fastest ciphers available for Secure Shell.**   **Note**

A simpler way to do this is to use the GNU tar program (it comes with Linux). All you need to do is pass the option --rsh-command=/PATHTO/ssh like so:

```
# tar --rsh-command=/PATHTO/ssh -cvpMf remote-
host:/source/directory \
/destination/directory
```

This will back up everything in the remote host directory (this can also be a tape device, such as /dev/rst0) to the destination directory on the local host. This is another option you can use in a script to create remote tape backups or directory backups.

If you're just copying directories, there's a patch available for SSH2 for scp that supports wildcards. The patch is available on the CD-ROM.

Using Other Programs

Dave Cinege wrote a scp wrapper which uses both cp and scp. What it does is recognize whether or not to use scp or cp, depending on whether or not a remote host is given on the command line.

> **You can find scp-wrapper on the CD-ROM or at:**   **CD-ROM**
> http://www.psychosis.com/scp-wrapper.

If you don't want to write your own tape backup scripts, you can use Dave Cinege's Datbrk. According to the FAQ, it is "designed to provide seamless backups over an encrypted ssh (secure shell) link."

CD-ROM   You can find Datbkr on the CD-ROM or at:
http://www.psychosis.com/Datbrk.

You can also use rsync, which can use Secure Shell as a transport. The rsync application is a spiffed-up version of rcp, which incorporates additional features and speeds up any type of copying. To use rsync, it must be installed on both the local and remote hosts.

To use Secure Shell as a transport for rsync, you have two ways:

- Define the environment variable RSYNC_RSH as /PATHTO/ssh

- Use the -e command-line option

So, a command line for copying everything from the remote home directories using Secure Shell may look something like this:

rsync -avz -e ssh remote:/home/* /remote-home-backups/

CD-ROM   You can find rsync on the CD-ROM or at:
ftp://samba.anu.edu.au/pub/rsync.

Secure Shell and Other Authentication Methods

Even though using passwords and public key cryptography improves authentication, you have other means of authentication that you may like to use. Two of the more popular means of authentication are Security Dynamic's SecurID cards and one-time passwords with S/Key.

Note   These authentication patches work with SSH1 only (version 1.2.26 or higher).

S/Key

S/Key uses one-time passwords to authenticate. Fortunately, Steve Birnbaum wrote a patch for SSH1 version 1.2.26 to support

S/Key authentication. This patch affects quite a few files on Secure Shell to get it to work:

```
# cd /usr/local/src ssh-1.2.26
# patch -p1 < config.h.in.patch
# patch -p1 < configure.in.patch
# patch -p1 < configure.patch
# patch -p1 < readconf.c.patch
# patch -p1 < readconf.h.patch
# patch -p1 < servconf.c.patch
# patch -p1 < servconf.c.patch
# patch -p1 < ssh.h.patch
# patch -p1 < sshconnect.c.patch
# patch -p1 < sshd.c.patch
```

Next, you'll have to configure and rebuild Secure Shell with the option `--with-skey`:

```
# ./configure --with-skey
# make
# make install
```

After you have done this, you need to set up a configuration change on the Secure Shell server:

SKEYAuthentication This will enable or disable S/Key Authentication. Your choices are "yes" or "no."

SecurID Support

For full SecurID support with Secure Shell, Jean Chouanard wrote a patch that allows SecurID authentication including SecurID-only authentication, and supports next token and new pin requests. After the patch is applied, you need to configure Secure Shell with the appropriate options and install.

This patch is available on the CD-ROM or at:
`ftp://ftp.parc.xerox.com/pub/jean/sshsdi/`.   **Note**

To patch 1.2.26 with the SecurID authentication patch:

```
# cd /usr/local/src ssh-1.2.26
# patch -p1 < PatchSDI
```

Now you have two new configuration options for when you rebuild Secure Shell:

--with-sdiauth[=PATH] SecurID support for client and server. The PATH must point to the ace directory, which includes the `include` and `lib` locations.

--with-sdiclauth enables the new support for the client only. No PATH variable is needed.

To create Secure Shell with client and server support for SecurID:

```
# ./configure --with-sdiauth=/usr/local/ace
# make
# make install
```

To create Secure Shell with client-only support for SecurID:

```
# ./configure --with-sdiclauth
# make
# make install
```

After you have done this, you need to set up some updates on the server.

SDIAuthentication This will enable or disable SecurID Authentication. Your choices are "yes" or "no."

SDICompatforcemode Use if `SDIAuthentication` is set, and if the client has not tried `SDIAuthentication`. This forces the server to accept a `PasswordAuthentication`, but challenges the ACE server with the password as the passcode. This happens even if the `PasswordAuthentication` is turned off.

Problems with Multiple Methods of Authentication

With all of these different types of authentication available, Secure Shell can get confused. Carson Gaspar wrote a patch that will let you choose the order in which you want to authenticate by. This patch also includes additional fixes for SSH1 version 1.2.26, including Kerberos and privileged ports. Take a look at the README file for more information.

CD-ROM   This patch is available on the CD-ROM or at:
`ftp://ftp.cs.columbia.edu/pub/carson/`.

What this patch does is give you an additional option for the Secure Shell server called `AuthOrder`. This option allows you to

choose the authentication method you want to use first. Let's say
you want to use the UNIX password, then the Kerberos5 password:

```
AuthOrder password_unix password_krb5
```

Another example would be to use the SecurID password:

```
AuthOrder password_securid
```

> This patch does not currently support S/Key authentication if you **Note**
> choose to use it.

Future Authentication Methods for Secure Shell

So, with all the patches above, Secure Shell can support quite a
few means of authentication. This includes public key authentication, rhosts, password, Kerberos, S/Key, and SecurID cards. However, with new means of authentication always popping up, Secure
Shell is putting in some additional hooks for those as well.

One of those means is digital certificates. This is the X.509 standard for Digital Certificates that Secure Shell has the hooks for.
This way, you can incorporate vendor's products, including Veri-
Sign digital certificate products such as OnSite. This will enable
you to issue your own digital certificate by being a Certificate
Authority and provides a central point of trust for where the digital
certificates can be verified.

Smart cards, which are credit card-sized cards with a chip on
them, are becoming a popular way to authenticate users on systems. Also, smart card support is growing, particularly in Europe.
Secure Shell integrating with smart card technology could be a big
boost in the corporate sector.

Summary

Secure Shell can be used like a pocket knife for securing network
connections, including POP, X, PPP, and FTP. You can forward
these connections through a local port forward or even through
remote port forwarding—depending on what you're trying to
accomplish. Remote port forwarding is also good for creating a

proxy environment, whereas local port forwarding can also be used for creating a VPN by using PPP and Secure Shell.

Also, you can use Secure Shell with TCP wrappers to enhance the security of the connections. This will enable you to monitor the connections, log them, and even send countermeasures if you notice some form of attack. Also, TCP wrappers is a great way to control access to the Secure Shell application if you want added security.

Secure Shell is great for remote backups. Even though there is a secure copy command, scp, other network backup applications use Secure Shell for network transport. These applications include datbrk, which is used for network tape backups; GNU's implementation of tar, where you can define what the --use-rsh command can be; and rsync, which is a much faster implementation of rcp but can use ssh as a transport.

In addition, you can use Secure Shell for remote backups and additional authentication such as SecurID cards and S/Key authentication. As Secure Shell matures, future supported features include X.509 certificate support and possible integration with smart cards.

Troubleshooting Secure Shell

In this chapter:

- Things to help you troubleshoot

- Common problems

- What to do if this doesn't help

Now that you know how things are supposed to look, you may run across the way things aren't supposed to look. With a networking encryption application, you can run into all sorts of problems: everything from compiling problems to network connectivity problems to others that make you just go "huh?!"

This chapter covers some basic problems, but it doesn't cover everything you could run into. As both versions of Secure Shell have their share of quirks, you may run across a bug. If you do run across a bug, you need to contact SSH Communications at `http://www.ssh.fi/support/bug-report.html` or send email to `ssh2-bugs@ssh.fi`.

Each release of Secure Shell has its share of quirks. In this section, we cover the latest releases of both SSH1 and SSH2. If you are using an earlier version, you'll want to upgrade. For example, Secure Shell releases earlier than 1.2.23 Secure Shell have problems with an attack that allowed the possibility of executing arbitrary commands. Early releases have their share of problems such as host key access, root exploits, and Arcfour cipher issues.

Some Basic Troubleshooting Help

Sometimes you get so frustrated that you don't even remember where to begin. The first thing you do depends on the type of problem you're having. You should make sure you're network connection is working, the ciphers are compatible, and the version and protocol of SSH you are using is compatible. The following is a basic checklist for troubleshooting:

1. Check the network. (Is routing of various IP networks occurring?)

2. Check the ciphers.

3. Check the version.

4. Check and make sure you are using compatible SSH protocols.

It's important to remember that SSH1 and SSH2 are not compatible. Also, when you're troubleshooting and you need help, make sure you have as much information as possible about networking information, the cipher you're using, and most important—about the version of SSH you're using.

Things to Help You Troubleshoot

Even though you may feel frustrated and not sure what to do to get any information about what this mysterious application is doing and why it's not working, you do have hope—and help. You have two options that are built in directly to Secure Shell which can come to the rescue.

Your two options are to use the logging information, which doesn't require you to change any settings; or you can use the verbosity or debugging options, which provide you with lots of information. It's how your parents would see you when you got caught doing something you weren't supposed to—you spilled your guts. And when you did that, you told your parents way more than they wanted to hear.

Logging Information

A cool thing that can help you decipher what's going on is your system messages file. Even if you're not running in debug mode, it should provide you with lots of information about what Secure Shell is doing. Here's what it might look like:

```
Feb 4 12:05:24 tigerlair sshd[9303]: log: Generating 768 bit RSA key.
Feb 4 12:05:45 tigerlair sshd[9303]: log: RSA key generation complete.
Feb 4 12:06:01 tigerlair sshd[9303]: log: Connection from 1.2.3.4 port 777
Feb 4 12:06:33 tigerlair sshd[9303]: log: Password authentication for user stripes accepted.
Feb 4 12:07:12 tigerlair sshd[9303]: log: Executing remote command as user stripes.
Feb 4 12:08:49 tigerlair sshd[9303]: log: Closing connection to 1.2.3.4.
```

Every time a Secure Shell client is forked, a new 768-bit key is generated. This output you will most likely see for Secure Shell 1, unless you purchased Datafellow's commercial version of Secure Shell 2. You should be able to tell from this output that connection is made from a remote host and that the user is `stripes` (who is able to execute remote commands). After the remote command is executed, then the connection is closed.

Verbose Output

You can also get more information from Secure Shell by enabling debugging or verbosity options. This will provide you with more information to troubleshoot with than the logging information alone will give you.

The client has an option to give you: verbose output, -v. You can run ssh -v to see if the connection is doing funny things. Usually people on comp.unix.ssh are willing to help you with your problem, or you can check the FAQ. Most of the time it's a problem someone has already run across, and there is either a known solution or it may even be a known bug. If you run into a bug, you can email ssh-bugs@ssh.fi with a copy of the output and a description of the problem. If it can be re-created, a patch is made and is included in the next release. Here's what it looks like:

```
tigerlair:/home/stripes- ssh -v hobbes.tigerlair.com
```

Note

> Don't confuse the -v (verbose) with the -V (Version) options. However, they both provide you with information to help you troubleshoot.

The verbose option for the client will dump the debug output to your screen and look something like this:

```
tigerlair:/home/stripes- ssh -v -p80 tigerlair.com
SSH Version 1.2.22 [sparc-sun-solaris2.5.1], protocol version 1.5.
Standard version. Does not use RSAREF.
tigerlair.com: ssh_connect: getuid 348 geteuid 0 anon 0
tigerlair.com: Connecting to tigerlair.com [1.2.3.4] port 80.
tigerlair.com: Allocated local port 1022.
tigerlair.com: Connection established.
```

From here, you can see that the connection is made on the correct IP address on the correct port, and the client is connecting on port 1022. The server also has a verbose option, creatively named -d for debugging. This sends the verbose output to the system log and standard error. Also, this causes the server to not fork any additional processes, so that it's easier to chase just one process instead of multiple processes.

```
# sshd -d
```

The verbose option for the server will dump the debug output to the log files and look something like this:

```
debug: connecting to myhost.com...
debug: entering event loop
debug: ssh_client_wrap: creating transport protocol
debug: ssh_client_wrap: creating userauth protocol
debug: client_disconnect: Illegal protocol version.
Disconnected; protocol version not supported.
debug: uninitializing event loop
```

In case you're wondering, this output tells you that it can't connect because it doesn't support TCP wrappers. To make that happen, you have to recompile the Secure Shell application with TCP wrappers and configure it properly as shown in *"Other Cool Things You Can Do With Secure Shell"* on page 239.

> The debugging option for `sshd` and `sshd2` will not fork any pro- **Note**
> cesses. You can only run one connection to the daemon at a time in
> debug mode.

Common Problems

Like any application, Secure Shell has its share of known problems. Currently they relate mostly to compiling problems for all the different platforms that Secure Shell works on, connectivity problems with networking issues, and just some really weird problems that come up, but don't seem to fit into either of those two other categories very easily.

Compiling Problems

When you have an application that runs on multiple platforms, you're bound to have problems compiling. These problems vary from platform to platform. Some may be UNIX-specific; others may involve a specific quirk with a vendor's operating system. Some known problems include:

Secure Shell won't compile. You may not have a development environment on your computer. This means that you may not have the available libraries to get Secure Shell to work, even if you do have the compiler.

Solution: Try using a different computer with a known development environment and then moving the executables over to your working computer from the development environment, if you can't install the development environment directly on your computer.

Make or compiler doesn't work. This means you have an incompatible version of gcc, cc, or make. You need to make sure you have the proper version that will work with the Secure Shell code in the README file.

Solution: You need to upgrade your compiler to gcc 2.7.2 or to the latest release, or you'll need to use the GNU make instead of the version on your system.

Make fails during assembly optimizations: This is a known problem with some operating systems, including Solaris, BSDI, and HP-UX. The assembly optimizations improve the performance of Secure Shell, but it should work fine without it.

Solution: So the problem is caused by the optimization options? Remove them. To fix this, you'll need to turn off assembly language optimizations (ASM) in the configure script by passing the --disable-asm option.

SSH doesn't compile on IRIX. For running on 6.5, you need to have certain settings for the mipspro compiler. It comes with cc to compile with.

Solution: Make sure you set the compiler into the environment.

```
# env CC=cc ./configure
# make
```

Configure fails at X: I've had this one happen to me. You run the ./configure script, and it dies when it hits the xauth command.

Solution: You have a couple of possible solutions: you can either change your path while you're compiling (or permanently) to include the X binaries, or you can compile without X. If you don't want to run X connections through Secure Shell, you might as well not compile support in it.

The compiler dies at tgetent **and** tgetstr. You didn't configure the libtermcap library properly. This is external to Secure Shell, but Secure Shell uses it for pty allocation.

Solution: Define your location for libtermcap library, place it in the standard place on your system, or install it.

The gmp goes crazy on a recursive `configure`. Looks like you have the `configure` file left over from the original Secure Shell tarball.

Solution: Do `./configure` twice to make sure any residual `configure` files are removed. Otherwise, make sure you remove or rename any extraneous `configure` files. Another option is to run `make distclean` before compiling.

SSH doesn't compile on Solaris 2.6. Solaris takes some different options for compiling networking libraries into an application. You need to make sure all of your networking functions, such as the socket layer, are properly linked with the applications, including name resolution.

Solution: Replace the line "`-lsocket -lnsl`" with "`-lxnet.`"

Connectivity Problems

Networking does not suffer from the multiple platform problem when using the same TCP/IP implementation. However, networking by its nature breeds its own share of problems. You can have problems with the authentication, the socket connections, and compatibility. Common problems include:

Bad packet length. This is a compatibility problem between SSH1 and SSH2. In this case, a SSH2 tries to connect to a SSH1 and can't do it. The reason the connection does not go through is because the version of SSH1 is 1.2.25 or less. You'll see something like this in your messages file:

```
Feb 4 12:10:24 tigerlair sshd[9422]: fatal: Bad packet length 1397966893
```

Solution: The fix is easy—upgrade to 1.2.26 or higher.

Cannot log logins with SSH. This is a problem with the different versions of `login.c`. The problem is, not all `login.c` will compile properly with Secure Shell. Even if it does, it may not work properly with Secure Shell.

Solution: You may want to try to compile Secure Shell on a different computer running a development environment and double-check your environment variables.

Server dies or doesn't start. This is one where you would want to use `sshd -d` to see what's going on. This could be a variety of things.

Solution: The port that the Secure Shell daemon is trying to listen on is already in use by another program, you could have a bad host key on the local host, or it could be a new bug.

Connection is s- l- o-w. If this is SSH2, this is how the application is currently working. If it's SSH1 or SSH2, it could be that the CPU is not fast enough to compute the keys with the key size you have chosen. You may also want to consider whether it's your processor instead of the application.

Solution: Because cryptography applications are CPU-intensive, you may want to use a smaller key. Be aware, though, that this does have its security implications. The smaller the key, the easier the key is to break.

Port already in use. This means whatever port you have designated for Secure Shell is already in use.

Solution: You'll want to change ports (using the -p option), or if you're using the default port, make sure /etc/services looks like this:

```
ssh 22/tcp
```

Also, check the /etc/inetd.conf file to see if it's reserved any applications for port 22, or whichever port you defined for SSH.

Secure connection refused. You've installed Secure Shell, and you try to connect to a remote site and you get the following:

```
tigerlair:/home/stripes- ssh tigerlair.com
Secure connection to tigerlair.com refused; reverting to
insecure method.
Using rsh. WARNING: Connection will not be encrypted.
```

This could be any number of things. It usually means that your connection is blocked either through a firewall or router, or that the remote server is not accepting Secure Shell connections. It is most likely because Secure Shell is not installed.

Secure Shell does not start from inetd. It shouldn't. If you want to start it from inetd, be aware that it will be slower spawning off the server keys.

Solution: However, if you want to start Secure Shell from inetd, it is recommended that you use TCP wrappers as discussed in Chapter 9, "Other Cool Things You Can Do with Secure Shell."

Secure Shell connects on a weird port. In order to have RSA authentication, you need to connect on a privileged port. This is any port lower than 1024.

Solution: To fix this, the Secure Shell client needs to run as SUID root.

```
# chmod u+s /usr/local/bin/ssh
```

Debug information says the client connects, but it doesn't. This means that the client connection is not forked from the local daemon.

Solution: If you do not start up the sshd process, you cannot run any Secure Shell clients. So, before you do anything, you need to invoke the Secure Shell daemon.

Authentication Problems

You can get messages like "illegal host key" or "could not create user's ssh hostkey." This could be a problem with file permissions, an improperly configured host, or a corrupted key.

Problems with the host key. You may have problems getting the host key to authenticate either on the remote host or the local host.

Solution: Some options you have are to check the permissions on the key and the directory or regenerating the host key. Also, check to see that the versions of Secure Shell are compatible. The user that starts sshd or sshd2 should be the same user who owns the host key (both should be root).

Shadow passwords. There are some problems with some versions of shadow password files and Secure Shell. This includes the Trusted Computing Base (TCB) used by HP-UX, which divides the /etc/shadow file into a database with increased auditing information.

Solution: Make sure you are using the latest version of Secure Shell, because earlier versions of Secure Shell have problems working with the /etc/shadow file.

Problems with passwords in Expect. There's no special setting that you need to set, but you do have a better solution than sending a password in cleartext through a script.

Solution: Use ssh-agent and ssh-add to add keys to memory so that you don't have to type the passwords all the time.

Can't login with root. Secure Shell doesn't want to authenticate to a home directory that is not owned by the user. Check to see who owns the root directory "/". With AIX, it's usually `bin`. You may also have permission problems on the "/" directory as well.

Solution: Change the ownership of the directory. The group does not matter.

```
# chown root /
```

Can't use RSA authentication from a user to a another account. You can't log in to a remote account from two different accounts on the same host on Secure Shell 1. This is an authentication problem that differs from account to account, so it has to do with the user's Secure Shell configuration and key files.

Solution: Copy the `identity.pub` from the source account into the user's `authorized_keys` file on the target system.

I want to hide from `ssh-keyscan`. The `ssh-keyscan` only looks for host keys on port 22.

Solution: Move Secure Shell to another privileged port. You'll probably want to use an easy-to-remember port, such as 1022 or 222. This will make your life easier—since Secure Shell runs on port 22 by default—to remember where it's running. Don't forget to add this line to your `/etc/services` file:

```
ssh 1022/tcp # Alternate Secure Shell port
```

Weird Problems

Even though the basic problems that you might run into with connections or compiling are covered in the previous sections, you may run into other problems that we didn't cover, but which need to be discussed.

Won't accept "y" or "n" for an answer. You have to love software quirks. When you're trying to connect to an unknown host and Secure Shell is configured to ask whether or not to accept a host with a message like this:

```
Host key not found from the list of known hosts.
Are you sure you want to continue connecting (yes/no)?
```

it will not accept a partial word such as "y," "ye," or "n." As you can see from the output below, this doesn't work until you enter "yes" or "no."

```
Host key not found from the list of known hosts.
Are you sure you want to continue connecting (yes/no)? n
Are you sure you want to continue connecting (yes/no)? ye
Are you sure you want to continue connecting (yes/no)? y
Are you sure you want to continue connecting (yes/no)? yes
Host '1.2.3.4' added to the list of known hosts.
stripes@remote.hostname.com's password:
```

Solution: Make sure you type the full word: yes or no.

Wildcards don't work with scp **or** scp2. You're right, they don't, but wildcards can work for scp2.

Solution: For scp2, a patch is available.

> The wildcard scp2 patch is available on the CD-ROM that comes **CD-ROM** with this book.

Secure Shell daemon will not start. Check to see what it's complaining about. If you don't get anything in the log messages, run sshd in debug mode.

Solution: Most likely it can't find the host key. Check and see where /etc/sshd_config and /etc/ssh2/sshd_config have it set, depending on which version of Secure Shell you are running. Also, make sure the permissions are set properly, as well as the ownership. The root account should own the host key, and it should have permissions of 600, or owner read-write. Also, check to see who owns "/"—it should be root.

The scp **and** scp2 **clients do not implement** -p **correctly.** The file that is copied from the local host is now owned by root from the remote host. Also, in scp2, using the -p option and the -r option together will not modify the directory modification times properly.

Solution: If your remote account has permissions to change the UserID and GroupID of the file, it will. Otherwise, the UserID and GroupID will not change.

C2 security is not fully implemented. This is correct. This mostly has to do with the `login.c` and other logging information that needs to be provided.

Solution: Modify the Secure Shell code and other code including `login.c` to give the information you need for C2 compliance. This is out of the scope of this book.

What to Do If This Doesn't Work

Because Secure Shell is such a new application, there are still bugs that are yet to be discovered. As a matter of fact, you may have found a new one that isn't covered anywhere and there's no current available workaround.

If you do find a bug, you can let SSH Communications Ltd. know by going to the Web site at:

`http://www.ssh.fi/support/bug-report.html`

or by sending email to `ssh2-bugs@ssh.fi`. If you find a bug in the commercial version, you can let Datafellows know at:

`http://www.datafellows.com.`

If it's not a bug and it may be a configuration problem, you should do the following:

1. Call your computer ugly names.

2. Take a deep breath.

3. Have someone tell you a bad joke.

4. Read your logs.

5. Turn on debugging for both the Secure Shell client and server.

6. Contact the nice people on `comp.unix.ssh` or `ssh@clinet.fi`.

Many of the people on the mailing list or `comp.unix.ssh` (which are the same) can provide you with information or guidance to help you with your problem. Even the guys from SSH Communications Ltd. and Datafellows read the messages posted, so you can get some unexpected help—which is what makes Secure Shell so cool.

Summary

Despite Secure Shell's beauty, you can run into problems. Many times it's a matter of running the configuration script with the correct options, other times it may be your network configuration. Other problems can occur from improper networking configuration or even incorrect permissions or ownership on key files or directories.

Fortunately, Secure Shell has a nice built-in logging feature that provides you with enough information about what the client and server are doing. Sometimes, though, enough is not enough. You need more information than the logging feature can provide you. Fortunately, both the server daemon and the client have debugging features that make Secure Shell very chatty.

Even though this chapter provides you with some basic help, you do have some other options for getting further help. You can either file a bug report for SSH Communications Ltd. or Datafellows, depending on which release (freeware or commercial, respectively) product you are using.

A

Cryptography Basics

The thing that makes the Secure Shell application so cool is cryptography, which takes the clear information passing over a network and makes it unreadable. The clear information passing over the network is readable by anyone with a packet sniffer, which can pick up unencrypted passwords, and then all of a sudden, they have access to your account. In order to prevent a sniffer from getting your password and login name, you'll want to use a cryptographic application like Secure Shell. This chapter explains the basics of cryptography, without expecting an advanced degree in mathematics.

What Is Cryptography?

As a school kid, you probably played around with some way to put a private note into a code so that no one could read the message except for you and your buddy. That way, if you were passing the note via other classmates to get it to the right person, they couldn't read it. This brings us to the definition of cryptography.

Cryptography is the science of converting something readable (cleartext) into something unreadable (ciphertext) by using a code. These codes are cryptographic algorithms (also known as ciphers) or mathematical methods that convert *cleartext* into *ciphertext*. So, when you were coding messages with your friends, you were using very simple cryptography.

You have two basic studies that involve securing messages: *cryptography*, which is the study of securing messages; and *cryptanalysis*, which is the study of breaking the codes that secure messages. The study of both is *cryptology*. *Steganography*, which is an entirely different—yet related—field, is the study of hiding a message within a message.

To either encrypt a message or decrypt a message, you need to use a key, which is any large number of values. The larger the key, the stronger the encryption is generally.

We'll keep using the school kid example to illustrate encryption. So, let's say the kid uses a cipher that moves a letter of the alphabet over three (So, A becomes D, B becomes E, and so on). From this example, you can deduce that the encryption key is 3.

The encryption algorithm for this cipher looks like the one shown in Table A.1.

Table A.1 *The simple encryption and decryption algorithms used in the example*

Encryption algorithm	Decryption algorithm
Letter + 3 = Ciphertext	Ciphertext - 3 = Letter

So, how is the receiver able to read the message? The same methods that encrypt the message usually have a related function that decrypts the message. Basically, what the sender does to the clear text to get cipher text, the receiver must undo to get back to clear text. For example, if you have an encryption method that shifts each letter over to the right by three, you will have a related decryption method that shifts the letter to the left by three. See Table A.2 below for the example of how the shifting works.

So, "let's go to the toga party!" would look like this:

```
Ohw'v jr wr wkh wrjd sduwb!
```

Table A.2 *Encryption and decryption method applied to each letter of the alphabet*

Encryption method	Decryption method
A = D	A = X
B = E	B = Y
C = F	C = Z
D = G	D = A
E = H	E = B
F = I	F = C
G = J	G = D
H = K	H = E
I = L	I = F
J = M	J = G
K = N	K = H
L = O	L = I
M = P	M = J
N = Q	N = K
O = R	O = L
P = S	P = M
Q = T	Q = N
R = U	R = O
S = V	S = P
T = W	T = Q
U = X	U = R
V = Y	V = S
W = Z	W = T
X = A	X = U
Y = B	Y = V
Z = C	Z = W

In this example, your encrypted note is the message. Note that it looks like garbage and is unreadable unless you know how to decrypt it. In this case, the decryption mechanism isn't too difficult to figure out.

This method is known as *Caesar's cipher*—Julius Caesar used it as an encryption method. A similar cipher, ROT-13, or ROTate right 13 letters, was still popular with the UNIX folks as recently as a few years ago. With Secure Shell, an IP packet that has the data encrypted with a much more sophisticated algorithm is the message. The type of cryptography used in the note example—where both the sender of the message and the receiver of the message know the code—is called *conventional* or *symmetric key* cryptography.

Benefits of Cryptography

Cryptography, when used properly, should increase security in a computing environment. You have three aspects that cryptography can enforce: confidentiality, integrity, and authentication. All three of these together are referred to as CIA. From a technical standpoint, all encryption provides is privacy and integrity—everything else is derived from it. This include non-repudiation and authentication.

Confidentiality. Cryptography should be able to provide a way to transmit data without having any unintended party read it. In other words, no one except the receiver and the sender know the contents of the message. If the key is compromised, then the data can be read by anyone. The way that cryptography provides confidentiality is by encoding the message with either a key or a set of keys. For example, with Secure Shell, a packet is encrypted so that you can't see the contents without the decrypting key.

Integrity. You trust that the data arrives to you in the same condition that it left the source in. The data should not be corrupted during transit. The key should not be so easily broken that the data can be changed then re-encrypted by the intruder. Integrity is kept by picking strong ciphers and cryptographic keys that ensure that the intruder will have a difficult time breaking the key or finding an alternative cryptographic algorithm. Another form of data integrity is based on the knowledge that a message has not been altered in any way. Cryptographic hash functions are one-way ciphers that generate a unique "finger print" of the cleartext data. The cleartext data can still be intercepted and read, but modifying it changes the hash, and the intended receiver knows that the message has been modified. Merely adding a space to the message will change the resulting hash so dramatically that the intended recipient can see the difference between the hashes with the naked eye. Public-key cryptography is making this a popular form of verification. Using public-key cryptography is how Secure Shell ensures cryptography.

Authentication. It should be easy to verify who sent the message by whoever knows the key. A sender should not be able to deny that he sent it at a later date, as long as the key has not been compromised or shared with anyone else. This gets rather tricky when you're talking about bulk encryption or link-level encryption. Both can use a symmetric key and both can have information inserted into the data stream. Let's say that you have a cryptographic session established between two routers in order to send messages across the Internet. Computers attached to the network send cleartext to the routers, which convert it to cipher text, and then send it across the Internet to the other router. Any node on the inside, or unencrypted side, can inject a message. At this level of resolution, you can only determine if the message came from a particular network.

Non-repudiation. The example listed in the authentication section is a simple form of non-repudiation. The way this works is that someone who receives the data has received it from a trusted source. Modern strong authentication methods use cryptographic algorithms to compare some known piece of information such as a PIN. A relatively new example of how to determine if the source is trusted or not is by using digital certificates or digital signatures. Secure Shell uses a combination of public-key cryptography and passwords for authentication.

Cryptanalysis

The purpose of cryptography is to keep messages or data secret. The purpose of cryptanalysis is to find out what the cleartext is, either by figuring out the ciphertext or figuring out the key itself. Cryptanalysis has its good points too—it's like breaking into a computer system. If you can find the weakness before the attackers do, you can take steps to improve your algorithm. For this reason, cryptanalysis has some very important uses. However, if someone is doing a cryptanalysis attack on your system, you could be in serious trouble.

The attacker may or may not know the algorithm. For example, RSA Data Security is one of the many companies that has challenges to break different types of cryptography and offers a nice financial sum to those who do. At this time, the DES encryption algorithm was broken after only three days by a specially-designed computer. Both RSA and DES are well-known ciphers. As computers get faster and more powerful, the keys need to be harder to find and the ciphers need to get more difficult to crack.

You can face several different types of attacks. For illustration purposes, a simple mathematical function can illustrate how the attacks work. A cipher may look like this:

```
Encryption(plaintext) = ciphertext
Decryption(ciphertext) = plaintext
```

There are five basic cryptanalysis attacks: *ciphertext-only, known plaintext, chosen plaintext, chosen ciphertext,* and *chosen text*. These types of attacks are used by a cryptanalyst who has the encryption algorithm and the ciphertext to be decrypted.

Cipher-text only attack. Here's where the cryptanalyst only has the ciphertext of more than one message encrypted by the same key. The cryptanalyst tries to get as much of the plaintext messages as possible, or even the key. The key may be deduced from the ciphertext messages. A new method recently developed is called *differential* cryptanalysis and uses a complicated mathematical model that compares cryptographic text.

Known plaintext. Instead of looking for the plaintext of the messages, the cryptanalyst looks for the key. In this type of attack, the cryptanalyst has both ciphertext and cleartext of the messages. This is used to deduce the key by finding a pattern for encrypting the plaintext into ciphertext.

Chosen plaintext. This type of attack is stronger than a known plaintext attack. The cryptanalyst chooses the plaintext message (thus the name), along with the ciphertext generated with the key.

Here's where the strength of this attack comes in: the cryptanalyst can choose certain plaintext to encrypt, which may result in more solid results. This increases his chances of deducing the key.

Chosen ciphertext. A cryptanalyst has access to the ciphertext and the decrypted plaintext instead of the original plaintext. Again, the cryptanalyst is looking for the key used to generate the ciphertext.

Chosen text. An attack that combines both chosen plaintext and chosen ciphertext attacks. This makes the attack more effective than using chosen plaintext and chosen ciphertext attacks separately.

A popular method, and the one that broke 56-bit DES, is based on brute force. One method cryptologists use to measure the strength of their algorithm is called a 50% key space attack. The math of probability and statistics says that after you have looked at 50% of the possible keys for a particular algorithm, the chance of you finding the right key is very good. So a brute force attack starts with the first key, moves on to the next key, and does this until the message has been decrypted.

Strong versus Weak Cryptography

Defining strong cryptography and weak cryptography may cross a fine line. A strong cryptography implementation is one where the ciphertext or a key are not easily solved. What is considered "to solve?" It's relative and a matter of perspective. In algebra, people are given sets of equations that may form a geometric series, where the previous answer is used to determine the next number. In a sense, this is basic cryptanalysis.

A geometric series of 1, 4, 16, 256, and so on is easy to solve. All you have to do is square the current number in the series to get the next number. However, a series that looks like this may be harder to solve:

```
8, 5, 4, 9, 1, 7, 6, 10, 3, 2 . . .
```

This is a puzzle that I've seen in some seminars. If you take your mind out of how you would typically solve the puzzle (by using some mathematical function), you can see that the numbers are alphabetized. This may not be an easy thing to solve if you don't know the English language; thus making it "strong."

So, as computers get more computational power, the size of the key needs to get larger to stop a simple cryptanalysis attack. For example, the public key RSA algorithm uses prime numbers to create the key. If the prime number is small, then the key will be easy to break. If the prime number is large, the key is much harder to break.

Some very strong algorithms can be rendered rather weak by selecting the wrong key. This is referred to as a "weak key" and most algorithms have to deal with this problem. Making your DES key all 1s, for example, is a sure way for your private information to become very popular!

How Secure Is an Algorithm?

An algorithm is secure if the plaintext or key cannot be deduced from a cryptanalyst attack. The algorithm is unsecure if a key or an alternative key can be deduced from an attack. In addition, the algorithm is unsecure if the plaintext can be figured out from the ciphertext, or if the cryptanalyst figures out critical information about the plaintext or the key itself. This is why implementations of many popular algorithms add data to ensure that the length of the encrypted message does not increase or decrease with the size of the cleartext message. A 150-byte cleartext message will produce the same size block of crypto text as a one-byte cleartext message.

There are two types of algorithm security:

Unconditionally secure. No matter how much information is available, the plaintext cannot be recovered.

Computationally secure. The algorithm cannot be broken with today's resources.

Something an intruder also needs to consider is how much hardware is required to attack an algorithm, whether the cost of breaking the algorithm is more than the value of the plaintext, and whether it takes longer to break the algorithm than waiting for the key to expire or the value of the data itself to expire. It may not be economical to bother. For example, it might be worth attacking an encrypted IP packet that has the password belonging to a CEO of a corporation, if an attacker knows that the CEO does not use one-time passwords and rarely changes his login password.

What Cryptography Can't Do

Symmetric cryptography assumes trust between participants after the secret key or keys have been exchanged. Some algorithms assume trust between participants exists simply because they participate, such as some public key algorithms. Cryptography does have some wonderful uses; however, it can't do everything. One of the things cryptographic applications such as PGP and Secure Shell assume is that trust is already established. Also, when exchanging keys with someone, you are trusting that you are sending the key to the right person and that no one will intercept it. If it is intercepted, you are vulnerable to the "man in the middle" attack described earlier.

Cryptography cannot manage itself. All security comes down to whether or not the security tools and resources are managed properly (for example, key management and public key infrastructures or PKI). If your keys (or even passwords) get stolen, it is up to you to revoke or expire them and issue new ones.

Cryptography does not run hardware systems nor does it maintain patches to the software. Cryptography also does not notify you when you have a security breach. Other things to consider is how the security system that supports cryptography is being managed. If it is being managed poorly and trust is not checked, then the cryptography may lose its strength and subsequently its value as a tool.

Symmetric Key

Let's say you work at McDonald's. You've been working hard, and you get promoted to manager. What comes with being a manager? Aside from the usual headaches, long hours, and customer complaints, you get access to the safe, which contains lots of money. This safe is protected by a combination lock. How do you get the combination? Another manager gives that information to you, usually by word of mouth.

The combination is a shared key, which provides access to something valuable (lots of money). The combination is the same, no matter who has it. If that is compromised, then the safe is no longer secure.

This brings us to symmetric key encryption, or *secret key*, where all the parties involved with the cryptographic message share the same key. This is also known as *conventional encryption*. Knowing exactly what symmetric key encryption does involves a high-level knowledge of numerical analysis. Don't fear—the coverage of the symmetric key in this book is very conceptual, so that you have an understanding of how it works, not how to program it.

How It Works

A simple symmetric key could be a passphrase, PIN, or password that the trusted parties know. For simplicity, we'll use two trusted parties in this example. With symmetric key, both parties assume that they each have the key. When one of the parties starts a secure channel or session, the other one has to know the key or the session does not start. Figure A.1 shows how a symmetric key session may go.

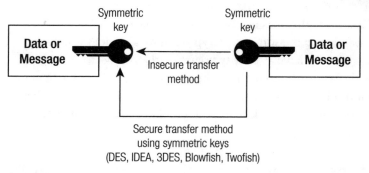

Figure A.1 *A symmetric key session.*

However, this does not take into account how the key exchange even happens. Keys may be passed directly from person to person without any third-party involvement, making less likely the possibility of an attack. Most experts will tell you that it is usually better to exchange the key "out of band" or through a different channel than the one used by the cryptographic session. In other words, you wouldn't email your key if you thought that your network was unsecure enough to warrant encryption. Also, if you use the same channel as the session, a lurker could snatch your key.

Another way that symmetric key exchange may happen is that a trusted third party may be used to exchange keys. This third party could be either another person or another computer that is trusted to handle the keys. This function is very similar to how a notary public works.

After the keys are exchanged, this third party is now partly responsible for the keys. However, if this entity is compromised, then we must destroy the symmetric keys and replace them with new ones, as well as replace the third party, because it is now also corrupt. Keep in mind that the participants can still compromise the keys and do so without the knowledge of the trusted third party. This process ensures that only trusted participants receive keys.

Weaknesses

The biggest weakness with symmetric key cryptography is the key exchange itself. If the keys are exchanged out in the open, then the keys are at risk of being discovered. Another problem with the key exchange is the trusted third-party involvement. If that third party is compromised, then the established trust is gone.

The other problem is to have someone masquerade as a trusted party. If a nefarious participant becomes the trusted third party for key exchange—be it either a "trusted" computer system or a person—the key is then compromised.

As you can see, symmetric key encryption has a fundamental flaw: the key exchange. However, if the symmetric key is used in conjunction with public key algorithm, then the key exchange can be made more secure.

Examples of Symmetric Key Cryptography

Because this book is about Secure Shell, it discusses the symmetric key algorithms found in the Secure Shell application. These are standard symmetric key algorithms found on many other cryptographic applications, including Kerberos, which "cryptifies" an application's access, as well as disk and file encryption software like Kremlin. Also, the UNIX password system, which stores the user passwords in /etc/passwd or /etc/shadow files, uses symmetric key encryption. Most of these applications implement DES, Triple DES, or IDEA ciphers. In the case of NIX, it's MD5.

DES and Triple DES (3DES)

Developed by IBM for the NSA, the Data Encryption Standard (DES) has been the de facto symmetric key algorithm worldwide for over twenty years. In the early 1970s, the National Security Agency (NSA) was the only United States government agency to have a knowledge base of cryptography. After the NSA created the algorithm, it was adopted as a federal standard in 1976 and approved by the American National Standards Institute in 1981.

However, DES is losing respect as a strong algorithm because of the recent successes by cryptanalysis contests on breaking DES. The most recent cryptanalysis on DES was done in less than three days, showing the weaknesses of sending encrypted messages with only the export standard.

Note   The results of the DES cracking contest are available at
http://www.rsa.com/rsalabs/html/challenges.com

In order to try to strengthen the security of DES, a method called Triple DES (3DES) is used in some implementations to improve the strength of the DES cipher. Although there is nothing that says that Triple DES strengthens security more than DES, this method is considered more secure than conventional DES encryption.

Despite its name, Triple DES encryption is not encrypting the information with three different keys. Triple DES uses a cryptographic method known as encrypt-decrypt-encrypt. In this method, the cleartext is encrypted, decrypted, and encrypted again. The key used to encrypt the first time and the key used to encrypt the second time are different keys. At least two keys are used; however, the more keys used, the more secure the ciphertext becomes. This method was selected to maintain compatibility with the 56-bit version. The same key is used for the entire 3DES operation, which means you've gone through a lot of CPU cycles to increase the strength of the cipher. If you use the same key to encrypt, decrypt, then decrypt again, you've gone through a lot of work to 56-bit strength.

Secure Shell uses both DES and 3DES; however, you're better off using 3DES instead of DES.

IDEA

Since DES has been losing popularity, other algorithms are starting to take its place. The International Data Encryption Algorithm (IDEA) is gaining ground. IDEA, which was created by Xueja Lai and James Massey, is one of the most secure symmetric key algorithms available. Secure Shell implements it as well as DES and 3DES.

Part of the appeal of using IDEA instead of DES is its speed and key length. IDEA is about twice as fast as DES and uses a 128-bit key instead of a 56-bit key—over twice as long as a DES key and does not require multiple keys like 3DES does.

Blowfish

Created in 1994 to be a secure and fast symmetric key cipher, Blowfish is not patented and is considered public domain. Bruce Schneier wrote this algorithm for applications like file encryption that do not require the key to change on a regular basis. The security of the Blowfish algorithm is dependent on the size of the key—the larger the key, the more secure the cipher. The key can be as large as 448 bits.

Because of its design, Blowfish is a compact algorithm, making it useful for applications like PGPfone and Secure Shell. Also, there is no known successful cryptanalysis attack done on the Blowfish cipher.

Others

Other symmetric key ciphers include RC2, RC5, and Skipjack. RC2 and RC5 are Ron Rivest's Cipher, which are trade secrets owned by RSA Data Security. Skipjack is an 80-bit classified algorithm that the United States government uses in hardware.

Because these algorithms are not implemented in Secure Shell, they will not be discussed in this book.

Public Key

Because symmetric key encryption has fundamental flaws for keys, public key encryption has grown in popularity for its usage of messaging and networking. Public key involves two keys belonging to the same party: a public key, which is shared by everyone, and a private key which is secret except to the owner. Like the description for symmetric key, this explanation is used for a conceptual understanding of public key encryption—no math will be used in the description.

How It Works

Unlike symmetric key encryption, public key encryption uses two keys to encrypt and decrypt. One of the keys is kept secret; this is the private key and is needed to decrypt the ciphertext. The ciphertext itself is created by a public key, which is distributed to those who want to send you an encrypted message.

Note   Do not distribute your private key. This defeats any security that public key encryption provides.

How does someone get your public key? Simple—you publish it. Many people have theirs listed in their `.plan` file, which is visible using the finger command on UNIX. Others may publish it on a Web page. Applications like PGP have servers which distribute public keys.

Note   The PGP public key server is available at `http://pgp.ai.mit.edu`

The only person who should be able to decrypt the message is you—the owner of the private key. However, if the private key can be retrieved from a network, then anyone who can access the private key will be able to read the messages. Figure A.2 shows how a message would be encrypted with a public key.

To decrypt a public key encrypted message, the decryption algorithm is applied to the message using your private key. This makes the key more secure and cryptanalysis a little more difficult.

You can have a collection of public keys, and some applications have public key rings, which is a collection of public keys. PGP and Secure Shell have a public key ring, and the public keys are usually stored as separate files or as part of the application.

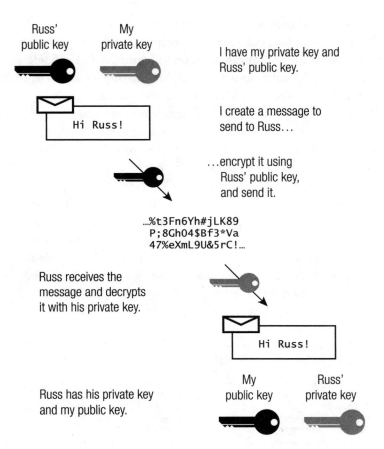

Figure A.2 *A public key encrypted message.*

Weaknesses

Public key cryptography does have its weaknesses, despite its improvement over secret key cryptography. You'll still find the third-party verification, such as a digital signature, which helps reduce disputes between "he-said she-said" types of arguments. Also, public key cryptography is still susceptible to the same type of cryptanalysis attacks that symmetric key cryptography is susceptible to.

Additionally, with public keys, you have to manage the keys. This includes issuing, authenticating, verifying, and revoking. Public key management introduces an entirely new weakness—management structure that can be compromised.

Examples of Public Key Cryptography

There are standard public key algorithms found in many other cryptographic applications in addition to Secure Shell. Diffie-Helman, RSA, DSA, and Elliptic Curve ciphers are implemented in many applications today, including PGP and Secure Sockets Layer (SSL). These ciphers are used for either encryption, digital signatures, key exchange, or a combination of uses. Additionally, Public Key Infrastructure products, including those produced by Verisign and Entrust, are based on the following public key ciphers.

One of the ways to distribute public keys is with *digital certificates*. Digital certificates contain a public key, the owner's name of the public key, and approval from the Certificate Authority (CA) that the public key is authentic. The CA is a trusted authority who issues, updates, validates, and revokes public keys. However, validation of a public key can be done by anyone who has the digital certificate. Figure A.3 shows how a CA can distribute the keys and verify CAs underneath it.

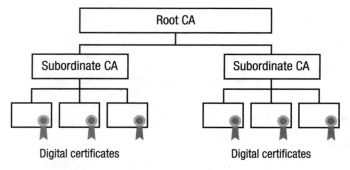

Digital certificates   Digital certificates

Figure A.3 *Certificate Authority hierarchy.*

Diffie-Hellman

Diffie-Hellman was the first public key algorithm published and is used only for key exchange. It is used for exchanging secret keys in symmetric key ciphers. It cannot be used for digital signatures or encryption and decryption of data.

Even though this is not used for encryption or authentication, the Diffie-Hellman cipher requires two keys for the secure key exchange. Both parties that are exchanging a symmetric key have both a public and private key generated by Diffie-Hellman. Diffie-Hellman in Secure Shell is used for key exchange only, not authentication. Even with ciphers such as RSA and DSA, Diffie-Hellman is used in applications today, such as Secure Shell, for key exchange.

RSA

In 1977, Ron Rivest, Adi Shamir, and Len Adleman of MIT developed one of the first public key algorithms based on Diffie-Hellman's key exchange. This algorithm is called *RSA*, using the first letter of the last names of the authors.

The RSA cipher is generated using very large prime numbers. The larger the primes, the more difficult the cipher is to break. The maximum key size in use today is 2048 bits. RSA is known to be the de facto for public key encryption and is the strongest public key algorithm available to date. RSA has not had a successful cryptanalysis attack to date. RSA is used in Secure Shell for authentication and for key exchange. Even though RSA can be used for encryption, Secure Shell uses a symmetric cipher for that instead.

As time goes on, the need for larger RSA keys increases. The larger the key, the longer it takes to generate—therefore eating more CPU cycles. This shows that the RSA cipher is starting to show its age. However, the RSA cipher is under a patent held by RSA Data Security's parent company, Security Dynamics, until 2000. Free implementation of the RSA cipher is available through RSAREF, which is RSA Data Security's unsupported cryptography library, and the code developed cannot be sold.

If you wish to create commercial code using RSA, you will need to license the cipher from RSA Data Security using one of their programming toolkits—and it's not cheap. But, when the patent runs out in 2000, there should not be an issue with running RSA encryption in the United States without a license. However, you'll want to stay up on it through Security Dynamics, which RSA Data Security is a division of.

DSA

The Digital Signature Algorithm (DSA) is used in the National Institute of Standards and Technology's (NIST) Digital Signature Standard (DSS). This type of public key is used in Secure Shell Version 2 (SSH2) for authentication. In addition, the DSS is being used in other applications today as an alternative to RSA because of RSA's increasing key size and licensing issues.

DSA is used in Secure Shell for authentication only, and not for key exchange.

Elliptic Curve Cryptography

Because RSA has an increasing amount of overhead to go with its increasing key size, *Elliptic Curve Cryptography* (ECC) is becoming appealing because it provides the same amount of security but with a much smaller bit size. Even though ECC has been around for a while, it does not "feel" as secure as an RSA public key, because ECC has not been implemented as much as RSA. In addition, ECC has not been subject to 20 years of cryptanalysis the way RSA has. Don't be surprised if more implementations of ECC emerge as RSA becomes less appealing because of the CPU cycles it eats.

Currently, Secure Shell does not use Elliptic Curve Cryptography for any form of authentication or encryption.

Digital Signatures

In the movie *Crimson Tide*, any message that was sent to the submarine had to be authenticated against an alphanumeric code. This alphanumeric code is issued by a third party as proof that the message was actually sent. In *Crimson Tide*, one of the messages was not authenticated. It was up to the officers to decide if that message was real or not, and that message contained information about a Russian nuclear submarine's possible attack on the United States.

Digital signatures provide a third party authentication to verify a message's contents, time and date of the message, and the author. Because public keys become more verifiable if signed by a third party, having a signature authority—similar to a notary public—helps guarantee the authenticity and resolve disputes.

Digital signatures commonly use public key cryptography such as RSA or DSA for creating signatures. Creating a digital signature with a public key works in the reverse of encrypting a message. Figure A.4 shows how the digital signature works with public key cryptography.

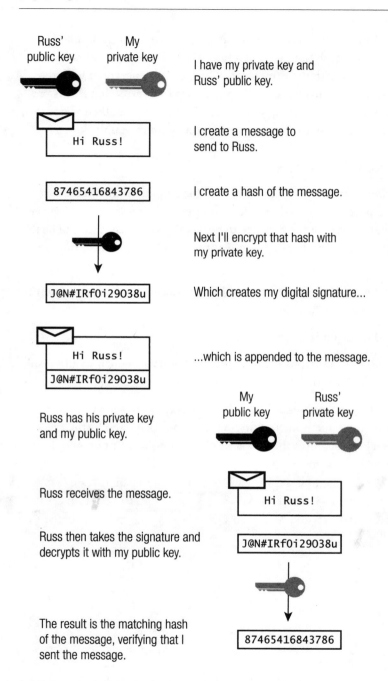

I have my private key and Russ' public key.

I create a message to send to Russ.

I create a hash of the message.

Next I'll encrypt that hash with my private key.

Which creates my digital signature...

...which is appended to the message.

Russ has his private key and my public key.

Russ receives the message.

Russ then takes the signature and decrypts it with my public key.

The result is the matching hash of the message, verifying that I sent the message.

Figure A.4 *Signing a message with a public key.*

What happens is the message is sent through a hash function (more on hash functions in a bit). That hashed message is then encrypted with the private key. Once data is encrypted with the private key, anyone with the public key can verify that it was created with the private key—as a result, the data is authenticated. So, the verification can be done by anyone with the public key.

Hash Functions

A *hash* function is a mathematical function that takes a message and produces a fixed-length thumbprint of a message. No matter what the size of the message to be hashed, the output should be the same fixed length. So, if you want to have a secure hash function, you need to make sure:

1. that reversing the function does produce the message, known as a one-way function

2. the output is a fixed length

3. no two functions produce the same output, which would result in a collision

These properties are used in cryptanalysis attacks, such as the brute force method, and finding collisions using the birthday attack, which uses the probability methodology of two people sharing the same birthday.

Hash functions are used in creating digital signatures. Hash implementations include MD5, Message Digest Algorithm created by Ron Rivest, and SHA-1, Secure Hashing Algorithm created by NIST.

International Cryptography Laws

Because exporting or even using cryptography software can be a sensitive issue in your country, please be aware of cryptography laws in your country and how they affect your usage or your availability of the software. This also affects whether or not the software can be included on the CD-ROM or if it has to be downloaded from the Web site directly.

These laws are in flux as the computer industry demands more and more secure connectivity over the Internet and other public networks.[1] Additionally, as more cryptographic ciphers become available, governments need to decide whether or not to allow cryptography to be used in an international environment. The CD-ROM accompanying this book does not include any software that is not legal in the United States, but it does contain software that is considered non-exportable.

---

1. This information from this appendix is derived from Bert-Jaap Koops' Crypto Law Survey at `http://cwis.kub.nl/~frw/people/koops/lawsurvy.htm`, which is updated on a regular basis.

International

The Coordinating Committee for Multilateral Export Controls (COCOM) was an international organization designed to make sure exporting cryptography only goes to countries who will be using it for legitimate purposes and do not have strong links to terrorism. Even though COCOM was disbanded in 1994, the member countries, including United States, Japan, and France, agreed to keep cryptography on export control.

The Wassenaar Agreement replaced COCOM in 1995, but kept its spirit. It controls the export of cryptography the same way weapons are controlled. The Wassenaar Agreement was revised in December 1998, which restricted some software, but on others, some of the laws were relaxed. As a result, the Wassenaar Agreement looks very similar to much of the United States' policy on cryptography. The following changed in the Wassenaar Agreement:

- All cryptographic products of up to 56 bits are legal to export.

- Mass-market (commercial) cryptographic software and hardware of up to 64 bits are legal to export.

- Products using encryption to protect intellectual property are relaxed.

- Export of all other cryptographic software still requires a license.

- No change on public-domain cryptographic software provisions; still free for export.

Despite the limits on cryptography export that the Wassenaar Agreement includes, it does not include export via the Internet—which is a major concern considering how popular electronic commerce has become. Table B.1 shows each nation or continent and what they allow for cryptography usage and export.

On December 3, 1998, the 33 countries that signed the Wassenaar agreement were convinced by the Clinton administration to impose strict export controls on cryptography similar to the United

Table B.1 *Cryptography laws and exports worldwide*

Country	Domestic	Import	Export
Australia	ok	ok	restrictions
Finland	ok	ok	restrictions
France	restriction	restrictions	restrictions
Germany	ok	ok	restrictions
Hong Kong	ok	ok	restrictions
Ireland	ok	ok	ok
Israel	ok	restrictions	restrictions
Japan	ok	ok	restrictions
Poland	ok	restrictions	restrictions
Saudi Arabia	restrictions	ok	ok
South Korea	ok	restrictions	ok
United Kingdom	ok	ok	restrictions
United States	ok	ok	restrictions

States' policy. This treats cryptography, otherwise known as "data-scrambling products," the same as weapons.

The countries in the Wassenaar Agreement now restrict general encryption products using more than 56-bit keys and mass-market products with keys more than 64 bits long for export. This is supposed to increase the level of security allowed previously; however, this brings the cryptography back to a domestic market in countries that develop the technology. Table B.2 on page 300 shows all the countries in the Wassenaar Agreement.

United States
The United States has some restrictive laws for exporting software. Certain types of encryption, mostly weak, are exportable; other types are not. For cryptography applications used inside the United States, any type of encryption is usable. This includes newly

Table B.2 *Countries in the Wassenaar Agreement*

Country	Region
Australia	Australia
Austria	Europe
Belgium	Europe
Canada	North America
Czech Republic	Europe
Denmark	Europe
Finland	Europe
France	Europe
Germany	Europe
Greece	Europe
Hungary	Europe
Ireland	Europe
Italy	Europe
Japan	Asia
Luxembourg	Europe
The Netherlands	Europe
New Zealand	Australia
Norway	Europe
Poland	Europe
Portugal	Europe
Russian Federation	Europe/Asia
Slovak Republic	Europe
Spain	Europe
Sweden	Europe

Table B.2 *Countries in the Wassenaar Agreement (cont'd)*

Country	Region
Switzerland	Europe
Turkey	Middle East
United Kingdom	Europe
United States	North America

created algorithms, as well as well-known strong ciphers such as RSA and elliptic curve.

The International Traffic in Arms Regulation (ITAR) follows the Wassenaar Agreement, where cryptography is treated the same as weapons. However, the United States does not include weak cryptographic keys like 40-bit DES in this rule. The ITAR was replaced with the Export Administration Regulations (EAR) in 1996 to favor export of cryptography for data recovery.

However, some particular ciphers as well as ciphers with a certain level of strength are not allowed to be exported outside of the United States. In the same way that 40-bit DES is easy to break, 56-bit DES is a bit stronger; however, it is not exportable. The RSA algorithm is also not exportable because of the cipher's strength.

Financial institutions are not subject to the same export restrictions as others. Because of the sensitivity of the personal data involved, banks and other financial institutions can use stronger cryptography. Additionally, the EAR provides for loopholes where other proposed encryption exports could be accepted on an individual basis.

With the recent cracking of 56-bit DES in three days, this is a hotly debated topic on whether to allow all cryptography through United States borders to other countries. Several legislation bills are proposed from both the cryptography business community and the United States government; however, nothing relating to this has been accepted and passed into law. The case study in this appendix goes further into the debate if you're interested.

Europe

The European Union (EU) regulates cryptography in a similar fashion to how the EAR regulates cryptography in the United States. For the most part, if a country is shipping cryptography, both hardware and software, outside of the EU, then it needs a license. The exception to this is public domain software like the SSH Communications Security version of Secure Shell.

Up until January 1999, a license was required for intra-EU cryptography shipments. But now a simple notification is currently all that is required. Also, encryption hardware and software is exportable in the intra-EU countries on laptops for personal use only.

Individual countries also have their own laws regulating cryptography. Ireland has no laws regarding cryptography. On the other hand, Spain, Germany, Belgium, Sweden, Denmark, and Austria all require licenses for exporting, but not for importing. The Netherlands has export restrictions; if cryptography hardware or software is found in a house that is searched by law enforcement, then police can order someone to decrypt the information.

Finland and Hungary have very similar laws for cryptography. They both require a license for exporting, but it's not needed for mass-market software. For Finland, the law also applies to software not needing extensive vendor support. Secure Shell is one of those applications that falls under this law.

Norway, Switzerland, Poland, and France have import and export regulations on cryptography. However, France has the most restrictive export laws in Europe. Import within the EU is free; however, outside of the EU requires a license. Also, a license is required for cryptography exports; and cryptography cannot be used for confidentiality without authorization. Key Escrow Agencies (KEA) have been set up by the French government so that keys may be handed over to law enforcement if needed. Cryptography software and hardware that have given keys to KEA can be used freely.

The United Kingdom only has export laws regarding encryption, but this includes other EU member countries. However, the United Kingdom is trying to relax its cryptography laws so that businesses will have an easier time exporting. Other members of the EU, including the United Kingdom, would like for the United States to soften its cryptography laws as well.

Asia

In Asia, there are some known export restrictions in Japan, Hong Kong, and South Korea. Singapore and Taiwan were members of COCOM. North Korea is not allowed by the COCOM and Wassenaar Agreement to have importation of encryption, because of its friendly relations with terrorist organizations.

For Japan, there are export restrictions that follow Wassenaar. Additionally, approval is required for cryptography export orders that cost more than 50,000 yen. Since Japan feels that cryptography is important for electronic commerce, there are no domestic restrictions.

China itself does not have clear rules regarding encryption; however, Hong Kong does. Hong Kong requires a license for exporting and importing cryptography. On the other hand, nothing is clearly stated about electronic regulations, such as sending encryption over the Internet.

South Korea does not have any regulations for using encryption within its borders. It does, however, have strong laws regarding importation of encryption. In fact, South Korea prohibits importing encryption, even for financial institutions such as banks.

Middle East

Depending on the country, the Middle East has several legal issues regarding encryption. Some countries, including Libya, Iraq, and Iran, are not allowed to have encryption exported to them because of their relations with terrorist organizations as listed in the COCOM.

Saudi Arabia prohibits use of encryption inside its borders; however, there are no laws regarding importing and exporting cryptography. Turkey follows the Wassenaar laws for exporting and importing cryptography; however, there are no known laws regarding domestic usage. Israel has both export and import controls on cryptography. It does issue licenses on an individual basis for exporting and importing; and strong encryption is widely used domestically.

Australia

Both Australia and New Zealand have cryptography export controls, but no domestic or import controls. New Zealand requires a license for exporting, as does Australia. However, Australia's export laws are much more stringent.

Australia requires written permission for cryptography exports, but this does not include electronic transactions such as those that take place over the Internet. A personal use exemption is available for cryptography but with strong restrictions. These restrictions include that the cryptography cannot be transferred anywhere and records must be kept for three years. Export controls in Australia include public domain and publicly available software.

Case Study: Do Crypto Laws Protect or Hinder?

The United States Federal government views strong cryptographic algorithms as a threat to national security. In Silicon Valley, the attitude is to let the cryptography laws relax so that the United States computer security industry won't fall behind other countries that are freely able to export any cipher.

Is the United States falling behind in the cryptography business because of its laws?

If you think about it, the United States government has a right to be paranoid—it's their job. The government feels that they need to be able to obtain all information that may be harmful to the United States. Currently, a bill is in Congress to allow government agents to wiretap the Internet or any other computer network that they feel is necessary. This goes for the Internet as well. Most traffic conducted over the Internet is not encrypted, and it would not be very difficult to sit online with a packet sniffer to read the network traffic anyway. This means that the government can be sitting there reading your connections—but so can a foreign spy.

In addition, the Federal government tried to pass into law the Clipper chip, a hardware chip that the government would issue and then be able to have your private keys and to incorporate key escrow. The Clipper chip would have allowed the Federal government to recover private keys when necessary. This bill did not pass because many privacy advocates and corporations were against it.

However, cryptography is commonly used in many security applications today, including VeriSign, Hewlett-Packard, Netscape, and Microsoft products. These companies conduct business on a worldwide scale—they have subsidiaries and close partners all over the globe. In order to export cryptography, a company needs to get special permission from the United States government.

Many corporations have received approval to export strong encryption algorithms. These corporations, however, are usually well-known companies. Many of the smaller companies have problems competing when they need to get special permission from the United States government to ship their product or to communicate securely with their subsidiary or business partner.

This could be much worse. France does not allow cryptography at all in its borders; thus, they do not allow any product like Secure Shell. Does this limit France in its ability to grow as a technological business stronghold? Quite possibly, especially with the increase of electronic commerce and credit card numbers floating over the Internet encrypted.

The United States government is beginning to relax some of its cryptography exportation laws. Congress is still battling with the benefits and costs of relaxing the laws completely. Hopefully, the United States government and technology businesses will find a way to allow cryptographic technology to grow in a worldwide economy and still protect the nation.

Here's an interesting case regarding how export laws can affect the industry. Phil Karn tried to export a disk with the same verbatim information in Bruce Schneier's book, *Applied Cryptography*; both contain source code for strong cryptographic algorithms. He was not allowed to export the disk, but the book is legally exportable. It's an interesting argument. To read more, take a look at:

`http://people.qualcomm.com/karn/export/index.html`

Tip

Glossary of Cryptography Terms

Algorithm: A procedure or function that takes some form of input, performs computational steps, and produces output. An algorithm is a precise recipe program developers use for implementation.

Arcfour: A symmetric stream cipher based on RC4 and SHA-1. This has a known hole that makes it unsecure for use with Secure Shell.

Asymmetric cryptosystem: A system that uses two different keys, a public and a private key. One is used for encryption and the other is used for decryption.

Authentication: Validating access to a resource.

Block cipher: A cipher which transforms a large block of data (often 64 bits) as a single unit into ciphertext.

Blowfish: A symmetric key block cipher designed by Schneier that uses a variable length key and a 64-bit block. Using a Feistal network, the data is passed through the encryption function 16 times. The key can be any length from 32 to 448 bits.

Caesar cipher: The most basic of substitution ciphers. It is also one of the oldest ciphers, from the time of Julius Caesar. The key dictates the alphabet rotation modulus 26.

CIA: Confidentiality, Integrity, and Authentication. The basic rules of security that cryptography helps to address.

Cipher: An algorithm for encryption and decryption. The goal of a cipher is to accept data (such as English text) as input and produce ciphertext as output so that the original meaning of the data is concealed.

Ciphertext: The text that is the output from an encryption algorithm. It is unreadable until it is decrypted with the correct key.

Cleartext: Also known as *plaintext*. This is the original data passed through a cipher. It should remain unchanged throughout the enciphering and deciphering process.

Confidentiality: Hiding the meaning of a message or senders of a message.

Confusion: A cryptographic technique in which the statistics related to the cipher text are made as complicated as possible, thus obscuring the relationship between the original message and the resulting ciphertext.

Covert channel: A way of sending information through a communication channel which bypasses the intended use of that channel.

Cryptanalysis: The study of breaking ciphers. You have four likely inputs to the analysis: plaintext (known, chosen, or neither), encrypted text, the key stream (often the goal of the analysis), and the algorithm.

Cryptology: The branch of mathematics that encompasses both cryptography and cryptanalysis.

Differential cryptanalysis: A cryptanalysis technique involving chosen plaintext and XOR difference calculations, which are studied in the hopes of determining the encryption key that was used.

Diffie-Hellman: The first public-key algorithm invented. It is often used as a key exchange protocol (the sharing of a secret key safely). The security of this algorithm is based on the difficulty of solving the discrete logarithm problem.

Diffusion: The technique of scrambling the statistics of the plaintext throughout the ciphertext so that attempts of frequency analysis and the like become useless.

DSA/DSS: The *Digital Signature Algorithm* and the *Digital Signature Standard*. DSA is an algorithm based on the discrete logarithm problem and is similar to signature schemes developed by Schnorr and ElGamal in the early 1990s. DSA uses SHA, and as an asymmetrical cipher, can only be used for signatures. DSA is contained in the DSS, the NIST reference, and is part of a government project called Capstone.

Exclusive-OR: A basic logical operation on bits. The result is one if two bits are different and zero if they are the same. This function is popular in cryptography because it has the property that x (xor) k (xor) k = x.

IDEA: The *International Data Encryption Algorithm* A block cipher developed by Lai and Massey in 1990. Originally called PES, for the Proposed Encryption Standard. IDEA is considered by some encryption experts as one of the most secure. IDEA uses a 128-bit key and XOR, modulo 2^{16} addition, and modulo $2^{16}+1$ multiplication to achieve encryption.

Information theory: A fundamental theory of cryptography. It is the way of understanding how much information is contained within a message by computing how many bits are needed to encode the message optimally.

Integrity: Detection of message tampering.

Kerberos: An authentication service that involves a trusted third-party arbitrator. Commonly deployed in campus networks to facilitate the authentication of users on a variety of hosts.

Message Authentication Code (MAC): A cryptographic checksum. This is a small block of data included with a message that has a fixed size. It is generated using a secret key.

Message Digest: A hash function. Mathematical calculations on a message to reduce the message representation to fewer bits. Used to detect message alterations.

MD-4: The first message digest algorithm developed by Rivest. This message digest accepts an incoming message and produces a 128-bit representation, the hash of that message.

MD-5: An improved message digest algorithm which supersedes MD4. Also designed by Rivest, the input is a message consumed in 512-bit blocks, and the resulting hash is a 128-bit unique representation of that message. The MD5 hash has the property that every bit of input is used to calculate every bit of output.

One-time pad: Virtually the only means to achieve perfect secrecy. Each key is used only once in the enciphering algorithm.

Perfect secrecy: No amount of ciphertext will reveal the original plaintext message or the key used. For this to be true, the number of keys must be a least as great as the number of possible messages to be encrypted.

Public key cryptosystem: See Asymmetric cryptosystem.

RSA: An extremely popular public key algorithm developed by Rivest, Shamir, and Adleman, which takes advantage of the difficulty in factoring large prime numbers for its security. The basic principle involves exponentiation in modular arithmetic.

Secure Sockets Layer (SSL): A protocol that utilizes both symmetric and asymmetric encryption algorithms to establish a secure connection between two computers. Initially exchanging a public key, the protocol switches to a symmetrical key after valid identities have been exchanged.

SHA-1: A *secure hash algorithm* developed at NIST and based on MD4. It was designed to be used with the digital signatures.

The maximum input accepted by SHA is a message less than 2^{64} bits long and outputs a 160-bit message digest. The input to SHA-1 is also processed in 512-bit chunks. Operates in a way very similar to MD5.

Steganography: The study of finding methods to hide information within blocks of data. For example, embedding a meaningful message within bits of a graphics or audio file.

Stream cipher: Symmetric encryption that operates on a continuous stream of input bit-by-bit.

Symmetric cryptosystem: A system that uses the same key for both enciphering a message and deciphering that message.

Twofish: An advanced version of the Blowfish algorithm designed by Schneier. Using a 128-bit block and 16 rounds, it has been submitted as a candidate for the Advanced Encryption Standard.

What's on the CD-ROM

This appendix tells you which applications are on the CD-ROM. The CD-ROM does not have as much software as it could, because of the United States patent laws that cover RSA. As a result, the software has already been approved to run in the United States because it either implements RSA through the correct channels or it does not implement RSA at all.

The good news is that this CD-ROM still has a lot of software—everything from the major releases of Secure Shell, to patches which improve the functionality, to releases on different operating systems. Even though the focus of this book is on the UNIX implementation of Secure Shell, some releases are also available for quite a few different operating systems that are listed in this appendix.

The directory structure has the top levels by operating system, followed by what's inside:

UNIX/ UNIX implementations and programs for Secure Shell. Under this you have three other directories: patches, tools, and applications.

Windows/ Windows implementations of Secure Shell. Under this directory you have evaluation copies of commercial software, including SecureCRT, F-Secure SSH Windows clients, and Sergey Okhapkin's NT port for ssh and sshd clients.

Others/ These are ports of Secure Shell for other operating systems. The VMS client and F-Secure SSH Macintosh clients are available on this CD-ROM.

UNIX

This section on the CD-ROM includes UNIX implementations of Secure Shell, as well as patches, applications, and tools that use the UNIX Secure Shell. The licensing agreement for each program or patch is included in the directory in order to save some trees. The actual filenames and release versions are in the README file for each directory.

Implementations

This directory includes the UNIX implementations of Secure Shell by SSH Communications Security and the General Public License (GPL) of SSH, lsh.

Secure Shell 1 The release of SSH1 from SSH Communications Security.

Secure Shell 2 The release of SSH2 from SSH Communications Security.

lsh GPL version of SSH

Patches

This directory contains patches that provide additional functionality for SSH1 itself. Many of the patches for SSH2 have been incorporated in the latest release. Other applications and tools are listed later.

S/Key authentication This patch enables SSH to support S/Key authentication.

SecurID authentication This patch enables SSH to support SecurID cards for authentication.

NFS patch This patch enables NFS to use SSH for authentication.

Authentication order If you use multiple authentication methods, Secure Shell can get confused. This patch allows Secure Shell to pick which form of authentication it's going to use first.

Kerberos buffer overflow This patch fixes a possible buffer overflow for Secure Shell implementations compiled with the Kerberos option enabled.

SGI project initialization This patch corrects the function call for setting up the project group on IRIX machines.

AFS/Kerberos 5 This patch enables an AFS token when a Kerberos ticket is passed or Kerberos password authentication is used.

AFS, Kerberos v4 support Enables Kerberos 4 authentication, Kerberos 4 password authentication, Kerberos 4 ~/.klogin authorization, AFS password authentication, AFS Kerberos ticket-granting ticket passing, AFS token passing, and AFS pts entry authorization.

Syslog open handle This patch opens the syslog and then closes it after logging.

IRIX bit mode compiling option This patch allows SSH 1.2.26 to be compiled with the 32, n32, or 64-bit mode flag on a IRIX 6.* machine. SSH 1.2.26 always assumes n32 when it compiles.

Static Linking This patch enables the binaries to be statically linked instead of using dynamic linking.

Tools

This directory contains tools that use Secure Shell for other applications, including Emacs, POP, FTP, TIS, and VPN. These enable you to use Secure Shell for uses other than what most people use it for.

ssh.el LISP programs that enable you to use Secure Shell and Emacs.

gwpop This program uses POP and Secure Shell to create a secure email gateway.

ftpsshd This program uses Secure Shell 1.2.26 for a secure file transfer.

tn-gw-nav This program allows you to use SSH to connect to a host that is on the outside of a TIS fwtk-derived Telnet gateway. The host on the outside must also be configured to use tn-gw-nav.

ssh-keyscan This program scans remote hosts for public host key on port 22.

VPS The Virtual Private Server (VPS) is a Linux-based VPN for connecting networks securely over the Internet.

datbkr A simple-to-use program that seamlessly does backups over a SSH connection.

ssh-tunnel.pl This Perl script will let you use SSH through an SSL tunnel. Remember that you need to have sshd listening on port 443 for this to work.

scp-wrapper This script allows you to use one command for cp and scp. If it sees a remote host on the command line, it assumes scp. Otherwise, it assumes regular cp.

Applications

This directory contains applications and toolkits to use with Secure Shell. They either help Secure Shell or use Secure Shell.

TCP Wrappers With this package you can monitor and filter incoming requests for the network services, including Secure Shell. This package provides tiny daemon wrapper programs that report the name of the client host and of the requested service.

rsync This program is an open source utility that provides fast incremental file transfer. You can make it use SSH as a transport.

Windows

This section on the CD-ROM includes UNIX implementations of Secure Shell, as well as patches, applications, and tools that use the UNIX Secure Shell. The licensing agreement for each program or patch is included in the directory in order to save some trees.

The actual filenames and release versions are in the README file for each directory.

F-Secure SSH Tunnel and Terminal Commercial evaluation version of the Windows client for SSH1 and SSH2.

SecureCRT Commercial evaluation version of the Windows client.

NT sshd and ssh ssh-1.2.26 precompiled binary and a diff to original ssh-1.2.26 package. This includes both the ssh client and sshd. sshd runs on NT only and uses NT's password authentication, not RSA authentication.

Tera Term Teraterm Pro is a free terminal emulator/Telnet client for Windows.

TTSSH Secure Shell plug-in for Tera Term.

Others

This section on the CD-ROM includes UNIX implementations of Secure Shell as well as patches, applications, and tools that use the UNIX Secure Shell. The licensing agreement for each program or patch is included in the directory in order to save some trees.

The actual filenames and release versions are in the README file for each directory.

OpenVMS Client FISH is a SSH client for VMS. It features the essentials for SSH1.

F-Secure SSH Tunnel and Terminal Commercial evaluation version of the Macintosh clients for SSH1 and SSH2.

If You're Not in the United States

Unfortunately, due to the restrictions on cryptographic software and hardware exports, the CD-ROM is not included for the exported copies of this book. To make up for it, I'm including the URLs where you can get the software from as of time of publication. Since neither McGraw-Hill nor myself maintain these sites they are subject to change.

Note that the commercial software included from Datafellows and VanDyke is evaluation copies, and therefore evaluation copies may not be available outside the United States.

Table D.1 *Secure Shell software and the URLs*

SSH Software	URL
SSH1	ftp://ftp.cs.hut.fi/pub/ssh
SSH2	ftp://ftp.cs.hut.fi/pub/ssh
lsh	http://www.lysator.liu.se/~nisse/archive/
NFS patch	http://fy.chalmers.se/~appro/ssh_beyond.html
S/Key patch	ftp://ftp.cs.hut.fi/pub/ssh/contrib
SecurID patch	ftp://ftp.parc.xerox.com/pub/jean/sshsdi/
Authentication order	ftp://ftp.cs.columbia.edu/pub/carson/

Table D.1 *Secure Shell software and the URLs (cont'd)*

SSH Software	URL
IRX bit mode	`http://www.ncsa.uiuc.edu/General/CC/ssh/` `patch_repository/`
Static Linking	`http://www.ncsa.uiuc.edu/General/CC/ssh/` `patch_repository/`
Syslog open handle	`http://www.ncsa.uiuc.edu/General/CC/ssh/` `patch_repository/`
Kerberos Buffer Overflow	`http://www.ncsa.uiuc.edu/General/CC/ssh/` `patch_repository/`
AFS/Kerberos4	`http://www.ncsa.uiuc.edu/General/CC/ssh/` `patch_repository/`
AFS/Kerberos5	`http://www.ncsa.uiuc.edu/General/CC/ssh/` `patch_repository/`
SGI Project Initialization	`http://www.ncsa.uiuc.edu/General/CC/ssh/` `patch_repository/`
ssh-keyscan	`ftp://ftp.cs.hut.fi/pub/ssh/contrib`
VPS	`http://www.strongcrypto.com`
gwpop	`ftp://ftp.internatif.org/pub/unix/gwpop/`
ftpsshd	`http://www.docs.uu.se/~pem/hacks/index.html`
ssh.el	`ftp://ftp.splode.com/pub/users/friedman/` `emacs-lisp/`
tn-gw-nav	`ftp://ftp.nlc.net.au/pub/unix/tn-gw-nav/` `index.html`
datbkr	`http://www.psychosis.com/datbkr`
scp wrapper	`ftp://ftp.psychosis.com`
ssh-tunnel.pl	`http://www.kluge.net/ftp/pub/felicity/`
TCP Wrappers	`ftp://ftp.porcupine.org/pub/security/`
rsync	`http://rsync.samba.org`
FISH	`http://www.free.lp.se/fish/`

Table D.1 *Secure Shell software and the URLs (cont'd)*

SSH Software	URL
NT sshd and ssh	`http://www.lexa.ru/sos/`
TeraTerm	`http://hp.vector.co.jp/authors/VA002416/teraterm.html`
TTSSH	`http://www.zip.com.au/~roca/`
SecureCRT	`http://www.vandyke.com`
F-Secure Tunnel and Terminal	`http://www.datafellows.com`

Index

About the Author

Anne Carasik is currently a Consulting Engineer with SSH Communications Security Ltd. in Mountain View, California, where she is working on network-security-related projects, including IPSEC Internet security packages.

Her previous experience includes network and system security at VeriSign, Inc. and network security consulting at International Network Services. Prior to that, Anne was at Hewlett Packard as a technical consult working with Internet infrastructure and Internet Security. Her experience includes penetration testing, incident response, network security architecture, and instruction. She is also the author of *Linux System Administration*, published in November 1998 by M&T Press.

Anne graduated from the University of Florida in Gainesville, Florida, with a Bachelor degree in Economics, while working at IBM and Northern Telecom. On sunny days, you can catch her roller blading or, on cold days, in Tahoe trying to learn to ski.